Tales Worth Telling

*Stories of Selected Heroes/Heroines
Who Define Us as Americans*

Tony Sanchez

University Press of America,® Inc.
Lanham • Boulder • New York • Toronto • Plymouth, UK

Copyright © 2014 by University Press of America,® Inc.
4501 Forbes Boulevard, Suite 200, Lanham, Maryland 20706
UPA Aquisitions Department (301) 459-3366

10 Thornbury Road, Plymouth PL6 7PP, United Kingdom

Library of Congress Control Number: 2013948038
ISBN: 978-0-7618-6224-6 (cloth : alk. paper)—ISBN: 978-0-7618-6225-3 (electronic)

For Nancy-
My extraordinary wife, companion, and best friend.
Your love and encouragement inspire me daily.

Contents

Acknowledgments   vii

Introduction   ix

  1   The Hero Concept and the Return of the American Hero   1
  2   "Tell Me A Story: Examining the Art Form of Storytelling"   17
  3   The Man Who Could Have Been King: George Washington   31
  4   The Father of the American Revolution: Samuel Adams   41
  5   The American Rascal: Benjamin Franklin   49
  6   The Surly Rebel's Defining Moment: John Adams   59
  7   Ahead of Her Time: Abigail Adams   67
  8   Champion of the Common Man: David Crockett   75
  9   The Conductor: Harriet Tubman   85
10   The Hidden Man: Abraham Lincoln   95
11   The Free Man: Frederick Douglass   105
12   Comforter of the Afflicted: Clara Barton   115
13   The Cantankerous Hero: Thomas Edison   125
14   The Birdmen: Wilbur and Orville Wright   135
15   Cultivating the Human Spirit: Jane Addams   145
16   Breaking the Barrier: Jackie Robinson   155
17   Always Do Right: Harry Truman   169
18   The Forgotten American: Dr. Tom Dooley   177
19   The Dream Keeper: Martin Luther King, Jr.   185

Contents

Postscript   195

Bibliography   197

Acknowledgments

A book is never the product of a single person's endeavors. Rather, it requires the encouragement and assistance of colleagues, friends, and relatives to truly see it to fruition. I was fortunate to have both during the lengthy planning, research, and writing phases of the manuscript.

Though I had the idea for this book firmly in my mind for some time and spoke of it often, I was greatly encouraged during the planning phase to pursue the project by the public school social studies practitioners with whom I have the pleasure to work, by my social studies colleagues in various universities who share my vision, and perhaps mostly by my social studies methods students, who strongly supported my motives for writing the book. Frequently hearing the phrase, "I'd definitely buy such a book" allowed me to keep my eye on the goal of providing a tool for future and present social studies educators to effectively use in the mission of teaching character/values education through historical storytelling.

During the research phase, financial assistance was provided to procure the numerous books I needed by the Department of Curriculum and Instruction in the Judith Herb College of Education at the University of Toledo. Several of my bosses graciously managed to adjust my teaching load to allow me additional writing time. I am indebted to those responsible.

It was during the seemingly endless but always enjoyable writing phase that I received the most encouragement. Keeping me on track were many relatives, friends, and colleagues whose unflagging support especially during the critical revision stages is greatly appreciated. Many thanks are due to many people who willingly took on the consuming task of reading various drafts of the manuscript.

Words cannot express my gratitude to University Press of America for publishing the book, which represents the culmination of a career dream of both writing a book and perhaps even in a small way advancing the mission of social studies education through the values of our heroes and heroines. Stella Donovan and Piper Owens provided valuable editorial guidance as well as encouragement during the final preparations for submitting the manuscript. They continually eased the doubts and frustrations of a first-time book writer and I extend my heartfelt thanks.

The author and publisher wish to acknowledge and thank those who have generously given permission to reprint excerpts and revisions of previously published articles:

It's Time Again for Heroes- Or Were They Ever Gone? (2000) and *The Story of the Boston Massacre: A Storytelling Opportunity for Character Education* (2005). Reprinted by permission of Copyright Clearance Center, Inc., Taylor and Francis Ltd.

Tell Me a Story: Becoming Reacquainted with a Neglected Art Form (2009) and *The Return of the American Hero* (2010). Reprinted by permission of the Ohio Social Studies Review.

The Man Who Could Have Been King: A Storyteller's Guide for Character Education (2006). Reprinted by permission of the Journal of Social Studies Research.

Harry Truman and the Atomic Bomb: An Excursion into Character Education through Storytelling (2006). Reprinted by permission of American Secondary Education.

The Remarkable Abigail: A Story for Character Education (2006). Reprinted by permission of the High School Journal.

The Forgotten American: A Story for Character Education (2007). Reprinted by permission of International Journal of Social Education.

There are no doubt others who have assisted me along the way who deserve acknowledgement. Though I may have left out their names, I trust they know who they are and how grateful I am to them.

Introduction

This book is organized into two parts. Part 1 features this introduction which relates why the book was written and how it was conceived to be used. Chapter 1 discusses the hero concept, its natural relationship to character/values education, and specifically the American hero. It concludes by proposing the storytelling strategy as an effective vehicle to teach the concept. Chapter 2 looks at the craft of storytelling through a brief history and suggestions for its effective implementation in the classroom. Both chapters are based upon several of my previously published articles and have been expanded and revised for this project.

Part 2 presents the individual stories of seventeen selected American heroes/heroines in condensed versions for practitioner use. Five of the stories were previously published in academic journals and have been expanded and revised for the book. The remaining twelve were written exclusively for this project. All of them are based upon comprehensively written, researched, and often celebrated books and additional sources. Each story also includes a set of guideline questions necessary for the crucial follow-up discussion as suggested in Chapter 2.

The inspiration to write this book began during my first tumultuous year as an 8th grade social studies teacher in an inner-city junior high school in Gary, Indiana. The entire landscape of the educational scene was a daunting experience for an idealistic beginner and I quickly found myself overwhelmed and despaired. My 8th graders were quite the challenge for several of the same reasons found in contemporary American schools: irregular attendance, significantly below grade level reading ability (if they read at all), and a short attention span. Perhaps most frustrating to me was their total disregard for history and an outright hatred for the subject. Making the common mistake of beginning teachers, I relied solely on what proved to be an inadequate textbook and religiously followed it in teaching the facts of the American adventure. It became a daily, desperate, and losing battle, not the least of which was basically my fault. In the "heat of battle" of adjusting to the rigors of the first-year teacher, I had neglected to fall back on my pre-service training and experience in how to teach history.

I harkened back to my days as an 11th grade history student in the class of Howard Jones. Mr. Jones was the consummate teacher who brought the subject alive and inspired me to pursue a career as a social studies teacher. He was my hero and it was as if I was letting him down. Then, of course, it dawned on me: I was failing because I wasn't doing what he had inspired me to do, what he had so effectively done to teach the essence of American history: storytelling. That sudden realization was an academic wake-up call and I vowed to try something new.

The opportunity first presented itself on an especially frustrating day in late September. I had finished dreary, fact-filled units on the Age of Exploration and the Colonial Era and was about to embark on the Revolutionary War. Student performance thus far had been dismal: they weren't getting it and, worse, they didn't care if they did. Using a recently read biography, I abruptly jettisoned the usual introductory lecture and accompanying worksheets and proceeded to launch into a story about George Washington, that famous resident of Mount Vernon and wooden teeth.

I began by showing them a conventional picture of him and asking students what they already knew about the man. Though it took much prodding, we amassed a short list of the "usual suspects": the first president, war general, lived at Mount Vernon, married to Martha, found on coin and bill, and the infamous wooden teeth. What was immediately apparent was the missing piece: their conventional but expectedly scant knowledge lacked the human aspect. To them, Washington was a flat, one-dimensional picture in a text-book. He had no human face to speak of and certainly had no relevance to them. They needed to be told the "real" story, the one not found in the textbook.

Primed and ready, I enthusiastically began the rendition with a pencils-down-just-listen approach. Weaved into the narrative were purposeful questions asked at key points to keep them engaged as I kept the story flowing. I could see their transformation as I humanized the man, especially by focusing on his character and values through details that no middle grades history textbook could relate. I was bringing him alive. The use of a few simple artifacts helped advance the mission: pictures of the man and his home, an example of a fashionable wig that he refused to wear, and a Brazil nut which allegedly contributed to his loss of teeth. They were attentive, even spell-bound, and readily responded to my timely questions, all of which gave me hope that they were learning something. The story lasted much longer than the fifteen minutes I had originally planned and I was even able to use it as a vehicle to "slip in" a few superfluous facts. But neither they nor I seemed to mind as they seemed to feed on my animated presentation. When the story concluded, I immediately transitioned into what turned out to be a follow-up discussion based on a set of questions which did not concern themselves with historical facts but instead delved into Washington's character and values. It was that discussion that allowed me to make a crucial past-to-present connection to the students.

It had all worked beautifully. Inspired, I told the story to my remaining four classes and though I was aware that each subsequent rendition altered slightly from the one before it, the result was the same: they paid close attention and got into the post-story discussion, further demonstrating a better understanding of the historical circumstances through talking about character and values. They were learning something about their own values in the process.

Prompted by this initial success, I took the textbook and began mapping out the next opportunities for stories. From that perspective, of course, they were endless. History deals with people and people have stories. I would not only have to be selective but would also have to find such stories outside the textbook. Finding quality sources to condense into accurate and multidimensional stories was not a problem as long as I was willing to devote the time and effort. My encouragement to continue my storytelling ways was bolstered by my students' reactions. What had enthralled them? The simple answer is that everyone loves a good story and it is all in the telling.

Storytelling thus became my most frequently used strategy and as my middle school career progressed, it never failed me. I became known as The Storyteller who told tales that weren't in the book. The more I told them, the more effective teller I became; and the more my students became involved. I even began convincing my colleagues of the benefits of storytelling, to the point where several borrowed my renditions for the effort. More or less convinced that my purported success could also be theirs, however, was their concern for the research factor; namely, they couldn't afford the time to research and construct comprehensive stories in addition to the strategies they were already using. Some also lacked the confidence and mechanics to be storytellers. But as long as I could supply the stories, many would at least attempt using them. So even then the idea for this book was brewing.

As I consistently utilized the storytelling strategy and the ensuing follow-up discussion, students began to realize two important points. First, everybody has a story simply because they are people. Indeed, history is a continuous story of individuals and groups tested by the trials of life. Students actually came to expect a story by relating their most frequently asked question upon encountering a historical figure: "What's his or her story?" Second, students not only learned the concepts of character and values but more importantly realized that they transcended historical time and were relevant to their personal lives as evolving citizens. It was this latter point that gave my stories the necessary human dimension that a textbook cannot do by its nature.

Invariably, I began to use the terms "hero" and "heroine" as a label to selected historical figures which prompted many post-story discussions over what the terms meant to individual students. While a consensus over a single acceptable definition was never actually reached, many other derived definitions allowed comprehensive examinations of the transcending values of the hero/heroine and their contemporary relevance.

My interest in the storytelling strategy and the hero concept continued as my career progressed to the high school level and finally to the university environment. In working with social studies practitioners and pre-service education students, promoting the storytelling strategy has been a relatively "easy sell." They recognize the potential of its effectiveness but also express the same concern; that is, there is little time to research and construct the great stories they would like to tell, especially in this era of standards-based education which too tightly structures teaching time and overly emphasizes factual knowledge acquisition. The purpose of this book is therefore to provide selected stories, not only to encourage their telling but also to encourage educators to research their own tales worth telling. One final word to practitioners or those simply interested in the lives of these selected Americans: These ready-to-be-told stories hopefully make an interesting and informative read that won't be found in a conventional textbook. More importantly, they are not simply meant to be read but rather to be rousingly told. It has been many years since I began my storytelling mission as a middle school/high school teacher and university professor. But I've had occasion to communicate with many former students from those years and every one of them tell me that they fondly remember my stories and learned something about themselves from them. I think Mr. Jones would be proud of me.

Chapter One

The Hero Concept and the
Return of the American Hero

INTRODUCTION

From the exploits of biblical times to mythological daring, from the obligations of valor to humanitarian sacrifice, and from famous and forgotten battlefields to the silver screen and the athletic arena, a place has always been
reserved for individuals known as heroes and heroines. [Note: the term
"hero" also designates "heroine"] Both history and literature abound with
such individuals who provide inspiration and hope (Walden, 1986). Though
the concept itself may be shrouded in ambiguity, cultures still provide an
arena for them (Sanchez, 2000).

The ambiguous nature of the concept nevertheless represents a measure of
character against which we evaluate ourselves, even as we question if heroes
are actually cultural necessities and products of historical events. But regardless of the possible debate over whether heroes create history or history
creates heroes, the fact remains that their perpetual existence seems to indi-
cate that we need them personally and collectively (Sanchez, 2000). Perhaps
it is indeed true as Robert Penn Warren (1972) noted that "by a man's hero
ye shall know him" (p.4). The essence may simply be in the timing: in
complacent times a Mickey Mantle or a Charles Lindbergh are relatively safe
choices, but in times of crisis an Abraham Lincoln or an Audie Murphy
might be necessary as objects of our worship. A time of crisis is no more a
prerequisite for the emergence of heroes than is a time of complacency, but
certainly a case can be made whereby the former circumstance frequently
brings to the forefront the appearance of the hero. A recent event in our own
history is testament of this assertion.

It has been over a decade since the generation-defining event of 9/11, a tragedy that changed the American nation to the point where nothing will ever be the same again, politically, legally, or socially. For social studies educators seeking to teach facets of citizenship, it also spurred the re-emergence and realization of the hero concept and the heroes among us:

> It took the horror of September 11, 2001, to remind us of just how special "unsung" heroes are. Many brave men and women sacrificed to help others. But that's what heroes do; whether they are personal or unsung or famous heroes. They give of themselves to make this world a better place (Denenberg & Roscoe, 2006, p. 10).

An implication is that the heroes of 9/11 suddenly re-emerged after a long absence. But in that eclipsing moment, we were reminded that heroes are not born; it is no genetic phenomenon. Rather, such status is earned through positive deed that makes a difference. But just as importantly, we were also reminded that such heroism is a potential within us all.

The patriotic zeal and unity that followed 9/11 seemingly disappeared in short order, but it also prompted social studies educators to consider where heroes have gone, their role in the curriculum, and the implications for advancing the moral/civic mission of social studies, which is "essential for the success of a democratic society" (Lickona, 1991, p.8). Do American heroes need to "return" and are they really necessary?

WHAT IS A HERO?

Inevitable in such a discussion is one's definition of a hero, which must precede any inquiry into the return or necessity of heroes. Historically, the hero concept/definition has always been somewhat shrouded in ambiguity, which may explain its alleged misconception and possible devaluing to the point that it may no longer mean something definitive, and which may contribute to the social studies educator's possible reluctance to teach the concept. But regardless of historical vagueness, the paradox is that such individuals have always existed which further infers that there has always been a need for them.

So what is a hero? The educator's personal definition is certainly crucial, as it may determine the presence or absence of heroes in a given historical circumstance. Definitions are as numerous as the years they span, yet they may be selectively gleaned for commonalities. Rzadkiewicz (2009) cites a conventional dictionary definition from Webster's (2004): "Any man admired for his qualities or achievements and regarded as an ideal or model" (p.657). Rolfe (2006) offers a personal definition of one "who performs an extraordinary, spontaneous act of bravery or sacrifice" (p. 1). Hakim (2006) believes that "real heroes are often those who quietly do what is right" (p.9). Sanchez (2010) defined a hero as "a person who performs a voluntary action that symbolizes the moral/ethical standards of the culture" (p.20). Finally, Weber (2009) perceives heroes as ..." [Those who] saw a real need for assistance and they rose to the occasion immediately" (p.6).

This recent set of definitions is probably as representative as any era could relate and in one form or another could transcend time in relevance. These diversely stated definitions also share at least five commonalities and implications that may lead to a more concise perception of the concept. The first and perhaps most obvious commonality among the definitions is achievement for the benefit of others. A hero must perform some specified deed that demonstrably helps others. Though the action may be the proverbial extraordinary or humanitarian feat, the hero's intent is to demonstrate- possibly through outstanding effort and/or uncommon ability- what is possible, thus inspiring those of lesser ability to change their behavior and attempt that which they may never have even considered without the hero's inspiration.

A second commonality/implication is that heroism knows no gender/race/ age limits. Virtually anyone can be a hero. Historically, the previously ill-perceived status of women and minorities often disqualified them from hero status in their own time. Changing social attitudes in the 20th century have enabled current generations to re-evaluate past generations whose selected individuals can now be viewed as the heroes that they are.

A third commonality/implication is that a hero's actions may be frequent. In many cases, a person need perform a single action to merit hero status. But in other cases, a hero's actions can be numerous and frequent. This is especially true for those who put their lives on the line on a daily basis to protect us, such as law enforcement officers, firefighters, and the military, as well as the daily sacrifices made by parents.

A fourth commonality/implication is the hero's pre-heroic status: fame is not a prerequisite for heroism and may not necessarily be the end result. In fact, a case to be made is that many heroes are "unsung" and remain so due to the deeply personal regard we have for them and the humbleness with which they regard themselves. He may simply be an ordinary person thrust into extraordinary circumstances and rises to the occasion. The hero does not ambitiously concern himself with being a hero and has no desire in being viewed as one. Rather, he is solely focused on achieving an action which may inexplicably put him in peril in order to benefit others, often without considering pros and cons beforehand; instinct may trump logic (Weber, 2009). But the admiration of others is not an objective of the hero and certainly the heroics of 9/11 serve as a prime example of the unsung hero.

A final commonality/implication is that the hero's actions exemplify those values which ultimately define a culture's character. In short, he does the right and necessary things which in turn reinforce the transcendental standards which perpetuate the culture and make it better (Sanchez, 2000a). This is the essence of operative values, or values in action, and acclaim is dependent upon advancing such values (Lickona, 1991). Thus, the hero serves as a model of and foundation for values/character education (Heching- er, 1987). Social studies educators may innately recognize that the best way to teach values/character is to teach about the people who exemplify them:

> In seeking the criteria that define the hero, we do not discover the "perfect" hero who transcends time, for such an individual remains in the context of his or her time. Rather, we find that the hero's values and character transcend the eras: courage, perseverance, truth, and daring to risk for the benefit of others. To promote a hero is to encourage the adoption of those values (Sanchez; 2000. p.59).

But in this regard, Lickona (1991) warned that a major obstacle for social studies educators to consider is the influence of the late-20th century move- ment of personalism, which stressed "the worth, dignity, and autonomy of the individual person" (p.9) and emphasized only the self through a "focus on expressing and fulfilling themselves as free individuals" (p.9) rather than fostering the values that perpetuated the culture. This led to resisting role models that legitimized cultural values and promoted a shallow moral relati- vism in the schools.

The history of every nation and culture is an adventure that demands and requires the accomplishments of heroes to solidify and advance it. With that in mind, a brief and cursory look at the history of the concept may further assist social studies educators with an additional foundation for understand- ing and teaching it.

A BRIEF HISTORY

Heroes originated in the distant mist of time (Jokinen, 1998). Biblical times presented the first opportunity for quintessential heroes who personified achievement and inspiration throughout the Old and New Testaments (Bald- win, 2008). Their spiritual, familial, and deeply personal exploits have never been equaled in Christian-Judeo traditions and they still serve as models of faith.

Though all cultures and countries have had heroes, the term itself actually originated with the ancient Greeks and then later directly adapted by the Romans (Bloomfield, 1975). In both Greek and Roman mythology and folk- lore, heroes were benefactors of mankind who, while facing adversity and danger, displayed great courage and sacrifice for the greater good. Though mortal, they achieved beyond the scope of normal humanity and were worshipped as were the gods (LaBarge, 2005). To be a hero was to go beyond what was perceived to be humanly possible. Thus, stories of heroes served as a moral compass in classical antiquity and played a crucial role in Greek and Roman religion. The realm of mythology was founded on the accounts of heroes (Rzadkiewicz, 2009). Epic poems relating heroic exploits further served to teach life lessons as they epitomized the ideals of the common person in the guise of both religious and literary figures (Leeming, 1990).

In medieval Europe, the epic hero of the Middle Ages had evolved primarily as a protector or helper in conjunction with the Greek "eroe," meaning "a superhuman or semi-divine being whose special powers were put forth to save or help all mankind or a favored part of it" (Bloomfield, 1975, p.27). This idea of the savior hero dominated early medieval epics, but soon gave way to the chivalric hero embodied in the courtly knight. The difference between the epic hero and the chivalric hero of feudal Western Europe was significant and indicative of the changing time; that is, the epic hero acted when circumstance required, while the chivalric hero set out to prove his valor through "the niceties of conduct" (Moorman, 1975, p.29) which reflected the values of courtly life (Auerbach, 1974).

Despite the differences among the mythological, epic, and chivalric heroes, they shared the common factor of an honorable heroic code which has endured through the ages: the hero did not act on his own behalf but always on the behalf of others, be they family, friends, community, or country, and without regard to glory, fame, or gain (Rzadkiewicz, 2009).

Like all cultures, the concept of the American hero similarly has a changing history (Sanchez, 2000a). But unlike many other cultures, America's younger history has focused much less on the literary figure and much more upon flesh-and-blood individuals who defined and advanced our ideals. During the late 18th century as the young republic was taking hold, we valued honor, duty, and patriotic virtue, traits that were necessary to sustain the goals of 1776. Symbolizing these traits were our first real American heroes: George Washington, Samuel Adams, Thomas Jefferson, Benjamin Franklin, and Abigail Adams, among others, certainly fulfilled those cultural needs. The 19th century took a different turn as American heroism was defined by humanitarianism, scientific achievement, economic attainment, and political or military exploits. Symbolic of these traits were such as Abraham Lincoln, Harriet Tubman,, Clara Barton, Frederick Douglass, Grant, Lee, and Thomas Edison, to name but a few. Interestingly, this phase of American heroism closely paralleled the European martial perspective personified by Carlyle's 1841 On Heroes, Hero Worship and the Heroic in History (1985), which centered upon military and political figures, such as Cromwell and Frederick the Great. But this same perspective explicitly lost favor during America's 20th century while continuing in Europe. America's 20th century heroes, on the other hand, magnified the physical attributes and sacrificial achievements of humanitarians, the self-made individual of the courageous deed, and the newly-admired sports/media figure. Symbolic of these traits were Babe Ruth, Charles Lindbergh, Jane Addams, Audie Murphy, Martin Luther King, and a multitude of athletes and media stars. For educators, the common-thread presumed a prevailing set of values that was subsequently advanced by such role models.

The American perception of heroes and what we both need and want them to be are intimately interrelated. For example, in his biography of Babe Ruth, Sobol (1974) stated:

Babe was a character, that's all. Something apart from every other human being you had ever met. And whatever your feelings about him you could never forget that he was the great, the incomparable, the idolized Babe Ruth... Only a Solomon could have looked at Ruth and separated the real man from the mythological hero (p.3).

Over time, the vagueness of the concept has probably resulted in the overuse of the term to a great extent. In that regard, Swindell (1980) noted in his biography of a movie great that:

Gary Cooper was idolized and admired but was also beloved, as perhaps no other contemporary screen figure was beloved... He was an encouragingly heroic image in an optimistic era of hero worship. He belongs to a very recent yet thoroughly bygone American eras such as many of our citizens yearn for (p.ix).

Time and maturity further affect our perception in that we "outgrow" some heroes {Sanchez, 1998). As we change, so may our heroes. New knowledge may also force us to reconsider objects of our worship. In examining the Custer myth, for example, Connell (1984) asserted that:

As values change, so does one's evaluation of the past and one's impression of long gone actors. New myths replace the old. During the nineteenth century [George A. Custer] was vastly admired. Today his image has fallen down in the mud and his middle initial, which stands for Armstrong, could mean Anathema... Thus, from a symbol of courage and sacrifice in the winning of the West, Custer's image was gradually altered into a symbol of the arrogance and Brutality displayed in the white exploitation... How odd that this consummate thespian's greatest role was a flop (pp.106-107).

Our perceptions must also take into account that heroes cannot be, and do not have to be, perfect, though more than a few have been disastrously construed as such. Time and new information reveal that all possess the proverbial feet of clay. Nonetheless, they all had a steadfast singleness of purpose, sometimes embodied in a single deed against overwhelming odds (such as Lindbergh and Murphy), sometimes over a lifetime of deeds (as with Helen Keller and Mother Teresa). Some made their appearance prematurely in that the context of their heroism was not recognized or acknowledged in their lifetime (as with Abigail Adams, who was basically excluded from wide recognition due to her gender). Some are simply forgotten for unknown reasons (Dr. Tom Dooley, though celebrated briefly in his own time as an embodiment of humanitarianism and self-sacrifice, merits reconsideration). In terms of consistency, few if any can be perceived as total successes. The rather arrogant perception of the mid-to-late 20th century that only "winners" can be heroes has evolved into one tempered by forgiveness and tolerance, especially if the potential hero in question has clearly risked everything against the odds or has been enveloped in the martyrdom of death (Warren, 1972).

HERO VS. CELEBRITY

It has been asserted that America has outgrown her old-fashioned belief in heroism and that "we as a nation seem to be losing both our sense of that heroism and our appreciation for it" (Rainey, 2007, p.3). In that regard, the most dramatic and perhaps disturbing turn in the history of the hero concept is the apparent disillusionment and cynicism of our times. Perhaps we became cynical because our ideals were so frequently betrayed (LaBarge, 2005). But if "heroes reflect the culture, and what the culture values will determine the type of heroic act to be rewarded" (Brodbelt & Wall, 1984, p.6), it is disconcerting to note that today's hero is too often the celebrity: a person of name value but little if any enduring substance performing media-based/media-inspired actions serving to entertain (Sanchez, 2010). The rise and powerful influence of popular media have made it decidedly easy for us to confuse celebrity with genuine heroism. As a result, sports figures and media stars meet the culturally misguided requirements for today's heroes: fame as a result of some physical prowess, beauty, constant media exposure, and ridiculously high incomes. Marginally talented though some- perhaps many- are, they can be mesmerizingly "mythological or pseudo-religious in their appeal and importance" (Walden, 1986, p. 12). How cruelly ironic in this regard that film and television actors are revered for portraying characters who are totally unlike themselves, a notion that once prompted the great Laurence Olivier to state that "acting is lying" (Channel 2 News, 1986). But publicized are their flaws, not their virtues. They are worshipped even though they may not only set bad examples, but also destroy the foundation of what a hero should be (Scott, 2008). Celebrities thrive on the admiration of the public, but this has never been the true hero's concern. In essence, if heroism reflects the highest standards of our culture, its displacement by celebrity now reflects a problematic and transient commercialism that has corrupted our national virtue (Rainey, 2007).

The celebrity ascent to hero status may well embody the disillusionment of current America and the media's power to make our choices for us. While this may be an indirect indictment against the institutions of family and school, this disillusionment has certainly led our youth to worship the imagery of the performer over the reality of life, thus valuing glitz over substance (Sanchez, 2000). Walden (1986) set forth an assertion in this regard that social studies educators need to seriously contemplate: such disillusionment is a distinct warning of a social identity loss due to a lack of effective guidance, a lack that Boorstin (1982) maintained leads to more and more of our heroes being performers or winners and fewer being those of social acceptability or servants of the group. Lickona (1991) asserted that "when [social studies educators] don't do moral education, influences hostile to good character push in to fill the values vacuum" (p.20); thus, the rise of celebrity influence. Lost is the perspective that "the hero reveals the potential of humanity and goodness of human nature; the celebrity reveals the potential of the media" (Sanchez, 2000, p.59). The hero is a role model who exists to make a difference by making the world a better place, while the celebrity exists merely for the camera and the box office (Rainey, 2007). The celebrity merely "is" by looking good or saying cleverly scripted words, while the hero "does" and inspires us to action.

HERO VS. ANTI-HERO

The disillusionment and cynicism of contemporary society has led to a move away from the more "traditional" hero to a more "nontraditional" role model: the anti-hero. If the hero symbolizes the moral/ethical standards that perpetuate the culture, the anti-hero seeks to undermine them (Sanchez, 2000). As the hero's nemesis, the anti-hero is not a new phenomenon. Indeed, they have stood side-by-side throughout history with the hero usually prevailing. But our recent history has seen a subtle but powerful revival of the anti-hero that has its base in popular media and changing social values. The social upheavals of the Vietnam era, assassinations of prominent cultural figures, the suspicions of and alleged betrayals by political figures and others in authority, and the accompanying accelerated rise of cable technology and its promotional power have all had a detrimental effect on the perspective of the hero (Sanchez, 2000).

The power of film and fictional book characters may be heavily responsible for the rise and current popularity of the anti-hero, though paradoxically the anti-hero has always been present in these mediums. Film heroes of the 1960s took a stronger nontraditional form that subtly and entertainingly began with the James Bond series and the ensuing international craze of the spy genre. These "different" heroes- though fictional- came to symbolize an often violent recourse to success, thus becoming anti-heroes in the process. Beginning late in that decade, the American public took the cue to glamorize

a new generation of both fictional and nonfictional anti-heroes whose vil-
lainy became celebrated. Three ground-breaking examples in film of this
trend in the late 1960s included Bonnie and Clyde ("They're young. They're
in love. They rob banks."), Butch Cassidy and the Sundance Kid (featuring
two handsome and popular actors who exchange cute one-liners as they rob
and kill), and The Wild Bunch (a film that also provoked much controversy
over its alleged glorification of graphic violence and prompted future films to
more graphically depict violence). So admired were their characterizations
that their ultimately well-deserved demises evoked great sympathy among
moviegoers. The antihero in film continues to be popular, case in point being
the various characters portrayed by action stars Bruce Willis, Arnold
Schwarzeneger, and Vin Diesel, among others. A further example is the 1999
Mel Gibson film, Payback, whose advertising line is "Get ready to root for
the bad guy." The film's box office popularity indicates that the public did.

Anti-heroes are certainly not limited to films and literature. They very
much walk among us. The media cannot be blamed for the rising "popularity" of youth gangs, a values-threatening social condition that is the bane of
many urban and suburban environments. As they undermine the legal and
moral foundations of a community, they classically represent the sobering
presence of the anti-hero. Only values re-examination and re-education appear to be the keys to this social dilemma, and since the base problem can be
perceived as a values issue, the hero concept may play a prominent role in its
solution.

Ultimately, any debate among hero, celebrity, and anti-hero must consider that only the life each of us chooses or is influenced to choose demon-
strates what each of us truly is: our deeds reflect our character in that the hero
gives, the celebrity takes, and the anti-hero deftly undermines. That has
always been the legacy, for the commercial fame of celebrity is fleeting and
momentary, while the ultimate fate of the anti-hero is often and justly sad,
both leaving an insatiable emptiness that cannot be filled.

HEROISM "GONE BAD"

Heroes may simply be individuals who inspire us to be better than we are.
Yet we must be cautious of who we elevate to that proverbial pedestal,
carefully and prudently choosing only those who reflect the qualities that
symbolize the very best of human nature (Wiesel, 2009). Yet even when we
acknowledge that our acclaimed heroes are indeed flawed, to bestow that title
gives tremendous power, power that may be used for good or power that may
be used to destroy (Wiesel, 2009; Dando-Collins, 2008). History unfortunately indicates that the problem is not one of strong devotion to heroes but

rather that such devotion may be directed to the "wrong" heroes (LaBarge, 2005; Hughes-Hallett, 2004).

In the realm of leadership, for example, heroes "serve as a powerful reminder that people are capable of resisting evil, of not giving into temptation, of rising above mediocrity, and of heeding the call to action and service when others fail to act" (Zimbardo, 2007, p.461). Yet history is riddled with heretofore proclaimed heroes who were not necessarily "good" people of character, but merely admired initially for their genius, creative achievements, or aggressiveness which were commanded and glorified. In these cases, heroism "went bad" and devotion led to idolatry and blind faith which ultimately proved destructive (Wiesel, 2009). These individuals took full advantage of our misplaced devotion and their "heroism" quickly gave way to an irreversible course of authoritarianism and dictatorship. Napoleon, Hitler, Stalin, Mao, Castro, and Chavez, among others, took heroic devotion and embodied, to an awe-inspiring degree, "force of will, energy, ingenuity, power, and an absolute recklessness about long-standing political, social, and legal conventions" (Egan, 1990, p.30).

Such individuals did not immediately betray our trust. Rather, we allowed them to dominate and define our morality and values when they committed unthinkable crimes. Forgotten was the notion that we define our ideals by the heroes we choose and emulate because our ideals define us (LaBarge, 2005).

A SOCIAL STUDIES MISSION

As noted earlier, to promote a hero is to encourage the adoption of the hero's values and character (Sanchez, 2000). Educationally, the paradox of sorts is that it is not really an individual that is promoted but rather his values. An individual must stay in the context of his time but his values transcend time. Thus for the social studies educator, the underlying issue becomes one of values education. The need to teach values and character in the social studies classroom is perhaps more important in post-9/11 America than at any time in our history and it purportedly remains a high priority in our standards-based mission (Sanchez, 2000). Yet the continuing debate over values education is too frequently deadlocked, even derailed, over the lack of agreement about whose values or what values should be taught. In many respects, this is a fruitless argument in that an "acceptable" core of values can be embraced: goodness, truth, responsibility, compassion, perseverance, work ethic, and courage, among others, are symbolic of the American character. Few would deny their cultural importance or their worth and priority to be taught in our educational institutions.

Social studies educators are therefore in an ideal position in the mission of guiding and inculcating our students to understand and identify with true heroes whose values reflect the best of what our culture offers:

> Citizenship education, the goal of social studies, is about the promotion of moral and ethical standards that symbolize and perpetuate a democratic citizenry. The standards are embodied in humanitarian endeavors that benefit others, that inspire and unite. We can inspire young people with the endeavors and values of authentic heroes who can be role models for the values, spirit, and traits that are necessary for our citizens in the twenty-first century (Sanchez, 2000, p.60).

If our students are to become the reflective and concerned citizens we need them to be, we must guide them in choosing and evaluating proper heroic models whose values can fulfill those citizenship obligations. The social studies mission thus becomes one of choosing those heroes who best model our moral/ethical heritage, engage and dialogue with students in a context-based examination of their exploits, and note the extent to which their prescribed values transcend time and become relevant for the contemporary student. Students will thus come to recognize not only that certain values are fundamental and not time-restricted, but also the heroic potential in themselves.

AN EFFECTIVE APPROACH

It has been asserted that if "the role of schools in creating knowledgeable and patriotic citizens is the vision of America" (Waltzer & Heilman, 2005, p. 156), then social studies should emphasize "true heroes of the American story" (p. 156). Indeed, America's story can be perceived as one continuous narrative of heroic individuals: ordinary people who rose to the occasion when thrust into extraordinary circumstances. Their transcending values represent a mother lode of opportunity for social studies educators. But if we are to teach those values we must further keep in mind that the American story is not a travelogue of purity to promote simple morality (Loewen, 1995).

Our goal must not be indoctrination that simply justifies the status quo, but rather to promote moral/ethical growth in students through a multidimensional examination of the positive and the imperfect. We cannot purify or romanticize our moral base by "removing our warts." The consequence of such is a culture drained of its essence, leaving cynicism in its place. It is crucial for social studies educators to present a critical self-examination of both the positive and negative aspects of the hero's life to promote the understanding that human imperfections are an integral part of the hero's character and may very well serve to enhance the fabric of heroism itself (Sanchez, 2010).

This begs the question of how to most effectively teach about heroes, which is crucial as educators may feel constrained by strict curriculum standards. Identifying a most effective pedagogy or implementation strategy will continue to be debated among researchers and practitioners, but certainly among the oldest and most effective approaches is the storytelling strategy (Sanchez, 2009; Sanchez & Mills, 2005). As a vehicle for teaching about heroes, storytelling can "empower the imagination, humanize individuals, promote empathy and understanding, reinforce values and ethics, and stimulate the development of critical/creative thinking" (Sanchez, 2009, p.25). Rousingly told stories about heroes engage students to reflect upon their values and analyze issues and choices made (Sanchez & Mills, 2005). How we tell historical and non-historical stories can crucially shape our perception of the past while at the same time defining our present with a powerful emotional appeal that prompts the listener/student to think critically from a moral perspective and work to extol a targeted value to inspire the modeling of a positive behavior (Sanchez, Zam & Lambert, 2009).

The stories of heroes establish a connection between the historical and the personal by acknowledging values and actions in context but in such a way as to transcend time for the contemporary student. We can thus better understand and conceptualize the basic dynamics of the hero's values, which in turn guides students to reflect upon and analyze pertinent values as they may relate to their own lives (Sanchez, 2000).

So where do we find these stories? Such stories are actually not difficult to find, but they will require the social studies educator to go beyond the conventional history textbook, which is too often by its nature broad and shallow to accurately and comprehensively relate a complete development of the hero (Sanchez, 2009). Dunn (1991) asserts that social studies textbooks notoriously neglect a comprehensive development and that "stories" of traditional heroes utterly lack depth and- in many cases- accuracy. Students are exposed all too frequently to a one-dimensional, overly positive, and ethnocentric depiction. The "ugly truth" about many has simply been glossed over or eliminated altogether. Perhaps in an effort to quantitatively include more of our heritage, the conventional textbook very narrowly presents accounts of traditional heroes without taking advantage of the opportunity for in-depth values or character education. This charge is further supported by the Brodbelt and Wall (1984) study of thirty-one selected social studies textbooks:

> The concept of hero/heroine typically was not utilized to illustrate those values and ideals necessary for the maintenance of a democratic society, nor were those concepts utilized in a manner which enables the student to better grasp democratic ideals... it would be beneficial if the values of society could be

presented, explained and integrated into the social studies context by focusing upon the hero/heroine. This study revealed that usually such was not the case (p. 12).

Educators must therefore pursue other avenues. More effective sources include trade books by notable authors, such as David McCullough, Joseph Ellis, Milton Meltzer, and Russell Freedman, among others, which offer detailed, accurate, and balanced treatments. There are also pre-written stories by educational researchers designed specifically for practitioners to tell within the parameters of the classroom (Sanchez, 2009). It is this latter point that represents the mission of this book. The hero concept symbolizes something much greater than the attainment of fame and wealth, performing death-defying or sacrificial acts, or acquiring media-promoted status. Heroes directly reflect our values, ideals, and dreams. Their qualities endure as a guide and inspiration for anyone to be a hero and therefore represent stories that are worth telling.

The storytelling strategy itself presents social studies educators with the pedagogical opportunity to make a true human connection with a lasting emotional impact; to reinforce what was possible for heroes and also what is possible for us. But in any case, our mission is clear: just tell the stories. In addition to telling these stories, however, is a crucial caveat necessary to fulfill the mission:

> ... Many historical and cultural stories [of heroes] have a moral or value perspective by their nature. As such, they cannot simply be told without a follow-up on the opportunity to more closely examine and share those perspectives. Failing to do this is the biggest mistake educators make in using this strategy. A well-told story will provoke both interest and debate in regard to relevant values for the contemporary student (Sanchez, 2009, p.27).

Thus, it is not enough to just tell the rousing and inspirational stories of heroes, but also to raise questions among students that lead to discussion and reflection. Only then can students comprehensively analyze pertinent values embodied by heroes and in turn relate them to their own lives.

THE RETURN OF THE AMERICAN HERO

Like all other nations, America has evolved through a number of historical phases. Each of these phases in turn featured at least three commonalities. First, each phase represented a nation in transition. Second, each successful transition required the adherence to a defining set of values and character, arguably and ably advanced by men and women we call heroes. Third, each of these sets features a common core of values that transcend time and uniquely define us as American. This feature alone justifies the study of yesteryear's heroes whose transcending values are still relevant to us today.

Post-9/11 America is a country in the throes of serious transition, as we always have been. Amidst this turmoil, however, is our historical/cultural/personal need for heroes, perhaps more than ever before. We need them, have always needed them, and need to be taught about them by our teachers. The ultimate paradox is that American heroes have no need to "return" for they have always been among us, yesterday and today. We need only to recognize them.

REFERENCES

Auerbach, E. (1974). *Mimesis*. Princeton: University of Princeton Press.

Baldwin, C. (2008). My heroes of history. *News With Views*, 1-4. Retrieved July 9, 2009, from http://www.newswithviews.com!baldwin/baldwin462.htm.

Bloomfield, M. (1975). *Concepts of the hero in the middle ages*. Albany: State University of New York Press.

Boorstin, D. (1982). *The image*. New York: Vintage Books.

Brodbelt, S. & Wall, R. (1985). An examination of the presentation of heroes and heroines in current (1974-1984) secondary social studies textbooks. *ERIC Digest No*. ED257726. Bloomington, IN: Clearinghouse for Social Studies/Social Science Education.

Carlyle, T. (1985). *On heroes, hero worship and the heroic in history*. Oxford: Oxford University Press.

Channel 2 News (1986). *Interview with Laurence Olivier*. WBBM, Chicago, IL, May 30.

Connell, E. (1984). *Son of the morning star*. New York: Harper & Row.

Dando-Collins, S. (2008). History without heroes: A case in point. *Home Newsletter*. Retrieved October 23, 2009, from http://hnn.us/articles/57696.html.

Denenberg, D. & Roscoe, L. (2006). *Fifty American heroes every kid should meet*. Minneapolis, MN: Millbrook Press.

Dunn, L. (1991). Teaching the heroes of American history. *The Social Studies,* 82(1): 26-29.

Egan, K. (1990). *Romantic understanding: The development of rationality and imagination, ages 8-15*. London: Routledge.

Hakim, J. (2006). Foreward. In D. Denenberg & L. Roscoe, *Fifty American heroes every kid should meet (p.9)*. Minneapolis, MN: Millbrook Press.

Hechinger, F. (1987). About education and values: Heroes and villains. *Science Times*. Retrieved May 10, 2009, from http://www.nytimes.com/1987/04/28/science/about-education-values-heroes-and-villains.

Hughes-Hallet, L. (2004). *Heroes, values, traitors and supermen*. London: Fourth Estate.

Jokinen, A. (1998). Heroes of the middle ages. *Luminarium,* 1-3. Retrieved July 9, 2009, from http://www.luminarium.org/medlit/medheroes.html.

LaBarge, S. (2005). Heroism: Why heroes are important. *Markula Center for Applied Ethics*. Retrieved April 21, 2009, from http://www.scu.edu/ethics/publications/ethicsoutlook2005/heroes.html.

Lickona, T. (1991). *Educating for character*. New York: Bantam.

Leeming, D. (1990). *The world of myth*. New York: Oxford University Press.

Loewen, J. (1995). *Lies my teacher told me: Everything your American history textbook got wrong*. New York: Simon and Schuster.

Moorman, C. (1975). *A knight there was: The evolution of the knight in literature*. Lexington: University of Kentucky Press.

Rainey, J. (2007). A time for heroes. *Anderson Independent-Mail*. Retrieved August 2, 2009, from http://www.independentmail.com/news/2007/mar/01/time-heroes.

Rolfe, D. (2006). Where have all the heroes gone? *The Dove Foundation*. Retrieved May 20, 2009, from http://www.dove.org/news.asp?ArticleID=80.

Rzadkiewicz, C. (2009). What is a hero? The changing concept of heroes. *Personal Development*, 1-2. Retrieved April 21, 2009, from http://personaldevelopment.suite101.com/article.cfm/who-are-our-heroes.

Sanchez, T. (1998). *Heroes/heroines across the life span*. Paper presented at the Indiana Council for the Social Studies Annual Conference, Indianapolis, IN, March 13.

Sanchez, T. (2000). It's time again for heroes- Or were they ever gone? *The Social Studies*, 91(2), March/April: 58-61.

Sanchez, T. (2009). Tell me a story: Becoming reacquainted with a neglected art form. *Ohio Social Studies Review*, 45(1): 24-33.

Sanchez, T. (2010). The return of the American hero. *Ohio Social Studies Review*, 46(2): 20-28.

Sanchez, T. & Mills, R. (2005). Telling tales: Teaching American history through storytelling. *Social Education*, 69(5): 269-274.

Sanchez, T., Zam, G. & Lambert, J. (2009). Storytelling as an effective strategy for teaching character education in middle school. *Journal for the Liberal Arts and Sciences*, 13(2), Spring: 14-23.

Scott, D. (2008). America's heroes. *ezineArticles*. Retrieved September 11, 2009, from http://ezinearticles.com/??Americas-Heroes&id=1063829.

Sobol, K. (1974). *Babe Ruth and the American dream*. New York: Ballantine.

Swindell, L. (1980). *The last hero: A biography of Gary Cooper*. New York: Doubleday.

Walden, D. (1986, January 25). Where have all our heroes gone? *USA Today*: 12-15.

Waltzer, K. & Heilman, E. (2005). *When going right is going wrong*. New York: Fordham Institute.

Warren, R. (1972). A dearth of heroes. *The American Heritage*, 23(6): 4-7.

Weber, A. (2009, April 9). What makes a hero? *The Toledo Blade*, B: 6.

Webster's new world dictionary (2004). New York: Simon and Schuster.

Wiesel, E. (2009). My hero's hero: The concept of heroes. *My Hero Project*. Retrieved April 21, 2009, from http://www.myhero.com/myhero/heroprint.asp?hero=Wiesel.

Zimbardo, P. (2007). *The Lucifer effect: Understanding how good people turn evil*. New York: Random House.

Chapter Two

"Tell Me A Story: Examining the Art Form of Storytelling"

"Do you remember the teachers that told you stories? I don't recall a single worksheet I ever filled out. And I did thousands of them. I don't remember the quizzes. I remember the teachers who told me stories. A bridge was created"
—Collins, 2003, p.128

"What a person usually remembers the longest is information that has an emotional impact"
—Abrahamson, 1998, p.443

INTRODUCTION

The previous chapter's discourse on the hero concept noted the benefits of its effective teaching via the storytelling strategy. This chapter takes an in-depth look at the history and mechanics of the strategy as a prelude for educators to confidently tell such stories.

Storytelling is as old as civilization. From the earliest cave markings to the advent of the written word into mass production and beyond, stories explained life, preserved history, and ensured the continuity of cultures (Abrahamson, 1998). Stories brought together human lives by creating a sense of belonging and understanding. As societies evolved and flourished, it became necessary to further document the historical account of events in writing (Chan, 1987). In this regard, the storyteller has always held a prestigious position by sharing, entertaining, teaching, and passing on the ways and wisdom of cultures and societies. The Egyptians were the first to allegedly record their stories, while the Greeks and Romans relied on nomadic troubadours to carry the tales of their cultures far and wide through a blend of fact, myth, and legend (Chen, 1987). But every culture seems to have invariably created stories, not only as a way to make sense of the world but also to foster a deeper understanding of self (Ellyatt, 2002). "Stories are the way we make sense of our lives; by telling them we tell ourselves who we are, why we're here, how we come to be what we are, what we value most, and how we see the world" (Columbo, Lisle & Mano, 1997, p.5).

Early generations were enthralled by stories heard directly, be they conceived from cave drawings of primitive societies, religiously-inspired exploits of sacred origins, hand-written manuscripts, and finally from books (Fulford, 1998). Some cultures would depend entirely upon stories as the vehicle for "passing down beliefs, traditions, and history to future generations" (Hamilton & Weiss, 1990, p.10). Native America in particular conveyed its numerous cultures through the simplest of narratives to give life to its numerous cultures and to persistently connect feelings and thoughts to bridge the past to the present to the future through converting stories into life lessons as the foundation of wisdom (Fulford, 1998). The 19th century's Industrial Age likewise industrialized the story through popular novels and magazines. The 20th century completely relegated the story to commercial prefabrication through film, radio, television, and the Internet. The 21st century will no doubt conjure new ways to relate stories, but the important point is that they will be told.

Amidst these technological advances, however, is a movement to providing the narrative of storytelling as a powerful teaching strategy in the classroom to empower the imagination, humanize individuals, promote empathy and understanding, reinforce values and ethics,, and stimulate the development of critical/creative thinking (Sanchez, 2009; Sanchez, Zam & Lambert, 2009; Sanchez & Mills, 2005; Mittelstadt, 2003; Ellyatt, 2002; Smith, 1993; Willis, 1992). History indicates that educators in and out of the conventional classroom have long depended upon storytelling as a historic foundation for teaching life lessons: "Great teachers, from Homer and Plato, through Jesus, Li Po, and Gandhi have used stories, myths, parables, and personal history to instruct, to illustrate, and to guide the thinking of their students" (Zabel, 1991, p.32).

But even as education became more formalized with an appropriate emphasis on literacy, storytelling continued to be a most effective strategy, especially for social studies educators (Barton & Levstik, 2004). Kennedy (1998) noted that "there is something innate in the human mind that makes the narrative form an especially attractive medium in which to contain, transmit, and remember important information" (p.465). Egan (1989) lauded the strategy for both the teacher/storyteller and the student/listener, referring to it as one of the most effective inventions of humankind. But what is really in it for the student/listener? Certainly more than mere entertainment; rather, it reduces depersonalization and serves as a powerful link to more meaningful learning within a historical context. That said, what is the benefit for the educator? It may perhaps represent something greater:

> Storytelling also encourages [students] to think of the curriculum as a collection of the great stories of their cultures. If one begins to think in these terms instead of seeing the curriculum as a huge mass of material to be conveyed to students, one can begin to think of instructors in society as connected with an ancient and honored role. Instructors are the tellers of culture's tales (Egan, 1989, p.459).

The power of the strategy is both simplistic and quite astonishing. Tellers and listeners find a reflection of themselves in a story by mutually creating an interaction and understanding between them (Sanchez & Mills, 2005; Ellyatt, 2002; Peck, 1989). A well-told story has a powerful emotional appeal that promotes the listener to think critically, especially from a moral perspective, and can work unconsciously to extol a targeted value and perhaps inspire the modeling of a positive behavior as a vicarious experience (Sanchez, 2009b; Willis, 1992; Casement, 1986). General principles of a story can be made easier for the student/listener to comprehend and apply to one's own life (Wells, 1986). Percy (1989) fervently argued that fictional stories portray a much clearer and cohesive picture of the human condition than any textbook could relate. That assertion provides the impetus for educators to seriously consider conceptualizing the American Experience as the story that it is (Sanchez & Mills, 2005). Viewing history as such and relating it through storytelling offer strong possibilities for both coherence and interest to the teaching of history and can also serve as a bridge to examining and understanding our pluralistic yet American society by providing opportunities through folktales, legends, myths, and epics that "touch on fundamental traits of human nature" (Bauer, 1993, p.139). But most powerful is the historical story (Sanchez, Zam & Lambert, 2009). Common (1987) noted the organizing power of using the metaphor of historical storytelling:

> Stories are narrative units. Because they are units, they speak forcefully to those who plan for teaching. Stories have particular clear beginnings, and particular, clear ends. It is their unity of wholeness and circumscription that distinguishes stories from other types of narratives (p.41).

Quite interesting in this foray is the emergence of a political viewpoint (Sanchez & Mills, 2005). Voices on the educational right and left have advocated for the teaching of history through storytelling, albeit for their own respective agendas. The conservative right has argued for a shift to what it terms the "traditional" social studies through the "simple" telling of the American story (Evans, 1989, p.85). Similarly, the liberal left also supports this shift, stating that history taught through storytelling:

... provides a basis for the subsequent development of an historical, dialectical conception of the world, which understands movement and change, which appreciates the sum of effort and sacrifice which the present has cost the past and which the future is costing the present, and which conceives the contemporary world as a synthesis of the past, of all past generations, which projects itself into the future (Gramschi, 1983, pp.34-35).

While it is initially perplexing that both political perspectives view the teaching of history through storytelling as the key to achieving their respective ends, that perplexity dissipates when one considers that historical stories can clearly convey the paradoxical need for cultural change and order, and how it may be accomplished. The historical story depicts an individual's values and character in relation to situations with active consequences. Quite frequently, these consequences are critical not only for the individual who personally experiences them but also for the listener who similarly experiences them. When presented by the teller in this fashion, the notions of history and story smoothly meld and are better understood.

EXTINCT OR MERELY HIBERNATING?

Despite these accolades, however, there is the rather tenuous assertion that the storytelling strategy has only recently been attempting to resurface from a long hibernation but from which it may never fully re-emerge (Sanchez, 2009b). Dubious as this assertion may be, three possibilities serve as explanations which may in turn hinder the educator from fully utilizing the storytelling strategy. The first is the increasing and over reliance on the history textbook as the sole source of knowledge and instruction, especially in this era of standards-based education and high-stakes testing which lead many an educator to believe that there is simply no time to be set aside for storytelling. It is certainly no secret that the history textbook has long been regarded with suspicion on both counts (Fitzgerald, 1979). Yet in spite of its acknowledged shortcomings and even affirmation from publishers that it was never intended to be the sole depository of knowledge and source of instruction, the history textbook continues to be misconstrued as THE curriculum (Sanchez, 2005). Consistent in being "little more than repositories of dates, names, and facts" (Tomlinson, Tunnel & Richgels, 1993, p.52), the potentially exciting stories of history are instead related in a decidedly broad and shallow nature that results in a flat, dull reading experience which may be further handicapped by historical/cultural inaccuracies (Sanchez, 2007). The conventional textbook tends to present content so superficially and briefly as to become only "a [chronological] dash through time" (Blount, 1992, p.221), morphing into a lifeless recitation lacking depth and humanity; and begging to be filled in by a knowledgeable educator. This perspective may not be as inaccurate as it is restrictive, a limitation leading to a too-narrow scope within which to work. In its defense, however, the history textbook does "do a good job with sequencing the facts of history, but poorly convey[s] the experiential feel of past events" (Sitton, Mehaffy & Davis, 1983, p.13). Storytelling, on the other hand, can relate history from multiple perspectives and gives facts meaning by creating "a structure for our perceptions; only through stories do facts assume any meaning whatsoever" (Postman, 1989, p. 122). As it stands, the conventional textbook does not truly reflect history as the real experiences of real people.

Storytelling offers the alternative of allowing history to rightfully take its place in the curriculum as a collection of great stories that not only inform but more importantly encourage students to relate and connect to the similarities between peoples of various times through transcending struggles and values (Sanchez, 2000b; Combs & Beach, 1994). The student/listener garners a crucial benefit from a well-told story; namely, if the "things" they did are similar to the "things" we do and/or are struggling with, an additional level of understanding and learning will occur; not only the technical learning processes, such as listening, speaking, sharing ideas, and accepting reactions, but also the shared experiences among a group that foster cooperation, and create bonds that transcend gender, class, and culture (Sanchez, 2000b; Hamilton & Weiss, 1990).

A second possibility is the status of values/character education, a concept that has historically and chiefly taught through storytelling (Sanchez, 2006; Sanchez & Zam, 2006; Sanchez & Mills, 2005). Though character education itself has a long and definitive history in American education, it is validly asserted that it is no longer the predominant issue in the curriculum (Sanchez, 2004). Rather, it has become a much lower priority in the focus upon academic competency in the midst of international competition and the fears wrought from legal issues separating church and state.

The currently questionable status of character education was of course not always so (Smith, 1993). Dewey (1934) noted the central role of character education in American schools from the republic's inception as the primary mission in the development of youth. It was a staple and expectation of the curriculum in light of the recognition that bias-free education or even neutral stance was neither desirable nor possible (Damon, 1988; Paul, 1988). Indeed, the mission of the American school stressed "character education as the objective of schooling and the resultant solution to social ills" (Sanchez, 2004, p.107). For the educator, the enduring success of integrating character education proved to hinge upon the method of historical storytelling, which related and promoted the moral/ethical standards that both symbolize and perpetuate our democratic republic (Sanchez & Mills, 2005; Sanchez, 2004).

Social and educational perspectives changed during the tumultuous post-World War II era and spawned the age of personalism and behaviorism

(Sanchez & Zam, 2006). The values clarification movement of the 1960s and Kohlberg's (1958) moral development approach had questionable results compared to the pre-World War II emphasis on character, but they did serve as a catalyst to finding more successful methods to teach at least the nuances of character (Smith, 1993). Ironically, the storytelling strategy remained in the hunt as a widely regarded impact method to balance many of the needs of moral education (Sanchez, 2004; Smith, 1993). Though hardly new from any perspective, storytelling began to experience a renaissance of sorts despite the fact that it had never actually been absent. But the damage, whether real or imaginary, nevertheless took its toll in that the strategy was too closely aligned with character education, which in turn generally scared off educators who feared crossing the newly drawn classroom line between church and state. Thus, storytelling seemingly took a back seat in the realm of effective methods.

A third possibility is put forth by Hamer (2000) who hypothesizes that the actual skill and artistry of storytelling has been devalued, culminating in a "deskilling" of the method among educators. That is, an underuse of the strategy has either resulted in or been the result of placing the power of teaching in the hands of curriculum specialists and textbook publishers whose only concern is content through standards-based education. This codependence has seemingly negated the value and use of historical storytelling in favor of a strictly parametered, student-centered perspective on learning. While this is not necessarily construed to be a disastrous situation, needlessly absent or at least underplayed is the magic to be experienced from a proven teacher-centered strategy.

From another perspective, Hamer (2000) reminds us that historical storytelling is an "oralized history that has been published (in textbooks) but is then told orally again" (p.21). It diverges from a standard, bland chronology of facts in that omits specific dates except as they may specifically relate to the rendition at hand. It is, in essence, actually "performed" rather than just "reported" as the teacher/storyteller "strives to create an oral presentation that will exist only in the moments of its being told in class" (p.22) while at the same time recognizing values and actions in a historical context. A connection is thus established between the historical and the personal in such a way as to transcend time through a rendition with a distinct moral message and characters to be emulated. Such is the power of storytelling that its effects may not be readily evident or measurable: "just because [students] don't speak of their reaction doesn't mean they haven't formed a relationship with that story" (Mittlelstadt, 2003, p.681). The history of the strategy indicates quite the opposite.

STATE OF THE ART FORM

For the social studies educator especially, a well-told story is an indispensable teaching strategy. It has the power to grab and hold interest, entertain, but, most importantly, instruct. Campbell (1988) noted the power of historical/cultural stories to impart important principles to a younger generation in that they are "about the wisdom of life" (p. 17). Storytelling differs from the conventional lecture in that it relates a deeply personal perspective: it literally becomes a psychological and emotional gift from the educator/teller to the student/listener (Lickona, 1991).

The historical stories comprising the American Experience have not only adventurous but also personal themes that transcend time in value relevance. Students are led to realize that heretofore one-dimensional figures experienced similar trials of anguish as they do. Such stories become value-laden tales of character whereby the central figures choose various courses of action that lead to certain consequences. Some choices proved beneficial while others did not, but they can serve as life lessons for the 21st century citizen.

Historical storytelling becomes more than teaching technology or solely relating information. Rather, it promotes conceptualization and understanding of the basic dynamics of an individual's values (Egan, 1989). Changes that occur during a character's life are due to decisions made regarding personal conflicts which in turn carry personally relevant truths for the listener (Sanchez & Zam, 2006; Henderson, 1964). The essence of the historical story compresses and emphasizes principles through dramatic action whose conditions enable students to examine and process issues brought forcefully to the forefront (Common, 1987). The organizing and teaching of history through storytelling becomes powerfully effective as the perpetuating adventure that it truly is. With citizenship education being the oft-stated goal of social studies, historical stories "are likely to attract the attention of teamers to arouse their interest, and to raise questions among them that lead to discussion and reflection about [citizenship] values" (Sanchez, 1998, p. 1). Such stories carry with them the explicit implication that humanistic decision-making resolves in one way or another the conflicts they contain in a way that establishes one's character as an American citizen. It is against the values and lessons found in historical stories that we have the opportunity to help guide our students in evaluating the landscape of American democracy itself, the very character of American culture, and, most importantly, the value implications for their own lives (Leming, 1996).

WHAT IS STORYTELLING AND HOW DO I DO IT?

Storytelling is the art form of using vocal skills of language, gestures, facial expressions, physical movement, and artifacts to effectively communicate a historical or cultural account in order to promote an audience's visual imagery in a co-creative process (Sanchez, 2009). This is based upon a prepared storyteller's rendition meshing with the audience's personal experiences and beliefs. The storyteller "tells" it, but the story "happens" in the mind of the listener who personally experiences it.

The bottom line, of sorts, is that the teacher tells a story, but there is certainly much more to this art form. To begin with, many social studies educators have the potential for being very good storytellers if they initially possess a passion for the historical which promotes a storytelling perspective; and that passion goes a long way. The teller in essence establishes a personal connection. But being a conventional historian- that is, one who relates the past to a relevant present- is not a prerequisite for being an effective teacher/ storyteller. While both are concerned with the story, a historian may be content with just recording the facts and letting the reader interpret the rendition. Thus, we have textbooks. The teacher/storyteller, on the other hand, verbally and passionately relates the tale through voice, gestures, and artifacts. It is not reading a story aloud, reciting a poem, or acting out a scene from a play, although historical and cultural storytelling does share some characteristics with these other art forms. Rather, the storyteller looks into the eyes of the prescribed audience and co-creates the tale with them (Ellyatt, 2002).

Such a narrative requires the listener to use imagery and imagination to co-create the rendition, in a virtual energy exchange between teller and listener, resulting in a true human connection. The intent is to promote the listener to personally experience the story, an event that will naturally vary from listener to listener, regardless of both the story itself and how it may be retold. The teller rarely imbues it the same way twice because the story will be embellished no matter how slightly from rendition to rendition, thus making it the "teller's own."

But if there are demands for more prescription to the method, there are some ground rules to consider. Outside of one's audience, of course, personal passion must be the first concern and is the prime difference between the effective storyteller and the ineffective one: he loves telling stories and loves the story at hand, which he can effectively use as a teaching/communication strategy. The teacher/storyteller, like the professional storyteller, does not read from a text and relies on the power of presence and the skills to promote narrative and visual imagery. But unlike the professional storyteller, the teacher/storyteller utilizes props such as pictures/photos, maps, or other artifacts to assist in the imagery. A picture of the central historical character, for example, is a vital reference point to help establish the evolution from one-dimensional to humanly multidimensional.

A GOOD STORY PLUS TECHNIQUE

Crucial to the mission of storytelling is initially having a good story to tell. Thus, there are technical elements to consider in organizing that good story amidst historical or fictional facts. Kennedy (1998) offers a perspective or general blueprint of five elements to consider:

- Characterization. The stories of history or culture are about real people, not abstractions, who are flesh and blood individuals with the same strengths and weaknesses of all humans. Unless the storyteller can imbue these individuals with dimension as the humans that they are, the audience will not be interested and will not identify with them.
- Connections. The storyteller must clearly establish the relationship between the character and the larger context of historical/cultural and personal significance. An example is John Adams's consequential role in defending the hated British in the Boston Massacre trial, a story that relates human strengths and frailties amidst an event that contributed to the birth of the republic and a future president (Sanchez, 2005).
- Conflict. There is usually a tense situation or dilemma leading the character to a showdown requiring value choices.
- Change. The conflict is resolved one way or another and not necessarily with a happy ending.
- Catharsis. There is a resolution often reflected by a dramatic release of tension that restores a balance of emotion.

The storyteller must sustain both the appeal and relevance of these elements through the connecting and transcending values inherent in the tale.

The technical elements of the story aside, memorization is an important initial issue in that a narrative should be comfortably memorized if it is not too long, though a comfortable length will vary from teller to teller. The problem with memorizing a "too long" piece is that the storyteller's focus tends to be merely on remembering the words in lieu of actually telling the story; and thus it becomes lost. Sanchez (2006) suggests that a pure story should not exceed fifteen to twenty minutes, unless the rendition features opportunities for listener interaction/involvement via strategically asked questions or comments by the teller, in which case the story could be significantly longer. Bauer (1993) further suggests that memorization of a story has a dependent factor: to make a story "your own" in the strictest sense by telling it in your own words is not recommended unless you are convinced that your phrasing is superior to the adapted version by a competent author. The teacher/storyteller should instead heavily depend on that version, but this does not imply that every word must be memorized. Rather, it may mean memorizing an introduction, conclusion, and specific key passages or phrases. A given story is plot-driven with a dependence upon specific actions and events. Familiarity with the plot solidifies the sequence of actions and events that in turn are related through the storyteller's own words. Visualizing the story as a set of pictures to be embellished into chosen words can be most beneficial to establishing this familiarity (Sanchez, 2009). Even as those words will experience some change with each subsequent rendition, there can be no mistakes per se and the story becomes your own.

There are also the purely physical elements to consider:

- The teacher/storyteller should manifest a confident presence (Sanchez, 2009b). Perhaps the greatest fear among beginning storytellers is forgetting something. Self-confidence should be promoted by the assurance that in all likelihood the teller is the only one who knows the story. The listener will thus not be cognizant of missing parts. In addition, the teller can always pick up a copy of the story for a glance that usually puts him back on track (Bauer, 1993).
- Voice inflection is a given. Even the most exciting story on paper can be killed by a monotone which will assuredly derail the endeavor. But it is highly recommended that the teller not take on any characterization of the central figure through accents or dialects (Bauer, 1993). The teller's modulation and inflection of descriptive language are enough to promote characterization.
- Eye contact is crucial and should be more or less constant. Looking into the eyes of listeners promotes both ownership and partnership in this co-creative endeavor.
- A selected set of facial expressions gives life to the story and interprets the multiple moods of the tale. Expressions allow the teller to give and express thought to "feeling" the events of the story, as well as showcasing the teller's personality to enhance specific moods (Bauer, 1993).
- Gestures in the form of a broad use of the hands and arms can assist in establishing the story's atmosphere and giving it psychological stability.
- The elements of pacing while utilizing the proper volume, modulation, and inflection, as well as strategically pausing are, needless to say, critical for dramatic effect and the mental digestion of the story itself.
- Physical movement may be debatable, but deliberate movement calculated to the point of being virtually choreographed is useful for plot-building, maintaining the flow of the narrative, and the physical comfort of the storyteller. Conversely, sitting while storytelling eliminates mobility but

may also help focus the listener's attention to the verbal impact (Bauer, 1993). It is strictly a matter of choice.

- A last element to consider is a fitting capstone to the others: practice. "No one can tell you how to learn a story or how to become an effective storyteller, for each of us has a method of his or her own. You will find, as in all endeavors, that the key lies in practice" (Bauer, 1993, p.54). But contrary to popular belief, practice does not make perfect; practice makes better.

Of great importance to the success of the storytelling strategy, however, is a point made in the previous chapter and bears repeating here: many if not all historical and cultural stories have a moral or value perspective by their nature. As such, they cannot be simply told without a follow-up on the opportunity to more closely examine and share those perspectives. Failing to do this is the biggest mistake educators make in using this strategy. A well-told story will provoke both interest and debate in regard to relevant values for the contemporary student. It will also serve to help conceptualize a complex set of ideas into an overall cohesive picture (Sanchez, 2009a; Cuban, 1984; Bowers, 1980; Ricoeur, 1977). Common (1987) further noted that:

> Our purpose as teachers of social studies is to create the conditions to enable our students to understand the issues and theories associated with the major themes in the body of knowledge we recognize as social studies... A story, through both its form and content, enables considerations clearly beyond those of process (p.41).

Thus, it is not enough to just tell a story that attracts the attention and arouses the interest of students, but rather to raise questions among them that lead to peer discussion and reflection (Sanchez, 1998). Only then can students fully analyze pertinent values as they may relate to their own lives and lead to humanistic decision-making that reflects the continuous efforts of our democratic society to perpetuate its citizenship ideals and create a basis for honoring diversity, promoting participatory citizenship, and encourage social justice (Sanchez, 2000a). As guides in this endeavor, however, educators must exercise caution by remembering that students will not, nor should they, have some moral authority looking over their shoulders dictating to them the right thing to do" (Lockwood, 2009, p. 89).

CONCLUSION

Storytelling may very well be the oldest and most effective of teaching strategies. It has linked humanity together through chains of narratives in which we are tellers or listeners or both (Fulford, 1998). It instructs by allowing values and belief systems to be examined and enforced, providing a sense of meaning and belonging (Ellyatt, 2002). "When stories are told, people react in subtle but shared ways to the message. That response is observed and felt by all in attendance. That is how the culture crafts itself over time" (Mittelstadt, 2003, p.682). The craft of storytelling in the social studies classroom is an art form that has an immeasurable payoff when properly executed and followed up. Like any other craft, the teacher/story-teller becomes more proficient with practice. The process of the craft re-quires an educator armed with the desire and knowledge to tell a story, but one that goes beyond the bland and claustrophobic textbook. To that end, Part 2 provides seventeen stories of the heroic lives of selected Americans needing only an effective teacher/storyteller to relate their tales. In the final analysis, a more comprehensive utilization of the storytelling strategy has the potential of two major benefits. First, history could regain its curricular prominence as an enduring, living discipline and a prime vehicle for citizen-ship education, instead of a perceived hodge-podge of names and dates to be memorized and tested. Second, educators can become reacquainted with an ancient but nevertheless enduringly effective teaching method.

Before proceeding to the stories, a word of explanation is merited con-cerning the subjects of this book. The choice of a hero/heroine is always a personal one for reasons that do not necessarily have credence with anyone else; in this case, the educators who will tell these stories or non-educators simply interested in these individuals. Not all of the set included represent my personal heroes/heroines. In point of fact, only two or three actually fall into that category. Rather, I have attempted to include a range of Americans whose lives and actions share the common factor of advancing the American Experiment and its ensuing values through their acclaimed heroism and in-formation not typically found in a textbook. Certainly others merit inclusion, but that is either the mission of another book or the choice of the teacher/ storyteller.

One will also note that none of the included individuals is a living, 21st century figure. This has been done purposively: "past" heroes/heroines re-veal transcendental links between their respective experiences and values and our own lives today. To promote their essence is to promote our own poten-tial. But why look back? As America entered the dark challenge of World War II, Wecter (1941) aroused a reeling country by stating that "a nation that cannot evoke the spirit of its dead heroes, in a time of crisis, is doomed" (p. 107). The purpose of this book hypothesizes that he is correct.

NOTES

Abrahamson, C. (1998). Storytelling as a pedagogical tool in higher education. *Education, 118(3): 440-459.*

Barton, K.C., and Levstik, L.S. (2004). *Teaching history for the common good.* Mahway, NJ: Lawrence Erlbaum, Assoc.

Bauer, C.F. (1993). *New handbook for storytellers.* Chicago and London: American Library Association.

Blount, H. (1992). Making history live for secondary students: Infusing people into the narrative. *The Social Studies, 83(5): 220-223. September/October.*

Bowers, C. (1980). Curriculum as cultural reproduction: An examination of metaphor as a carrier of ideology. *Teacher College Record, 82: 270-271.*

Campbell, J. (1988). *The power of myth.* New York: Doubleday.

Casement, W. (1986). Literature, irrationality, and the prospect of didacticism. *The Journal of General Education, 37:261-279.*

Chan, A. (1987). The art of the storyteller. *The Leader, 1: 1-6.*

Collins, R. (2003). Bridges, bull's-eyes, and dreams: Can the stories we tell make a difference? *Communication Studies 54(2): 121-131.*

Colombo, G., Lisle, B. & Mano, S. 1997). *Framework: Culture, storytelling, and college writing.* Boston: Bedford Books.

Combs, M., and Beach, J. (1994). Stories and storytelling: Personalizing the social studies. *The Reading Teacher, 47(6): 464-471. March.*

Common, D. (1987). Stories, teaching, and the social studies curriculum. *Theory and Research in Social Studies Education, XV(1):41.*

Cuban, L. (1984). *How teachers are taught.* New York: Longman.

Damon, W. (1988). *The moral child.* New York: Free Press.

Dewey, J. (1934). *A common faith.* New Haven: Yale University Press.

Egan, K. (1989). Memory, imagination, and learning: Connected by the story. *Phi Delta Kappan, 70: 455-459. September,*

Ellyatt, W. (2002). *Learning more about the power of narrative and storytelling.* New York: EBSCO Publishing.

Evans, R. (1989). Diane Ravitch and the revivals of history: A critique. *The Social Studies, 80:* 85-88.

Fitzgerald, F. (1979). *America revised.* Boston: Atlantic Monthly Press/Little, Brown.

Fulford, R. (1998). The heritage of storytelling. *Maclean's, 111(4): 80-84.*

Gramschi, A. (1983). *Prison notebooks.* New York: International Publishers.

Hamer, L. (2000). Oralized history: History teachers as oral history tellers. *The Oral History Review, 27(2)]' 19-37.*

Hamilton, M., and Weiss, M. (1990). *Children tell stories: A teaching guide.* Katonah, NY: Richard C. Owen.

Henderson, J. (1964). *Ancient myths and modern man.* New York: Doubleday.

Kennedy, D. (1998). The art of the tale: Storytelling and history teaching. *Reviews in American History, 26(2): 462-473.*

Kohlberg, L. (1958). The development of modes of moral thinking and choice in the years ten to sixteen. Unpublished doctoral dissertation, University of Chicago.

Leming, J. (1996). Paradox and promise in citizenship education. In Callahan and Banaszek (eds.), *Citizenship for the 21st Century, Bloomington, IN: ERIC.*

Lickona, T. (1991). *Educating for character: How our schools can teach for respect and responsibility.* New York: Bantam Books.

Lockwood, A.L. (2009). *The case for character education: A developmental approach.* New York: Teachers College Press.

Mittelstadt, J. (2003). Why I have spent my time in such ways: The ways of the storyteller. *The Reading Teacher, 56(7):680-682.*

Paul, R. (1988). Ethics without indoctrination. *Educational Leadership, 45(8): 10-19.*

Peck, J. (1989). Using storytelling to promote language and literacy development. *The Reading Teacher, November: 138-141.*

Percy, W. (1989). Interview. *The Chronicle of Higher Education,* May 10, 1989: A3-A5.

Postman, N. (1989). Learning by story. *The Atlantic, 264:119-124.*

Ricouer, P. (1977). *The rule of metaphor: Multidisciplinary studies of the creation of meaning of language.* Toronto: University of Toronto Press.

Sanchez, T. (1998). Using stories about heroes to teach values. *ERIC Clearinghouse for Social Studies/Social Science Education, EDO-SO-98-10.*

Sanchez, T. (2000a). It's time again for heroes. *The Social Studies, 91(2): 58-62. March/April.*

Sanchez, T. (2000b). Heroes, values, and transcending time: Using trade books to teach values. *Social Studies and the Young Learner, 13(1): 27-30. September/October.*

Sanchez, T. (2004). Facing the challenge of character education. *International Journal of Social Education, 19(2): 106-113. Fall/Winter.*

Sanchez, T. (2005). The story of the Boston massacre: An opportunity for character education. *The Social Studies, 96(6): 265-270.*

Sanchez, T. (2007). The depiction of Native Americans in recent (1991-2004) secondary American history textbooks: How far have we come? *Equity and Excellence in Education, November, 40(4):311-320.*

Sanchez, T. (2009a). Character education: A middle school responsibility? *Michigan Middle School Journal, 33(1):17-20.*

Sanchez, T. (2009b). "Tell me a story": Becoming reacquainted with a neglected art form. *Ohio Social Studies Review,* 45(1): 24-33.

Sanchez, T., and Mills, R. (2005). "Telling tales": The teaching of American history through storytelling. *Social Education, 69(5): 269-274.*

Sanchez, T., Zam, G., & Lambert, J. (2009). Storytelling as an effective strategy for teaching character education in middle school. *Journal for the Liberal Arts and Sciences, Spring, 13(2): 14-23.*

Sitton, T., Mehaffy, G. & Davis, O. (1983). *Oral history.* Austin: University of Texas Press.

Smith, R. (1993). An old moral education method rediscovered. *Education, 113(4):541, 550.*

Tomlinson, C., Tunnell, M. & Richgels, D. (1993). *The story of ourselves.* Portsmouth, NH: Heinemann.

Wecter, D. (1941). *The hero in America.* New York: Charles Schreibner's Sons.

Wells, G. (1986). *The meaning makers: Children learning language and using language. to learn.* Portsmouth, NH: Heinemann.

Willis, J. (1992). Lives and other stories: Neglected aspects of the teacher's art. *The History Teacher, 26(1):33-43. November.*

Zabel, M. (1991). Storytelling, myths, and folk tales: Strategies for multicultural inclusion. *Preventing School Failure, 32.*

Chapter Three

The Man Who Could Have Been King: George Washington

He is in many respects the quintessential American hero, but he humbly considered himself to be an ordinary man thrust into extraordinary circumstances requiring moral/value choices that we all similarly face. However, George Washington was much more. From many perspectives, Washington has earned his historical immortality in spite of his human frailties, his lifelong desire for status, and his disillusionment over the price he had to pay for it. But as one learns more about him, it becomes clear that "...[He] seems to be one of those illustrious heroes whom Providence raises up once in three or four hundred years..." (Butterfield, 1951, p.92), yet paradoxically he was also "a man imprisoned by his own celebrity" (Smith, 1994, p.6). Although there is much credence to the assertion that America might never have been without him, his life and deeds have come under close, scrutiny, but unlike most prominent figures he amazingly emerges mostly unscathed and above reproach (Parry, Allison & Skousen, 2009; Flexner, 1974).

The man who could have been king began his ascension to hero status as the third of seven children, but the first by his father's second wife. He was not born into wealth or a ruling family by any stretch of the imagination but rather into a very modest environment. His father was a successful land trader but also an insecure and restless man. But he adored George and George adored him. His self-centered mother, however, gave George little reason to love her, but love her he did. Though he remained devoted and respectful of her, they would clash over the years and long into his adulthood. Ironically, "he learned early from his mother how one's own actions affect the feelings of others. It was a lesson in decent human behavior that stood him well in his future career" (Meltzer, 1986, p.21). Living a fairly normal childhood, the opportunity for formal education bypassed him. This would remain the biggest regret of his life, no doubt magnified by future association with the intellectual giants of his time. What education he did receive was through informal tutoring and self-teaching, but he was always sensitive about his lack of a formal education (Parry, Allison & Skousen, 2009).

The first major turning point in his life came at age eleven when his beloved father suddenly died. Seemingly lost and seeking guidance, the youth turned to his older half-brother Lawrence, who readily took on the role of George's guide and benefactor. It would be Lawrence's consistent interventions that would open many doors to get him through the early rigors of growing up.

Washington's formal career began at age sixteen as a surveyor for the Virginia colony, a job that taught him, among other things, to be a great outdoorsman. The measure of land also taught him the value of it and though he lacked the funds, he became obsessed with its possession as the means to

social prestige (Ellis, 2004). It also honed one of his great talents. Few "had a passion for counting equal to [his]. During his whole life, he kept his eye on the number on the number of things. Every penny he owned and every foot of land was set down...in the most orderly and meticulous way" (Woodward, 1926, p.24). But after a few years, the surveying job wasn't working out, as he longed for something better. After careful deliberation, George decided he wanted a life of public service and proceeded to enlist in the British Army at the age of 19.

Historically, he first appears on the scene two years later at age 21 as a military messenger for the British, a position he attained not through merit or experience but by Lawrence's social conniving on his behalf. It was not the first or last instance of Lawrence's intervention, as it can be asserted that virtually every occupational and financial position he ever assumed found him unqualified and inexperienced (Ellis, 2004). Set at this stage of his life to being a soldier, Washington continued to display the self-proclaimed philosophies that not only set the standard for his values and character but also made him stand out from others. He firmly believed that one must "take care to perform the part assigned to us in a way that reason and their own consciences approve of" (Meltzer, 1986, p.61). His credo emphasized that "every action done in company ought to be done with some sign of respect for those that are present" (Ellis, 2004, p.9) and that character was not simply who one was but also what others thought one was. His character was exemplified by respect, responsibility, but mostly a deep faith in God (Lilliback, 2006). From his early upbringing, he embraced what would be a lifelong dedication to Christian faith which strongly influenced "his passion for self-discipline, self-control, and rectitude" (Lilliback, 2006, p.17). His faith in God ran deep and he never wavered to trust in divine intervention in his life pursuits (Parry, Allison & Skousen, 2009).

He was no saint, however, and could accurately be accused of "bottomless ambition and near obsession with self-control" (Ellis, 2004, p.38) that capped a keen desire for fame on his own terms, which is one avenue where he went wrong. He was about to learn that life does not play by our rules but rather its own. But there was no question of his intractable honor, duty, and integrity. Acquaintances could be assured that "Washington could be counted on to say little, but do the right thing" (Ellis, 2004, p.64). It quickly became evident that he could never refuse the responsibility and obligation to duty, a trait he would carry to the extreme.

Despite a decent but not spectacular military record, Washington felt slighted and unappreciated by the British, for whom he had bravely fought as a colonial in the French and Indian War. He summarily resigned from the military to pursue social status. Lawrence's death had netted him the eventual inheritance of Mount Vernon and he now devoted himself to being its squire, yet another position for which he totally lacked experience. Though

not knowing the first thing about farming or managing even a small operation like Mt. Vernon, he nevertheless looked the part. Physically majestic at
six-feet, four-inches tall (the average height being five-feet, six-inches), the
reddish-brown-haired but socially stiff gentleman took advantage of the opportunity to compete for and win the hand of Virginia's wealthiest widow,
Martha Custis. That arrangement sealed his stature with instant wealth and
social credibility, but it also proved to be a genuinely affectionate union with
a respected partner (Sanchez, 2006). Much has been made of Washington's
life-long infatuation with Sally Fairfax, his best friend's wife, but there is no
evidence that anything ever came of their relationship, nor of the three wom-
en who rejected his marriage proposals before Martha (Meltzer, 1986).

Life can indeed be grand and certainly those early years with Martha were
that: he became skilled at farming, expanded the acreage of Mount Vernon,
and thoroughly enjoyed the role of husband and step-father. He was also
losing a sizable amount of money on gambling. But the Squire of Mount
Vernon was about to enter the most tumultuous period of his life and, arguably, of the future of America. The American Revolution may arguably be
considered the most consequential event in our history, "the crucible within
which the political personality of the United States took shape. In effect, the
character of the man and the character of the nation congealed and grew
together during an extended moment of eight years" (Ellis, 2004, p.73). After
the first shots had been fired, the Second Continental Congress met to determine our course of action and all eyes were on him during the discussion for
appointing a military leader. Humbled and embarrassed by the open talk of
his qualifications, he left the chamber only to be dragged back in and was
unanimously elevated to the position of Commander-in-Chief of the yet-to-
be-created Continental Army, a position he reluctantly accepted. There was
an intense need for a symbol of colonial unity "who could consolidate the
disparate and even chaotic response of thirteen different colonies to the British threat... [H]e satisfied the requirements visually and politically more
completely than anyone else" (Ellis, 2004, p.69). It was readily conceded that
Benjamin Franklin was wiser than Washington. John Adams was better read.
Alexander Hamilton was far more brilliant. Thomas Jefferson was more
intellectually sophisticated. James Madison was certainly more politically
astute. Yet each of these men acknowledged that George was their unques-
tioned superior because they knew that he possessed the character necessary
for the struggle ahead (Ellis, 2004).

The Revolution would witness bleak moments, but "wherever history was
headed, he and America were going there together" (Ellis, 2004, p.74); and it
would be a bumpy ride. No military historian would ever rate him as a
genius. Lacking essential experience and knowledge of his British adversaries, he would lose far more often than he won in the early years. But "he was
blessed with personal qualities that counted most in a protracted war. He was

composed, indefatigable, and able to learn from his mistakes" (Ellis, 2004, p.74). His was "the triumph of a man who knows how to learn, not in the narrow sense of studying other people's conceptions, but if the transcendent sense of making a synthesis from the totality of the experience" (Flexner, 1974, p.82). Sharing his men's hardships through the incredibly desperate winters at Valley Forge and Morristown (where the desertion rate neared fifty percent) netted him universal respect and admiration. Against tremendous odds, his personal character roused the spirits of his troops and subordinate commanders, inspiring through his peerless though sometimes reckless courage. He refused to despair, believing that "Divine Providence will not permit [us] to fail" (Parry, Allison, & Skousen, 2009, p.155). He also began using creative and different battle strategies than those of the British, and timely victories emerged. As he relentlessly drove and inspired his way into the American pantheon, friend and foe alike realized "he could not be bribed, corrupted, or compromised" (Ellis, 2004, p.74).

Ultimate victory was, by many perspectives, miraculous. The reasons are numerous, but at the heart of them all is George Washington: he was the force that kept a ragtag army of farmers and patriots together through unthinkable trials; Washington's was the mind that saw the way to victory. "With faith and steadfastness he varied neither to the right or left. He pursued the ideal of liberty despite the dreadful trials of hunger, death, and freezing winter, despite mutiny and inconstant militia, despite deceit and severe financial loss. If Washington had done nothing more than lead his countrymen to victory, if his public life had begun and ended with the turbulent years of the Revolutionary War, his name would deserve to be celebrated and revered for countless generations to come (Perry, Allison & Skousen, 2009, pp.416-417).

Though several of Washington's worthy adjuncts merit some credit, he remained the human symbol that embodied the liberty we had just won (Ellis, 2004). A man of lesser integrity might easily have allowed his ego to preside, but it underlined the rare and exceptional character of the man to refuse to regard himself as the indispensable power of the Revolution. The reasons for his stellar behavior were so deeply ingrained in his character that they functioned like a normal biological condition that required no explanation (Ellis, 2004).

With the conflict over, the man who now regretted being a living legend and arguably the most famous individual in the world retired to Mount Vernon. But it would be impossible for him to remain a private citizen, as he had become "a figure deliberately set apart, wrapped in a paternal mystique until it became a psychological straightjacket" (Smith, 1992, p.3). His desire for fame was more than ever at odds with his disillusionment over its consequences.

The post-Revolution period would witness the rise of myths and legends that have pervaded time, but the true nature of Washington involved a reserved dignity that forbade familiarity and was sometimes interpreted as aloofness but mixed with a formal affability that inspired love and reverence (Lilliback, 2006; Smith, 1994). He was now a man who was also keenly aware that he was past his physical prime. His hair had turned white after eight years of virtually daily service but he still refused as always to wear a fashionable wig. His eyesight was failing and his hearing was unreliable, though few outside of Martha were aware. He had few intimates and preferred farming and gambling, losing much on both accounts. But he was also enjoying life again as a man who loved dancing, parties, hunting, his vintage Madeira, and- thanks to Jefferson- ice cream (Meltzer, 1986).

Two of the more enduring myths surfaced at this time. First is the issue of whether he ever told a lie. He not only told lies, he lived them. Indeed, no small part of his genius as a future statesman was his ability to convince everyone, including himself, that he was no leader (Smith, 1994). This deception was further fueled by his continuing sensitivity over his lack of formal education in regard to his personal writings, which had to be "intellectually sanitized" by himself and others before he would allow any publication of them.

Then there is the matter of his teeth; or, rather, the lack of them. He began to experience dental problems while in his 20s though it is unknown what those problems were. What is known is that he began losing teeth and eventually opted for dentures. The condition forced him to endure "near constant toothache caused by ill-fitting dentures that cause[d] his mouth to bulge and his lips to clamp shut in unsmiling repose" (Smith, 1994, p.3). John Adams, who had a love-hate relationship with Washington, claimed that Washington lost his teeth as the result of cracking his beloved Brazil nuts between his jaws (Smith, 1994) (there is an irony in this assertion in that Adams had no teeth himself). By the time of his presidency, he had one tooth left and alternated using dentures fashioned from cow's teeth, hippopotamus teeth, and even human teeth, but not from the wood of lore (it is interesting to speculate about his apparent vanity over keeping one tooth). The dentures were constructed to fit over his one remaining tooth but caused more or less constant pain for which he regularly took (and may have been addicted to) laudanum, the most powerful painkiller of the time. Such was his discomfort that when posing for numerous portraits or busts, he removed the dentures and stuffed his mouth with cotton.

As to Parson Weem's imaginative rendition of the cherry tree, it can unhesitatingly be dismissed. Likewise, it is also easy to dismiss the tale of his hurling a dollar across the Potomac, not only because of the physical impossibility but due to the fact that he was a most frugal man.

Washington did not believe the Revolution was over simply because the fighting had stopped. By 1787 it was clear that the Articles of Confederation could not sustain the new nation, which was basically operating as thirteen separate nations; and not very well. He believed that America was destined to be "a historical experiment in representative government larger than any single person, larger than himself..." (Ellis, 2004, p. 143) and that only a powerful but limited and small central government derived from the consent of the people could secure the goals which we had fought for in 1776. To that end, he began hosting informal gatherings to convince others that a new government should be the goal. His singular stature played a decisive role in the calling of the Constitutional Convention and his subsequent and necessary appointment as its chair. His character and credibility were stabilizing factors though he was the least involved in the proceedings. He had to be there if America was to have a future. His very presence not only radiated authority but helped secure the creation of the U.S. Constitution (Ellis, 2004; Meltzer, 1986).

If the concept of America was a work in progress, he also realized that the ratification of the Constitution would require his further service as the first president (Ellis, 2004). His public modesty kept him from readily seeking the office but he was ready to serve for one reason: considering himself first and foremost an American, "his one concern was to make American succeed and to do it peacefully" (Meltzer, 1986, p. 152). Only as proof against all tyranny would he consider to be the first chief executive, knowing he would forge it based upon his own high standards with interests greater and nobler than self-interests, and in constant fear that failure would destroy the new fragile republic. His unanimous electoral selection demonstrated that one individual could provide a symbolic solution acceptable to all sides. He was not chosen for what he thought, but only for who he was (Ellis, 2004).

As both a symbol of continuity and an instrument of change, Washington was his country's greatest asset and in many respects its only glue. His goal was to make the promise of America survive and prosper. At the outset, the American Experiment was all hope, looking for a leader "to transform the improbable into the inevitable" (Ellis, 2004., p. 189). He was that man. The specter of monarchy would plague his administration, especially as the political culture became partisan. But the republic would succeed because of his stature and devotion. He believed that he had earned the right to be trusted with national power without abusing it, as he had proven before, and he was always aware that his responsibility was to the fledging nation. Also aware that every move would be a precedent, his leadership skills centered on delegating power to qualified minds and seeking counsel when necessary, but he was no bit player or puppet in the wings, as some historians describe him (Smith, 1994). He was sufficiently confident in his abilities and knew when to avoid conflict as the essence of executive leadership. In the end, he would prove to be more visionary than any of his battling subordinates and contemporaries.

With his highest public priority being the creation of a unified American nation, he very reluctantly agreed to pursue a second term on the belief that his country needed him to serve again (Parry, Allison & Skousen, 2009). That too would set a precedent for all future two-term presidents, as his second electorally unanimous term proved to be far more difficult and disappointing than the first, engendering political and public criticism over foreign troubles and domestic strife (Ellis, 2004). But he was obsessed with the importance of leaving office alive. "Washington believed that by stepping down [after a second term] instead of dying in office, he would create a peaceful turnover of power by election, unlike the monarchy who handed down power" (Flexner, 1974, pp.260-261). Despite the exaggerations of his age and alleged diminished mental powers, he left office as he came in: dignified, defiant, and decisive; and confident about where history was taking us (Ellis, 2004). It was his sheer character alone that decisively guided the republic the crises of the early years by stressing, his "deep feelings about the need for morality and virtue among Americans" (Parry, Allison & Skousen, 2009, p.496).

Retired to private life once more, Washington was cognizant that as a living legend he would remain public property. One last but enduring issue of "moral numbness" now consumed him. Like many of the Founding Fathers, he remained a slave-owner despite his support that "all men are created equal." Posterity's judgment of him depended on setting this issue right as much as any decision he had made as president (Ellis, 2004). He would maintain that his hesitancy- past and present- to free his slaves was a matter of economic considerations outweighing moral considerations. To successfully compete in the agricultural economy, he concluded that he had no viable choice but to own slaves, even though it was morally reprehensible to Washington for one human to own another (Parry, Allison & Skousen, 2009). His ultimate reasoning to this dilemma evidently eased his suffering conscience: Mount Vernon would persistently run in the red (it rarely showed a profit), mostly because he was supported his approximately two hundred slaves and refused to sell them for fear of breaking up families, a practice that allegedly almost mined him financially. This economic "solution" does not exonerate him and is somewhat contradictory in that although he had a cash flow problem, he was still a wealthy man, probably America's first millionaire (Sanchez, 2006). Ultimately, the issue was resolved when his slaves were freed under the terms of his (and Martha's) will as a final testament to the human values he espoused most (Ellis, 2004). The slavery issue, however, still remains a controversy in his overall evaluation.

Upon his death, the eulogy .of "first in war, first in peace, and first in the hearts of his countrymen" elegantly summed up the achievements upon which his legacy rests: leading the victory for American independence, securing the principles of '76 by supporting the creation of the Constitution, and overseeing the birth of the republic as it first chief executive. He was the central figure in early America and performed as no one else could have. The minor misjudgments he made were outbalanced by his major military/political decisions which proved to be invariably correct, and he was that rarity who devoted himself to getting the big things right (Ellis, 2004). In short, George Washington was the strong leader of a weak nation. His vision of the American republic was in many ways an extension of his own character. Because he credited harsh self-discipline in realizing his personal destiny, he embraced an energetic government as the only means of protecting the American union from flying apart. Because he balanced executive vigor with personal restraint, he gave us a government strong enough to lead and wise enough to listen (Smith, 1994).

Certainly Washington was no saint, but despite his personal shortcomings he singlehandedly redefined the idea of greatness and heroism. The man who could have been king believed that ultimate power lay with the people and proved it by calmly walking away from it without regret. His enduring values were demonstrated in conceding his humanity to the final judgment of the people and faith in God. Thus while in his own mind he may have been an ordinary man thrust into extraordinary circumstances, he was possessed of values and character that prompted him to rise to the occasion.

DISCUSSION GUIDELINE QUESTIONS

1. How does the story reflect more dimension and humanity in Washington? Why was it evidently necessary to invent myths concerning him?
2. What values were depicted in his life that won him the support of others?
3. Where did he learn his values?
4. Are these values still important today?
5. What may have been his greatest character trait?
6. What evidence is there that indicates that Washington struggled with certain moral dilemmas? Are they similar to moral decisions that must be made today?
7. Did he make any wrong moral/value choices? If so, what were the consequences?
8. Doing the right thing was obviously important to him. Is this value as important today?
9. Why might Washington's character be important enough to examine or model today? Are there any individuals on the scene today who are similar in character to him? Why or why not?

REFERENCES

Ellis, J. (2004). *His excellency George Washington.* New York: Alfred J. Knopf.

Flexner, J. (1974). *Washington: The indispensable man.* Boston: Little, Brown.

Lilliback, P. (2006). *George Washington's sacred fire.* Bryn Mawr, PA: Providence Forum Press.

Meltzer, M. (1986). *George Washington and the birth of our nation.* New York: Franklin Watts.

Parry, J., Allison, A. & Skousen, W. (2009). *The real George Washington.* New York: National Center for Constitutional Studies.

Sanchez, T. (2006). The man who could have been king: A storyteller's guide for character education. *Journal of Social Studies Research, 30(2): 3-9.*

Smith, R. (1994). The surprising George Washington. *Quarterly of the National Archives, 26:3-11.*

Woodward, W. (1926). *George Washington: The image and the man.* New York: Boni and Liveright.

Chapter Four

The Father of the American Revolution: Samuel Adams

He is best known today as a beer, which is a most unfortunate misnomer, for Samuel Adams was much more than a brewer. He is not as renowned as his contemporaries, such as Washington, Franklin, Jefferson, or even his second cousin John, yet in his own time he was widely considered worthy of the title of Father of the American Revolution (Puls, 2006). His life would exemplify patriotism, religious spirit, and virtue of character, and the religious over-tones he embodied are crucial to understanding the winning of American independence. Liberty, virtue, and piety underscore the reason why Colonial America continually fought in the face of despair and defeat yet ultimately triumphed (Stoll, 2008). History has more or less consigned Adams to an undervalued place but modem America can identify in his mixture of religion with politics, his skepticism of a powerfully large federal government, his warnings of extravagance and the influence of money on elections, his recog-nition of the power of a free press, and his spirited endurance to win a war for freedom (Stoll, 2008).

He was born quite inauspiciously in 1722 in Boston, the fourth of twelve children but only one of three who survived beyond age two. His father was involved in local politics as a representative to the provincial assembly which proved to be a harbinger to Samuel's future, as the younger Adams's political views would parallel his father's orientation towards colonial rights (Miller, 1936). Though Harvard-educated, he bucked the family hope of becoming a Protestant minister and instead unsuccessfully attempted various commercial business ventures (Stoll, 2008). His apparently utter disinterest in making money or keeping it led to bankruptcy (Maier, 1980). Samuel would then work briefly as his father's partner in the family malthouse business, but only as a malster and not the contemporarily portrayed brewer of beer (Baron, 1962).

To support his young wife and family, Adams ironically became a Boston tax collector for twelve years. Yet he often failed to collect designated taxes from his fellow colonists, a move that made him popular while at the same time making him personally liable for shortages (Alexander, 2002). But it was this position that led him simultaneously down the path of politics and newspaper writing. Recognizing the power of the press as a political weapon, Adams quietly acquired stature in Boston politics, proving early on that he was a significant writer and thinker but more so a very practical politician. Through the key positions as a Boston clerk and the Massachusetts House of Representatives, he firmly established himself as a force to be reckoned with.

The major turning point for both Adams and the future America was the end of the French and Indian War in 1763 which led to England's ensuing attempts to pay for it. It would be the reaction to the Stamp Act (1765) and the customs crackdown that propelled Samuel Adams to first burst onto the

public scene as an opponent of Parliament. He was more than eager to lead the gathering clash with George III, asserting correctly that the taxation without representation issue would inevitably reduce colonial rights and lead to conflict. Perhaps above all other colonials, Adams worked feverously on the political and press fronts to constantly defend and advance colonial liberty from the threat of burdening taxation (Fowler, 1997; Stoll, 2008). Bolstering his stance was his alliance with James Otis, who was also emerging as a bold defender of colonial rights, though Adams would far surpass him in such boldness (Alexander, 2002).

As events which would lead to open conflict took their turn, Adams advanced his great enthusiasm for freedom through the press: "For true patriots to be silent is dangerous" (Cushing, 1908, p.74). His writings clearly reflected his unwavering belief that "the laws of God and nature are the only true basis of all government" (Cushing, 1908, p.153), yet though he was "the symbol of the religiously passionate Founding Father, the flaw of his religious perception was not accepting or being tolerant of all religions (Stoll, 2008). This was his dark side, as he openly resented Catholicism as well as non-believers with near hostility. But for depth of purpose and zeal, Adams had no equal as the pillar of the colonial cause. In our darkest moments- and there would be many- he was a man of "deep religious conviction whose confidence, zeal, and endurance in the struggle for freedom were grounded in a belief that an intervening God was on [our] side" (Stoll, 2008, p.9), and never believing for a moment that we stood alone. George Washington may have been destined to be the fighter and human face of the struggle, but Adams would be our moral conscience.

The Boston Massacre (1770) and the Boston Tea Party (1773) provided Adams with the opportunity to take the colonial lead in arguing, organizing, and blatantly planning against the British (Stoll, 2008). Seizing the moment with the former incident, he immediately and aggressively pressed to wring every possible ounce of political advantage from the bloodshed to rouse the colonial ire. The latter incident, which featured his "offspring," the Sons of Liberty, presented itself as yet another opportunity to advance the cause of independence and a fervent yet nonviolent colonial opposition to ensuing British reprisals. But these events were merely a prelude.

Gathering to formally make their case against taxation without representation and infringements on religious freedom, the First Continental Congress (1774) showcased Adams's stance of being further down the road to independence at this point than many of the delegates who later became known as Founding Fathers (Stoll, 2008; Raphael, 2004). That body's willingness for more serious action was indicated by the agreement to meet again in 1775, but a peaceful conclusion was not to be and Adams' life was about to drastically change.

By the time of the "shot heard 'round the world," the "slightly heavy, gray-haired fifty-five-year-old with large dark blue eyes, prominent nose, and high forehead" (Stoll, 2008, p.3) had suffered personal losses that would have deterred many a man: his first wife and four of their six children had died of natural causes and he was increasingly forced to spend prolonged amounts of time on colonial business away from his second wife and surviving children. In addition, Adams had aligned himself with John Hancock to become in the eyes of the British the leading rebels in the Colonies. Their strange political partnership would serve many purposes and benefit both men, but it would soon inexplicably unravel, probably due to the wide disparity in their economic status (in point of fact, Adams was probably the most financially poor of the Founding Fathers). The rift would eventually be mended near Hancock's death, but for the moment, this tandem was viewed as the most serious rebel threat to colonial subservience. The British attempt to capture them in April 1775 prompted Paul Revere's famous ride. "Paul Revere's primary mission was not to alarm the countryside. His specific purpose was to warn Samuel Adams and John Hancock, who were thought to be the objects of the [British] expedition" (Fischer, 1994, p.95). Though the two rebels escaped, the opening shots of the Revolution were fired, ushering in a new phase of the struggle and making Adams both a virtual refugee and a hunted man (Stoll, 2008).

Undaunted, Adams's role as a prominent leader became clear as the Second Continental Congress began the task of managing a war. This cumbersome, consuming effort sorely affected his unwavering faith in God and a seven-year separation from his family; and only his great and unwavering Puritan faith allowed him to cope. Faith and family were his constants and he openly stressed and lived the connection between private virtue and public action (Stoll, 2008). Stating that "we shall never be abandoned by Heaven while we act worthy of its aid and protection" (Puls, 2006, p.44), Adams was certain that God would intervene in our behalf but only if we did our share by action of virtue.

The fight for independence would demand a high price of courage, sacrifice, and time. Adams's bold assertion that "we have proclaimed to the world our determination to die freemen; rather than slaves" (Hosmer, 1980, p.336) had been preceded by the Declaration of Independence, which formally rationalized our course of action. Jefferson, of course, merited most of the credit for its writing, yet much of the content followed phrases and arguments advanced by Adams in his newspaper writings for more than a decade before 1776. But it was Adams who openly expressed the understanding that declaring independence was dependent upon winning and maintaining it. That, in turn, would require behaving in a manner worthy of the freedom that they sought as the freemen that they purported to be and the grueling military endeavor that would indeed try men's souls (Stoll, 2008).

As the war raged, Adams's abilities, judgments, but mostly his patriotic reputation propelled him to leadership, but as a result his health and strength began ebbing and in no small manner helped by the long separation from his family. Still he continued, asserting that he would never decline serving his new country (Cushing, 1908). That service would see him take on the additional burden of formulating the constitution of Massachusetts, an endeavor that required his active participation on twelve separate committees (Stoll, 2008). Though Cousin John handled the brunt of the proposal, Cousin Sam authored the controversial section concerning the relations between church and state. The resulting document not only featured more checks and balances than any previous charter, but would also prove to be "one of the great enduring documents of the American Revolution" and "the oldest functioning written constitution in the world" (McCullough, 2001, p.225). Indeed, it is still referred to by the U.S. Supreme Court on matters of national importance and legal implications (Stoll, 2008).

Just before the Battle of Yorktown (1781) ended the military aspect of the war, Adams finally left the Second Continental Congress after prolonged service, but he would immediately return to Massachusetts under its new constitution as state senator and president of the state senate. He was not yet sixty years old and had devoted over twenty-three years of public service, ranging from tax collector to newspaperman to battling taxation acts to forging the foundation of a new nation. Yet he would have almost twenty years more of serious work ahead, which would entail securing a proper course for his home state while helping to establish a new country.

From Adams's perspective, the new America faced two main threats under the guiding Articles of Confederation. The first would be local uprisings, which in his mind would be prompted by the second: a decline of character among the citizenry (Stoll, 2008). The former would be embodied in Shay's Rebellion in his own beloved Massachusetts, even while he was determined to stave off the latter through a continuing campaign on virtue and religion which were consistent with his professed principles of civic behavior. He urged a hard stance against the uprising while emphasizing the impact of character on our new foreign relations. But America was floundering for another reason.

The utter failure of the Articles led to the Constitutional Convention in 1787, but Adams would be conspicuously absent, even though he knew and agreed that revision of the Articles was necessary. He had always been a staunch defender of state/local rights (a stance so radical that modern historians have compared his vigor to Malcolm X) (Stoll, 2008). He further held a deep skepticism of a revised and more powerful central government, even though the framers would fashion a structure remarkably similar to the one that Adams had helped draft for Massachusetts more than seven years earlier (Stoll, 2008). That skepticism would be tempered by his realization of the proposed U.S. Constitution's ultimate worth to the American Experiment along with the knowledge that if Massachusetts rejected it, the fledging nation would be doomed. For this reason and the promise of a proposed Bill of Rights to which he contributed, Adams used his exceptional influence to support ratification, asserting that "it is essential that the people should be united in the federal government, to withstand the common enemy, and to preserve their valuable rights and liberties" (Cushing, 1908, p.244).

In the meantime, Adams had assumed the Massachusetts governorship upon the death of his former rival John Hancock's death in 1783 and would be elected in his own right three more times. He fervently continued to promote property rights, religion, and liberty, extending the latter to those who would be deprived of it in other states due to racial prejudice (Stoll, 2008). Unlike many of his Founding Father contemporaries who owned slaves or waited until their deaths to free them, Adams demonstrated through action that liberty must also apply to African- Americans (Wells, 1866). He additionally viewed education as "an engine of egalitarianism [to demonstrate] the moral and religious duties [people] owe to God, their Country, and to all Mankind" (Cushing, 1908, p.351), taking the radical step of making provisions for the schooling of females, though that endeavor was still not equal to males.

Adams's palsy- probably essential tremor, a nerve disorder causing uncontrollable shaking- had worsened over the past twenty years and he had long had to dictate his writings and correspondence. But he continued to be a challenge and moral conscience to his opponents even in his fading years. Upon his death in 1803, Adams was fittingly buried in Boston near Hancock and the victims of the Boston Massacre. Even his detractors had to concede that no individual contributed more to achieving American independence, prompting at least one historian to later note that this great rebel had "the greatest part in the greatest revolution in the world" (Bancroft, 1866, p.59).

Though he never held national office or even served as an ambassador, the character and values of Samuel Adams reflect the true history of the American Revolution. Following his steadfast defense of religious freedom, property rights, limited government, and taxes imposed only by elected representatives, America has prospered like no other nation. His Puritan influence may make him remote in a past to present connection, but he has given modern America a vital legacy:

> We can see Samuel Adams today when we see Americans for whom religion is central to their lives. We can see him when we encounter Americans who have higher values than material possessions. We can see him when we see what leaders and individuals around the world endure amid great risks in revolutions for freedom. These may not be qualities that correspond neatly to today's political factions, but they are aspects of the American spirit and, Samuel Adams would add, of the human one (Stoll, 2008, p.265).

DISCUSSION GUIDELINE QUESTIONS

1. What values are specifically depicted in his story?
2. Where did he learn his values?
3. Are his values still important today?
4. What may have been iris greatest character trait?
5. What was his greatest flaw?
6. What evidence is there that indicates that Adams had to struggle with certain moral dilemmas?
7. Are our value struggles similar to the ones he experienced?
8. How and why might Adams have compromised his values?
9. Why might his values and character be important enough to examine or model today?
10. Are there any individuals on the scene today who are similar in character to him? Why or why not?

NOTES

Alexander, J. (2002). *Samuel Adams: America's revolutionary politician.* Lanham, MD: Rowman & Littlefield.

Bancroft, G. (1866). *History of the United States from the discovery of the American continent.* Boston: Little, Brown.

Baron, S. (1962). *Brewed in America: The history of beer and ale in the United States.* Boston: Little, Brown.

Cushing, H. (ed.) (1908). *The writings of Samuel Adams.* New York: G.R. Putnam's Sons.

Fischer, D. (1994). *Paul Revere's ride.* New York: Oxford University Press.

Fowler, W. (1997). *Samuel Adams: Radical puritan.* New York: Longman.

Hosmer, J. (1980). *Samuel Adams.* New York: Chelsea House.

Maier, P. (1980). *The old revolutionaries: Political lives in the age of Samuel Adams.* New York: Knopf.

McCullough, D. (2001). *John Adams.* New York: Simon and Schuster.

Miller, J. (1936). *Sam Adams: Pioneer in propaganda.* Boston: Little, Brown.

Puls, M. (2006). *Samuel Adams: The father of the American Revolution.* New York: Palgrave.

Raphael, R. (2004). *Founding myths: Stories that hide our patriotic past.* New York: The New Press.

Stoll, I. (2008). *Samuel Adams: A life.* New York: Free Press.

Wells, W. (1866). *The life and public services of Samuel Adams.* Boston: Little, Brown.

Chapter Five

The American Rascal:
Benjamin Franklin

The Founding Fathers are frequently viewed as a formally stiff band of near-mythological beings descending from Mount Olympus to engage in extraordinary events before retreating back to hallowed ground for commoners to worship from a distance. Benjamin Franklin, however, presents an alternative picture as a man different from the others and in a class by himself. He relates far more humanity and approachability than his counterparts, allowing us to accept him as one of us. He literally winks at us through a chattiness and rascality that enable us to readily identify with him today (Isaacson, 2003). His life gives us many opportunities to perceive him in contemporary terms, for he was most certainly the most transcendent and versatile of his generation. During his eighty-four years, he was our leading scientist, inventor, diplomat, writer, and business strategist, all of which were underlined by his strongest suit: being a practical thinker. But perhaps his most interesting invention was his keen ability to perpetually reinvent himself.

Though "born and bred a member of the leather-aproned class, Franklin was, for most of his life, more comfortable with artisans and thinkers than with the established elite" (Isaacson, 2003, p.3), a stance that allowed him to comfortably straddle both sides. Yet his self-identity was always grounded in a common perspective: he always preferred to be referred to as "B. Franklin, printer." It was this common stance that supported his most important vision and philosophy of life: an American identity solidly based on the virtues and values of its middle class (Isaacson, 2003). This vision provides a contemporary connection to us but it was further bolstered by his life-long belief that his morality was dependent on a sincere belief in leading a virtuous life, serving the country he so loved, and hoping to achieve salvation through good works (Isaacson, 2003).

He was born on January 17, 1706, as the eleventh of thirteen children and the youngest son of the youngest son for five generations. His family's migration from England was predictably motivated by both religious freedom and economic desire. Young Franklin was originally slated to study for the ministry, but it quickly became apparent that he was totally unsuited for it

due to his increasingly wide variety of interests, all of which he approached from a practical perspective. Such a perspective would serve him best as a future inventor but it would first crucially hone his training and experience as a printer, publisher, and newspaperman. Indeed, he would become the most popular writer in Colonial America with a self-taught style of rascality and conversational prose that was powerfully direct. That, however, was only his immediate future.

After five years as an apprenticed printer in New York, Franklin took the risk of becoming a runaway to Philadelphia where his future awaited him. His initial struggle upon his arrival was smoothed by his character. Even at age seventeen, "his most notable trait was a personal magnetism that attracted people who wanted to help him and he proved to be a consummate networker. Never shy, and always eager to win friends and patrons, he consistently and gregariously exploited his charm" (Isaacson, 2003). Though he was "a self-centered and self-willed man [he] moved through life at a calculated pace toward calculated ends" (Franklin, 2001, p.79). He benefited from a self-deprecating humor with an unpretentious and disarming conversational approach that garnered him many friends. He made fewer enemies than most, but enemies he would have. But though he easily made friends and acquaintances, Franklin was far less adept at forming bonds that required deep emotional commitments, especially within his own family. He would painfully find that this flaw would haunt him throughout his life.

Like most of the Founding Fathers, and contrary to current academic belief, Franklin had a deep faith in God. However, he abandoned common Puritan theology in that he believed one discovered God's truth through reason and studying nature; that religious ceremonies/practices were beneficial if they encouraged good behavior and morality (Isaacson, 2003). God was best served through good works and helping others. His was not a profound moral or religious philosophy, but he nevertheless repeatedly and increasingly asserted his creed of a virtuous, moral, and pragmatic belief in a supreme God for whom the most acceptable service was doing good for one's fellow man (Isaacson, 2003). Religion was therefore fine with him but only if it made men better and improved society. It is no surprise then that religion, virtue of character, and civic virtue merged into a single philosophy that became his essence: being civic-minded, caring about public behavior, and valuing collective action (Brooks, 2000; Schneider, 1958). It would be with this organizational/collective attitude that he would help galvanize the American Experiment (Isaacson, 2003).

Franklin never wavered in his advocacy of truth and sincerity, and was a virtual "patron saint of self-improvement guides" (Isaacson, 2003, p.48). His ascension to publisher of the Pennsylvania Gazette provided him an initial vehicle with which to seek and promote truth, virtue, and social betterment. An additional vehicle in this mission was his soon-to-be-published *Poor*

Richard's Almanac (1732), which not only promoted virtue but also made him money. Its twenty-five-year run would prove to be Colonial America's first great humor classic. But perhaps inevitably, he was also becoming increasingly political in the pursuit of truth: "Printers are educated in the belief that when men differ in opinion, both sides ought equally to have the advantage of being heard by the pubic" (Franklin, 2001, p.75).

Ever the practical man, it was only after he established himself in the printing business at age twenty-four that he took a wife, the faithful Deborah. Lore relates that she had laughed at him seven years before when he stumbled upon entering Philadelphia as a runaway (Isaacson, 2003). But Deborah had an estranged husband, and the couple feared possible or unexpected bigamy charges. Though it never materialized, their resultant forty-four-year marriage remained common law, an arrangement that symbolized Franklin's adversity to deep emotional commitments. Their union was less a marriage than it was a mutually collaborative partnership, and certainly not as celebrated as the model marriage between John and Abigail Adams (Isaacson, 2003). Benjamin and Deborah's enduring union was based upon a respect for each other's independence, but to a miserable fault: for fifteen of the last seventeen years of their union, Franklin would be conspicuously absent, even when she died.

Two major complications arose early for the couple and would have a profound effect on them both. The first was the "great inconvenience" (Isaacson, 2003, p.101) of the illegitimate birth of Franklin's first son, William, whose full paternity would remain a mystery. Though William would represent a perpetually dark episode in Franklin's life, Franklin must also be given credit at the outset for taking financial responsibility for him, something that understandably cannot be said for Deborah.

The second complication was initially joyous: the birth of their son, Francis (called Frankie). The child would tragically die at age four, creating a void in Franklin that he was never able to fill. Frankie's memory was one of the few to cause him ongoing anguish. But eleven years after their son's death, their daughter Sarah (called Sally) arrived and would be Franklin's pride and joy. His uncharacteristically close emotional relationship with her symbolized his lifelong habit of nurturing non-family youth, especially females, as if they were his children.

Growing restless by age forty-two, Franklin "retired" from the printing trade to pursue the interests that would bring him both personal satisfaction and international fame: politics, diplomacy, and especially science. His scientific interests were driven by pure curiosity and the sheer thrill of discovery and he would be celebrated as the most famous scientist of his time, on the same level as such notables as Newton and Watson (Isaacson, 2003). He would take such pleasure in his discoveries and inventions that he refused to patent them, wishing instead to share them with all. This was especially true with his Franklin stove, bifocal glasses, and the first urinary catheter used in North America (Isaacson, 2003).

But it was his practical approach to proving the connection between lightning and electricity that led to a breakthrough of historic significance; namely, that electricity is a single fluid and that lightning is a form of it that could be harnessed via a lightning rod. This was aptly but dangerously demonstrated by his 1752 kite/key/wet string experiment, an event from which he luckily emerged alive. The resultant lightning rod invention made him worldfamous and ensuing honorary degrees would follow to net him the distinguished title of Dr. Franklin (which was always how he was addressed by the Founding Fathers).

Politically, Franklin espoused "volunteerism and limited government, but also that there was a legitimate role for government fostering the common good" (Isaacson, 2003, p.148). Though his strength as a political thinker was far more practical than abstract, what made him a rebel was his natural resistance to authority. He was among the first to view the Thirteen Colonies as a potentially unified nation, that colonists might have to go it alone without reliance- or subservience- to Britain, and that the Colonies could certainly accomplish more if they were united. From this sprang his civic belief in encouraging and providing opportunities for all to succeed based on their ambition, virtue, and hard work, all of which would enable them to rise socially. Thus, before it even had a title, Franklin espoused the American Dream.

Always eager to promote colonial unity, Franklin helped devise the Albany Plan of Union, which featured a representative congress and a president based on the concept of federalism. Though it was rejected, its principles would later resurface to make Franklin a major player in the American Experiment.

Despite being a sloppy, disorderly man, Franklin's personal virtue would come under considerable attack due to his flirtatious nature with young women (some would say all women), enough to earn him a reputation for lecherousness yet not infidelity to his wife (Isaacson, 2003). But it was apparent that it was only with females that he could approach any semblance of a lasting relationship (Lopez and Herbert, 1975). Interestingly, Franklin thrived on this repute and continuously exploited it to his advantage throughout his life.

Perpetually torn "between his professed desire to acquire the virtue of humility and his natural thirst for acclaim" (Isaacson, 2003, p. 171), Franklin now moved confidently forward into the diplomatic arena. It appeared to be a natural role for him, as he was famously proficient at defusing turmoil. But this skill would initially fail him as a pre-Revolution diplomat to Britain, though he persevered there virtually fifteen years. Franklin correctly assessed that the increasing tension between Britain and the Colonies was due to the latter being shamelessly exploited as a market. He thus proposed that the Colonials be treated as full citizens of the Empire with equal liberties, rights, and economic considerations. Of course, it was soundly rejected but Franklin's position was clear and he continually but futilely pressed the issue right up to the Revolution.

Then he stumbled. The Stamp Act (1765) was the first major internal tax imposed on the Colonies and while Franklin clearly recognized the impending danger of "taxation without representation," he disastrously misplayed his stance by agreeing with it, a move that seriously tarnished his credibility at home. For the first time, the Act transformed and galvanized the Colonies into thinking and reacting as a collective unit. Facing the daunting task of diplomatic damage control, Franklin took advantage of a chance for redemption by dramatically and brilliantly presenting the colonial case against the Act directly to Parliament, an event that led the British to repeal it and restored his reputation as an effective ambassador. He had risen to the occasion- and not for the last time- but he further erred by basically recognizing Britain's plan to impose external taxes.

By the early 1770s, separatist sentiments were rapidly growing and though Franklin considered himself "too much of an American" (Smyth, 1970, p.234) and too little of a British subject, he was not yet willing to advocate a total break from Britain. Perhaps it was because his mind and efforts were on other endeavors. At age sixty-five, he had written *The Autobiography of Benjamin Franklin,* a work in letter form that "flowed as a string of wry anecdotes and instruction lessons.., with a mix of wry detachment and amused self-awareness" (Isaacson, 2003, p.256). Popular as it was, its simplicity was interestingly its shortcoming as Colonials were more focused upon the approaching break. But as was the case with all of his writings, what endured was the promotion of a new American society built upon middle-class virtues of hard work, frugality, volunteerism, and ambivalence to unnecessary luxury, and privilege (Isaacson, 2003).

As national issues were coming to a head that would consume him, so also were personal events to which he would apparently give short shrift. Deborah died in1774 and he predictably was not at her side, foreshadowing a related event with his son. The ever more probable clash between Britain and the Colonies matched the personal one between patriotic father and loyalist son. William had long played upon his father's considerable fame and his obsession with political success and social stature far exceeded his father's. A showdown was inevitable and resulted first in a more serious estrangement between the two and later an irreparable rift (Lopez and Herbert, 1975). Franklin did not need any additional reasons to virtually disown William and he would unapologetically miss his son's momentous life events. The battle between father and illegitimate son would continue with a different weapon. William would himself father an illegitimate son- Temple- who became a treasured grandson to Benjamin but perhaps only in the sense that he was used as a pawn against William (ironically, Temple would also father an illegitimate son).

Franklin had also changed his political stance. While voyaging home in 1775, war officially broke out. For at least the previous decade, he had hoped and despaired that a break was avoidable, but precisely a year before his fellow patriots, Franklin had taken the crucial step of publicly calling for full independence. Despite being the oldest member of the Second Continental Congress, he was now at the forefront of ardent opposition to Britain and a new diplomatic challenge.

There was an immediate need for a formal declaration, which had been deftly spurred by Thomas Paine's *Common Sense,* a pamphlet that many believed Franklin had written; and in point of fact, he had offered Paine some revisions to the piece. But Franklin was now assigned to a declaration committee which included Jefferson, Adams, Sherman, and Livingston. Jefferson's superior philosophical depth enabled him to write the majority of the Declaration of Independence, yet the document Jefferson drafted was in more than a few ways similar to what Franklin would have written (Isaacson, 2003).

Using the previously rejected Albany Plan, Franklin again proposed a post-war union based upon the principles of a federalist system that would begin initially as the ill-fated Articles of Confederation. The roots of the American Experiment were planted, but a war would have to be won first.

Now regarded as the world's most famous American, Franklin was assigned the crucial task of procuring a reluctant France as an ally. With his fame came influence, and the fate of America was as much in his hands as it was with General Washington's. His resulting success firmly solidified his stature as "America's first great image-maker and public relations master" (Isaacson, 2003, p.326). So brilliant was this diplomatic coup that despite the underlying intrigue and controversy over the alliance, Franklin continued as a minister to France while additionally spearheading a commission that would eventually negotiate a peace treaty with Britain, a task he initially handled alone. Amidst complications and in-fighting among the American negotiators (especially the surly and jealous John Adams, against whom Franklin's endearing but sometimes frustrating charms rarely worked), it was Franklin who shrewdly appeased all sides to an agreement.

Franklin could now claim direct involvement in shaping the three major documents of the Revolutionary War: the Declaration of Independence, the alliance with France, and the peace treaty with Britain. But one last challenge lay on the horizon and it would arguably prove to be his signature political accomplishment. Now diplomatically stationed permanently at home, Franklin was among many who saw the need to replace the failing Articles of Confederation in 1787. On the original premise of merely amending the

Articles, the mission of the Constitutional Convention would produce the most successful and enduring governmental document ever written and in no small part to his contributions. At age eighty-one, he was the senior member by at least fifteen years and twice the average age of the members (Cart, 1990). His frail health (he could not walk by this time due to debilitating kidney stones and had to be carried in a chair to and from the proceedings) kept him from pursuing the chairmanship and he instead supported the selection of George Washington who was the better choice for stability purposes (Sanchez, 2006; Cart, 1990).

Over those historic four months, Franklin offered three crucial strengths that highly influenced the final product. First, he was far more comfortable with the concept of democracy than the other Founding Fathers. Second, because he was by far the most traveled, he was thoroughly familiar with the commonalities and differences between European nations and America. Third, and most important as it turned out, he embodied the tolerant spirit of Enlightenment and pragmatic compromise (Isaacson, 2003).

With tensions mounting daily, his calming influence extended to the practice of opening each session with prayer, which promoted his belief that "the longer I live, the more convincing proofs I see of this truth- that God governs in the affairs of men" (Smyth, 1970, p.310). This was not lost on the delegates who were quick to realize that they must be awed and humbled to succeed (Isaacson, 2003). Following Madison's lead, perhaps Franklin's greatest contribution at the Convention was his timely support and ushering through of the delicate legislative branch compromise that ultimately "sealed the deal." Franklin was justifiably proud that the Constitution reflected his life-long philosophies and activities. Together with the three documents of the Revolution, his signing of the U.S. Constitution made him the only American to sign what were to become the Four Founding Papers (Isaacson, 2003).

Old and ill, Franklin could have and should have retired a revered hero, but he stubbornly continued into his last year working in the Pennsylvania Assembly on the moral crusade that had engaged him for decades: slavery. As with most of the Founding Fathers, he continually wrestled with this moral dilemma, even though he had once owned a slave couple and periodically used a slave as a personal servant. His dogged efforts to abolish the institution made him a leading and controversial abolitionist, but it was one of the few endeavors of his life in which he failed.

Franklin's death in 1790 fittingly earned him widespread praise, but the future generation historian Frederick Jackson Turner may have stated it most succinctly by referring to him as "the first great American... whose life is the story of American common sense in its highest form" (Turner, 1887, p.234). Over the past two centuries, Franklin's values have directly affected succeeding generations. His promotion of frugality and industriousness, for example, made him the patron saint of the Great Depression generation. By relating morality to daily human consequences, Franklin laid the foundation for the most influential of America's homegrown philosophies: pragmatism (Isaacson, 2003). Politically and diplomatically, he further demonstrated that a compromiser may not make a great hero, but a great democracy resulted. In the final analysis, he had his share of personal flaws, but he helped create and symbolize a truly American environment based on merit, virtue, and hard work, traits that best served God and country. The practicality and usefulness that distinguish the American Experiment can thus be found firmly rooted in him.

DISCUSSION GUIDELINE QUESTIONS

1. What values are specifically depicted in his story?
2. Where did he learn his values?
3. Are Franklin's values still important in contemporary America?
4. What may have been Franklin's greatest character trait?
5. What was his greatest flaw?
6. Were there moral dilemmas with which he struggled?
7. Did he make the right value choices?
8. Why might his values and character be important enough to examine or model today?
9. Are there individuals on the American scene today who are similar in character to him?

REFERENCES

Brooks, D. (2000, October 23). Our founding yuppie. The *Weekly Standard*, p.7: 1.
Carr, W. (1990). *The oldest delegate*. Newark: University of New Jersey Press.
Franklin, B. (2001). *The autobiography of Benjamin Franklin*. New York: Penguin Putnam.
Isaacson, W. (2003). *Benjamin Franklin: An American life*. New York: Simon and Schuster.
Lopez, C. & Herbert, E. (1975). *The private Franklin*. New York: Norton.
Sanchez, T. (2006). The man who could have been king: A storyteller's guide for character education. *The Journal of Social Studies Research*, 30 (2): 3-9.
Schneider, H. (1958). *The Puritan mind*. Ann Arbor: University of Michigan Press.
Smyth, A. (ed,). (1970). *The writings of Benjamin Franklin*. New York: Haskel House.

Chapter Six

The Surly Rebel's Defining Moment: John Adams

Many heroes in the American pantheon attained such status through a single action. Others had a celebrated life that featured a series of heroic actions spanning years of their lives. These latter individuals, however, also had a defining moment that clearly reflected the character and values that set their soon-to-be heroic lives in motion. Such is the case with John Adams, a man not frequently associated with hero status. He was a successful lawyer, a fiercely devoted patriot, a contributor to and signer of the Declaration of Independence, a foreign ambassador and treaty negotiator, one of the Founding Fathers of the Constitution, the second president of the United States and its first vice-president, father of another president, and one of the most brilliant minds to ever grace the republic. But a closer look beyond these stellar achievements also reveals an often bitter and stubborn man whose desire for distinction and the esteem that came with public life were frequently personified by his angry disposition (McCullough, 2001; Smith, 1962). Among the early presidents, Washington was called the Great One; Jefferson was the Smart One; Madison was the Quiet One; and Monroe was the Common One. Adams, however, was the Grumpy One (McCullough, 2001). Complicating things was his paradoxical nature. He was brilliant and honest, yet vain and cranky. He was a devout Christian yet a sensibly independent thinker, never seeing any contradiction between the two (McCullough, 2001). His marriage to Abigail was legendary and he was the most devoted and loving husband and father one can imagine. But as a colleague, few called him friend. Although he cared deeply for the friends he did have, he made it difficult to be liked. He thought he was better than everyone else and kept people outside of his family at arm's length, but then could not understand why he wasn't loved (Sanchez, 2005).

But twenty-six years before he attained the presidency as the heir-apparent to the immensely popular George Washington and the culmination of an extensive political life, John Adams experienced the defining moment of his career, a moment that long presaged all of his future triumphs and failures, and would symbolize the values he demonstrated throughout his long life. It was an episode that could have easily destroyed a lesser man of character, but instead established the young lawyer-patriot's reputation as a man of integ-

rity and successfully launched a political career that coincided with the birth of the republic itself.

The atmosphere in 1770 Colonial America was decidedly tense and in Boston, Massachusetts, it was outright hostile. The reason: two regiments of British troops had been quartered in the city, first in order to establish a royal presence, but also to keep order amidst a rising tide of colonial discontent and resistance to the Crown. Although the soldiers had been ordered not to fire upon colonists without the expressed permission of the royal governor, there had already been a number of incidences in which several colonists had been shot (Storey, 1975). Gangs of young men and mere teenagers roamed the streets, spoiling for a fight. Wherever these gangs encountered soldiers, there were always minor skirmishes, all of which were a foreboding to something explosive. The mood of the snow-covered city was especially antagonistic on the cold moonlit evening of March 5th, when a group of Bostonians began pelting a small detachment of British soldiers with snowballs and garbage, allegedly in response to the soldiers' harassment of a colonist. But prodded by the crowd's blatant refusal to disperse, seven soldiers under the command of Captain Thomas Preston were ordered to fire upon the unarmed crowd. It was a catastrophe resulting in eleven casualties: three colonists were immediately killed, two more were mortally wounded and would die shortly, and six additional colonists were wounded to varying degrees. Among the fatalities was a mulatto sailor named Crispus Attacks, whose death elevated him to hero status as an early casualty in the patriot cause.

This was the story told to thirty-four-year-old John Adams the next day when he was approached by British officials about defending eight soldiers and their captain. But why approach Adams, of all people? Surly, arrogant, and sometimes detestable, he was even then regarded as an up and coming patriot for the cause of independence, but he was also reputed to be the finest lawyer in Massachusetts. Numerous rumors readily circulated, prompting the British to genuinely fear a colonial uprising. There was war in the air. The colonists were not ready for it, but it was in the air and wars had been fought for less provocation.

The fires of hatred and hostility were being constantly fanned in the colonial press by the three leading patriot/rebels of the time and now they moved swiftly into action. First and foremost there was the feisty leader, the man of action, the "go-to" man, the man who would soon be called the Father of the American Revolution: Samuel Adams. He was John's second cousin by blood but the number one rebel in the Thirteen Colonies. Second only to the great Benjamin Franklin himself in name recognition, he was the acknowledged leader of the brewing tensions with Britain. Seizing the moment, he called the incident a "bloody butchery" (McCullough, 2001, p.66) and officially dubbed it the Boston Massacre. Then there was James Otis, a fascinating character whom history has long forgotten. Just three months before this incident, he had been so brutally assaulted by British officials that he was left with a fractured skull. His brilliant brain was never the same afterwards and for the remainder of his thirteen years he drifted in and out of insanity. One never knew which Jim Otis would show up from one day to the next: the spirited and outspoken patriot who never feared to lead, or the incapable victim who was totally out of touch with reality. Finally, there was Paul Revere, a practicing dentist and silversmith, five years before his famous ride into history. Revere's famous engraving of the Boston Massacre-which depicted the incident as "a slaughter of the innocent [and] an image of British tyranny" (McCullough, 2001, p.66)- was widely circulated and further infuriated the colonists, even though Revere was not present at the time and based his engraving on hearsay, second-hand accounts, and pure conjecture. This, however, was an era where communication was limited to word-of-mouth and newspapers, and it was thus viewed as truth. But the fact remained that colonists had been killed- murdered in the street- and the people would demand the blood of the perpetrators.

Dare he take the case? Though he "relished the sharp conflict and theater of the courtroom" (McCullough, 2001, p. 19) that showcased his portly frame, sharp nose, and glaring blue eyes to full effect, there was a decidedly ominous nature about this case. Only one year before, he had successfully defended four American sailors charged with killing a British naval officer who had boarded their ship with the intention of impressing them into the British navy (a principle that would ironically be a major factor in the future War of 1812). However, public opinion had been firmly behind him in that case but it certainly would not be this time (McCullough, 2001). To take this case would surely turn his fellow-patriots against him, brand him a traitor, endanger his family, and destroy the legal future he was so intent to have. Knowing that the soldiers could not possibly get a fair trial, considering the colonial mood, Adams nevertheless accepted the case despite the agony he knew would be forthcoming. He based his decision on one simple principle: equal justice before the law was the sole consideration a lawyer must put above all others and "...no man in a free country should be denied the right to counsel and a fair trial" (McCullough, 2001, p.66). In point of fact, he accepted the case almost immediately and for a mere fraction of his usual fee (Sanchez, 2005). He also accepted the case with or without consultation or advice from Cousin Sam, who apparently had no public objection to John's action. In any case, John was not the type of man who sought advice. He had no doubt that this course of action was simply the right thing to do and had been the guiding principle his entire career. Besides, Adams reasoned, if these soldiers were tried fairly, would it not prove that the colonists valued righteousness above hatred and prejudice? It now became a matter of who would risk demonstrating that justice stood higher than personal safety and a legal future. The most important trial in colonial history was about to take place and the patriot John Adams would be defending the enemy.

Assisted by another lawyer, Josiah Quincy, Jr. (who was also his cousin), his first move as chief counsel was to postpone the trial for seven months, first, in hopes that the hostile atmosphere might subside (the colonial press would squash those hopes) and second, to allow him ample time to gather evidence for a proper defense. He knew he could not claim the incident was an accident. There were two pieces of circumstantial evidence that would prevent such a defense: one, there had been an order to fire; and two, seven soldiers had inflicted eleven casualties, meaning that several of them had fired and then reloaded to fire again. Both circumstances hardly constituted an accident. Yet he was perplexed at Captain Preston's adamant claim that he had never given an order to fire, a claim widely refuted, even by some of the soldiers involved who claimed they heard one. The reaction in the press to the postponement was expectedly bitter, claiming it was a blatant attempt to avoid justice. Tellingly, however, there was no mention of John Adams directly, though "the defense was accused of conspiring to save the soldiers from their just due" (Sanchez, 2005, p.268).

As the evidence mounted from numerous witnesses gathered during that tumultuous summer, Adams began piecing together an emerging story quite different from the one promoted in the press and by the prosecution. By the time the trial opened that October, Adams had been enduring unrelenting threats from his fellow-Bostonians. "Criticism of almost any kind was nearly always painful for Adams, but public scorn was painful, in the extreme" (McCullough, 2001, p.66). Never overly popular because of his perceived unpleasantness even before the trial, he could now not walk the streets without being spat upon or having rocks thrown at him. Only the support of his wife and equal partner Abigail and his own sense of righteousness kept him going (Withey, 2001). Daily threats against his life, family, and home were unnerving, to say the least, but he remained steadfast in his determination to secure a fair trial for his clients. Trying to remain above it all as best he could, Adams began his defense by unveiling a different perspective to the Boston Massacre.

Early on the evening of March 5th, he began, a young apprentice barber followed a British Officer to the main barracks in front of the British Customhouse, calling him insulting names for not having paid the barber for services rendered. Amidst a tolling church bell that apparently served as an alarm, a large crowd immediately gathered as the sentry on duty swung his musket at the youth and knocked him down. As the boy fell to the ground, the crowd began to pelt the sentry with snowballs and garbage and then menacingly closed in on him from all sides. Unable to escape, the sentry shouted for help and Captain Preston and seven soldiers came racing from the barracks.

Refusing to disperse, the crowd continued to close in and pelted all of the soldiers while shouting threats to kill them and daring them to fire. They proceeded to knock down one soldier while another soldier had to wrestle several colonists who were trying to grab his musket. Refuting the prosecution's claim that Captain Preston then gave the order to fire, it was asserted that in the ensuing struggle a shot was fired; a single shot that must have frozen time. But who fired the shot? Probably one of "them" and maybe one of "us," but what difference did it make? The soldiers reacted accordingly. Defense witnesses then testified that the soldiers were actually being engulfed and attacked by two crowds, a second one attempting to move on the barracks while carrying clubs. None of the witnesses heard a command to fire. In addition, Adams established that one of the fatalities was a gang member and known trouble-maker who had been part of an assault on some soldiers just days before the Massacre, while another of the fatalities had been involved in several brawls with soldiers.

But perhaps his best witness was a dead man. One of the mortally wounded colonists had told his doctor shortly before his death that he believed the soldiers had acted in self-defense; that he had never seen such abuse as that heaped upon those soldiers; and that he forgave whoever had shot him. This was the basis of Adams's defense: he maintained that British law justified killing in self-defense, be it by civilians or soldiers. The soldiers had been attacked by a mob and because their lives were in eminent danger had the right to defend themselves. A mob—colonial or otherwise—had provoked a justifiable action of self-defense.

The colonial jury acquitted Captain Preston in less than two hours of deliberation. Two weeks later in a separate trial, two of the soldiers were convicted of manslaughter and subsequently branded on the thumb (which was a common punishment) and discharged from the army. The remaining six soldiers were found not guilty. Adams had won his case but more importantly had remained true to his principles. He now prepared himself for the repercussions as the press expectedly denounced the verdicts as a travesty.

Though Adams himself was never publicly criticized for his role in the trial, the months immediately following the verdicts found him daily preparing for the worst. But the worst did not happen. His fellow-patriots respected him for the integrity that he demonstrated; indeed, the integrity that he lived, even though he was widely disliked. His fellow-colonists gradually understood that a dedicated patriot had done the right thing, despite the fact that he had represented the hated British. Over fifty years later, Adams would review the events of his long public life and pay homage to the significance of the Boston Massacre by calling it "one of the most gallant, generous, manly and disinterested actions of my whole life, and one of the best pieces of service I ever rendered my country" (McCullough, 2001, p.68). But for now, a new

era of respect had begun for John Adams, for his character was above reproach and his American adventures were awaiting him.

DISCUSSION GUIDELINE QUESTIONS

1. If Adams had opted not to take the case or had withdrawn under
   pressure, what effect would such an action have had on him personally
   and on the tense British-colonial relationship?
2. Would a political figure today dare risk a similar stance in the public
   eye? Why or why not?
3. What values are depicted in the story?
4. What was his greatest character trait?
5. What was his greatest flaw?
6. Is doing the right thing worth the risk of possible public condemna-
   tion?
7. How important is doing the right thing for one's character?
8. Are there circumstances when not doing the right thing is acceptable?
9. In the story, Adams is depicted as surly and arrogant, personality traits
   that endured throughout his life. His decision to do the right thing in
   this situation (and subseqently in others as well) evidently had no
   effect on his personality. How are personality and values related? Can
   an "unpleasant" personality still demonstrate the character of an effective citizen?
10. Are there any individuals on the scene today who can be compared to
    Adams?

REFERENCES

McCullough, D. (2001). *John Adams*. New York: Simon A Schuster.
Sanchez, T. (2005). The story of the Boston massacre: A storytelling opportunity for character
    education. *The Social Studies*, 96(6): 265-269.
Smith, P. (1962). *John Adams (volume: 1735-1784)*. New York: Doubleday.
Storer, D. (1975). *Amazing but true! Stories about the presidents*. New York: Pocket Books.
Withey, L. 2001). *Dearest friend: A life of Abigail Adams*. New York: Simon Schuster.

Chapter Seven

Ahead of Her Time: Abigail Adams

She was a small, diminutive woman with piercing dark eyes, a sometimes overbearing and forceful personality, and an independent spirit that fueled her devotion to family and friends, all of which garnered love and respect from nearly everyone she encountered (Withey, 2001; Osborne, 1989; Levin, 1987). But Abigail Adams was not simply the wife of a Founding Father whose name and exploits dwarfed hers in an age when disfranchised women were hardly more than second-class citizens (Sanchez & Stewart, 2006). Educated and outspoken, Abigail was not a passive, reticent bystander but rather an important participant in the development of the republic in a time when few women were acknowledged. Her entire life is instead a stand-alone testament to the fact that America was not built solely upon the backs of white males. Though underappreciated during her lifetime, her clamor for gender equality and standing up for what one believes solidly illustrate the heroic character that presaged the political and social freedoms we currently hold dear.

Abigail could be something of a contradiction. She advocated improved legal status for women and espoused that "women were the intellectual equals of men and had the right to an education" (Withey, 2001, p.xi). There was also her less than subtle hint at the right for women to vote (Butterfield, Friedlaender & Kline, 1975). But she somewhat paradoxically believed the chauvinistic view that a woman's place was in the home and that women were best suited to be housewives and mothers. Though she accepted those prevailing but confining social standards and never personally stepped out of them herself, she would take them to the limit and use them as a base from which she expressed her view that improved legal status and education would better define the American woman (Withey, 2001). It was a classic example of working within the system and changing it without undermining it.

She was born in 1744 in Massachusetts, the second of four children, and would be "raised with a firm but gentle hand" (Withey, 2001, p.5) in a somewhat unconventional manner: she was home-schooled by her parents and though she bolstered her education with self-teaching, she became and remained extremely sensitive of her educational limitations, even though she would become one of the best-read women of her time. Her values would be based on a deep Christian faith in a loving God, believing that religion was

the most important foundation in providing a set of moral standards to guide one's behavior (Withey, 2001). Religion and family would be the pillars of life and serve as her personal foundation to fight the injustices she perceived.

The turning point in Abigail's life was, of course, meeting and marrying the brash and arrogant John Adams, who was nine years her senior. John discovered early in their courtship that this woman was his intellectual equal; and to his credit, he nurtured Abigail's intellectual growth (Withey, 2001; Shaw, 1976). They were also different. While Abigail could be as temperamental as John, whose public persona was one of crankiness, hers was of a private nature, and she was publicly regarded as a generous and loving woman (Withey, 2001). She made it clear, however, that "she was not content with the lot of an ordinary woman" (Withey, 2001, p. 17), but neither of them knew just how extraordinary and sacrificing their life together would be. Nevertheless, theirs was a love story for the ages and their deep love for each other never wavered during their long life together.

The arrival of children and the managing of their farm would soon be eclipsed in importance by the Boston Massacre (1770), which heralded the beginning of John's ever-increasing involvement in the political arena. It would also mark the beginning of long separations and personal sacrifices. As history happened around them, their marriage would have to be maintained through informative and supportive letters of correspondence, which especially in Abigail's case would not sooth her depressed spirits over being separated from John (Butterfield, Friedlaender & Kline, 1975).

Their separations did not, however, affect her domestic self-sufficiency and her opinions on perceived injustice. As she expressed more interest in gender equality, Abigail became enamored with the anti-British writings of Mercy Otis Warren and Catharine Macaulay. She would increasingly align herself with their similar views and eventually forge close friendships with them which further strengthened and inspired this female triumvirate (Withey, 2001). Despite the revolutionary bravado of Abigail's writings, she believed that American virtue would ultimately aid their cause (Withey, 2001). However, the feared but necessary Revolutionary War would intervene to test that virtue.

As the war raged, Abigail more seriously questioned the legal and political position of women in an American society now needing every person for its survival (Withey, 2001). Her most famous statement— suggesting that John "remember the ladies" in considering their future role after independence—gave her the reputation as an early feminist, but her purpose was to shrewdly link the cause of women to the base of national independence (Thompson, 1998). Hers was not a call for a radically different social position but rather an increased female "influence" enhanced by improved legal statute and educational opportunity.

Sometimes to her regret, Abigail never discouraged John's increasing involvement in politics, even though it meant unbearably long separations. At one point, "they spent the better part of ten years living miserably apart" (Withey, 2001, p. 115). His sense of duty could be outright unnerving, but she believed that supporting him was a necessary patriotic sacrifice, however aggravating her anxieties were as a result. She understood him intimately and loved him as deeply as a woman could ever love a man. Their letters to each other were their only consolation and yet their love strengthened through sharing and depending solely upon each other through the written word.

Her letters to him began to serve another purpose. "Abigail listened to opinions expressed around her and passed them on to John" (Withey, 2001, p.73). As her written observations and personal perspectives became increasingly clear and confidently expressed, he grew to depend upon her as his "unofficial, unpaid, but most influential political adviser" (Withey, 2001, p.xi). No other Founding Father would be able to make such a claim and it was a crucial role that she continued to fulfill for the remainder of his political life.

As the war ended, she went to Europe to finally be reunited with John for four years as he continued his diplomatic duties. Returning home together in 1788, the new Constitution would again dash their hopes of a simple life as John was elected the first vice-president. Though that eight-year period for them was a comfortable yet hectic routine, Abigail had also grown accustomed to public life as a political wife and basked in it. But John's election to the presidency in 1796 renewed all of the ambivalence that Abigail felt about political life (Withey, 2001). As always, she had total confidence in his abilities, but John had become "a cantankerous, unpopular man of little flexibility" (Withey, 2001, p.243). She also knew that following Martha Washington as First Lady was no easy task.

It was during this time that a little-known incident occurred in Abigail's life which illustrated her character in action and the importance of standing up for what one believes in (Sanchez & Stewart, 2006). Shortly after John had been elected the second President of the United States in November of 1796, Abby, as he affectionately called her, knew that there was much to be done to prepare for their presidential home in Philadelphia before his presidency would officially begin the following March. John let her know how desperately he needed her help in setting up their future household. Living life as a lawyer and politician left the future President with little practical knowledge or experience in setting up and caring for a home. This had been one area where John had always and completely relied upon his wife, as he knew that this task was beyond the scope of his talents. Still, Abby decided that her first priority was at their home in Quincy, Massachusetts, and so she left the housing decisions to John until she had completed her work and could join him. After all, Abby mused, John had lived abroad for long periods of time and had handled political opponents and situations without her being constantly at his side. Certainly he could manage to pick out a house and a few furnishings. Besides, Abby was adamant in her belief that Congress should be responsible for procuring and furnishing a home for the elected leader of the country, and she was not shy in expressing that opinion, much to John's amusement and regret (the newly-planned White House would not be ready for occupancy until his last year in office). Abby had more important responsibilities caring for the properties that she and John owned in Quincy; she could not be bothered with Philadelphia just yet. There were plenty of things yet to be done. She knew from previous experience of running the farm that the main issues in Quincy were problems with laborers.

Abby had grown accustomed to dealing with the tenants that worked the Adams farm. She felt proud in having personally chosen their overseer, a man named French, but Abby knew that she would have to bargain with him to keep him from leaving at the end of his contract. Inflation was creating havoc with the dropping value of money, and other landowners were only too happy to have an overseer as knowledgeable and reliable as French running the labor operations. Although she had proven to be a very shrewd business-woman, Abby was also practical and reasonable. She therefore decided to provide him with a business arrangement that profited both parties. At the same time she found herself dealing with another tenant on a most unpleasant matter. The man had a reputation for being lazy and drunk, both attributes that Abby did not condone in a person and certainly not an employee. It was in her personal handling of this situation that her focus shifted to a matter of greater importance to her: the subject of educating one of their servants.

James Prince was a reliable indentured servant to John and Abby. He was the youngest of their servants and Abby felt a special fondness for him. She was sufficiently impressed with James when she had met him in Philadelphia a few years earlier that she offered him a position on the Adams farm. As an educated woman in her own right, she strongly believed in all people having at least the right of an opportunity to an education, especially women and minorities. To this end, she had taught James and several other servants to read and write. Abby was most pleased and surprised when James approached her for permission to formally continue his education at a local school offering evening classes for apprentices. James wanted to attend even though he would have to pay for it himself. He had learned from Abby that education was the key to opportunity, and as an indentured servant he would be free from obligation someday. Thus, an education would greatly help him to earn a respectable living. After giving James her blessing, he began school while Abby turned her attention to the issues of the tenant farmers and preparing to go to Philadelphia.

Shortly afterwards Abby had a visit from a neighbor who asked to speak with her on what he described as a most delicate matter. Abby was surprised yet curious, as she was not accustomed to having her neighbors simply stop by without cause. After exchanging pleasantries, the neighbor, quite aware of Mrs. Adams' personality and the strength of her convictions, stated that he had come to discuss the boy James. This immediately piqued her curiosity, as she knew James to be a fine, respectable young man and faithful servant. She could not imagine what he might have done to bring this neighbor to her door. The neighbor requested that Abby insist that James immediately cease attending school. He went on to say that if James continued, the school would have to close. Abby, perplexed, wanted to know why on earth the school would possibly close. From all indications, James was doing as well as the other students and was progressing as expected. Had James done something inappropriate, she asked? The neighbor replied that it was not a matter of misbehavior. Then the true nature of the visit became clear: it was because James was black. The neighbor proceeded to explain that the other boys attending the school, who, he reminded her, also paid tuition, were uncomfortable having to sit in the same classroom with a black, and therefore he should not be allowed to attend.

Abby was inwardly outraged but tactfully maintained the decorum and manner of her status. While the culture of the time dictated that blacks (and women, for that matter) were ultimately inferior, she understood from experience that education was an equalizer. Thus to deny James the opportunity of education in order to find a just position in society based upon his race was tantamount to denying opportunity based upon gender as well. On this subject she would refuse to remain passive. She quietly turned to her formidable logic and fairness to make her point. Abby asked if the boys objected to sitting in the same church with James, knowing of course that they didn't, and the neighbor agreed that they didn't. She continued this line of questioning by asking if he had also seen these same boys at local dances when James routinely played his fiddle. Once again the man agreed that the boys in question had attended the dances. Abby then stated that "the boy is a freeman as much as any of the young men, and merely because his face is black is he to be denied instruction" (McCullough, 2001, p.480)? The man had no reply and shifted slightly with the uncomfortable turn that the conversation had taken. Abby was not about to stop: "How is he to be qualified to procure a livelihood? Is it the Christian principle of doing unto others as we would have others do to us" (McCullough, 2001, p.480)? She then further defended James' right to attend school as attacking the very principle of liberty and equality on the only grounds for which it ought to be supported: an equality of rights. Abby then politely requested that the boys attending the school come to visit her so she might discuss the issue directly with them. The neighbor thanked her for her time and excused himself. Confident that the issue was resolved, her parting words to her neighbor were "tell them... I hope we shall all go to Heaven together" (McCullough, 2001, p.480; Withey, 2001, p.246).

Abby, ever vigilant in her correspondence with her dear husband to keep him updated regarding the family and the farm, related this event in a letter. She was pleased to report that not another word was ever said about James Prince attending school. It remained open and all of the students continued to attend.

John's term as president was not a success, even though his leadership kept the young republic out of a direct conflict with France. There were petty and inevitable political squabbles that, among other things, caused a rift of silence with their mutual friend, Thomas Jefferson. John failed in his re-election bid in 1800 and Abigail dwelled obsessively on what she perceived to be the ingratitude of the voters who had turned him out of office (Withey, 2001).

They now began the difficult adjustment to retirement which was compli-cated by personal problems and tragedies with their grown children, the barrage of post-presidential criticism against John, and the ascension of their son John Quincy into politics. Their ten grandchildren were a never-ending source of pride and diversion, but the infirmities of advancing age were taking a toll. Advancing age also inspired Abigail to repair friendships that had been damaged by political differences, especially with Jefferson. It was Abigail's initial correspondence with him following his presidency which led to the end of the long silence between the two former Presidents. The re-newed correspondence between John and Jefferson proved that the deep friendship they had felt for each other trumped the political animosities of years past and it lasted until both men famously died on the fiftieth anniver-sary of the Declaration of Independence. But it was Abigail who merited credit as their mediator.

After a brief illness, Abigail died in 1819 at age 73, leaving John alone and lost. Fifty-four years of marriage had not diminished the intensity of their love. Abigail would probably be surprised at her contemporary status of heroine, instead believing that John or John Quincy would be more worthy. But she certainly would have approved of the reasons for her fame; namely, "the interest of a later age in the history of family and domestic life, as well as the history of politics; and, above all, its interest in the emancipation of women in the past who spoke out on behalf of their sex" (Withey, 2001, p.317).

DISCUSSION GUIDELINE QUESTIONS

1. What values are depicted in the story?

2. How important is it to do what is right and to take a stand for what one believes?

3. What was her greatest character trait?

4. What was her greatest flaw?

5. In the major incident of the story, she did what she considered to be the right thing. Are there circumstances when not doing the right thing is acceptable?

6. How difficult must it have been for Abigail to assume various roles that were considered to be exclusively male?

7. Is education held in the same high regard as it was in Abigail's time? How might it have changed? Though American society has certainly changed, are there any females on the national scene that are reminiscent of Abigail? How is a woman of her character viewed today?

REFERENCES

Butterfield, L., Friedlaender, M: & Kline, M. (eds.). *The book of Abigail and John: Selected letters of the Adams family.* Cambridge: Harvard University Press.

Levin, P. (1987). *Abigail Adams.* New York: St. Martin's.

McCullough, D. (2001). *John Adams.* NY: Simon & Schuster.

Osborne, A. (1989). *Abigail Adams.* New York: Chelsea House.

Sanchez, T. & Stewart, V. (2006). The remarkable Abigail: Story-telling for character education. *The High School Journal,* 89(4): 14-21.

Shaw, P. (1976). *The character of John Adams.* New York: Norton.

Thompson, C. (1998). *John Adams and the spirit of liberty.* Lawrence: University of Karakas Press.

Withey, L. (2001). *Dearest friend: A life of Abigail Adams.* NY: Simon & Schuster.

Chapter Eight

Champion of the Common Man: David Crockett

One of the more prevailing tenets of 21st century America is the increasingly distrustful perception of our elected officials. Such suspicion has probably existed much longer than we imagine, perhaps from the beginning of the democratic system. But the early 21st century has witnessed a decided and frequently justified disillusionment toward politicians. We complain that our elected officials are out of touch with our needs and problems, that they do not put our best interests ahead of their own or their party, that they do not truly serve us, and are only concerned with their own power base and re-election. In many respects, these allegations are quite accurate and as a result we continually long for the model politician who as a true statesman seeks only to serve the electorate. Asserting that such a person never existed in the annals of American government would be cynical and wrong, for history indicates otherwise.

A heretofore unlikely example of what we seek may be found in one of America's celebrated folk heroes who is acclaimed for other reasons. He is David Crockett, more commonly referred to as Davy, and he is renowned as a pioneer, Indian fighter, and martyr. But he was also an elected representative of Congress who believed that political loyalty should never be placed above duty to his constituents (Boylston & Wiener, 2009). Always keeping attuned to the electorate's views, he never forgot that he was a public servant and emerged as a true champion of the common man. Fiercely independent, his conscience always outweighed politics and he refused to compromise his core beliefs in serving the people of his home state. The problem with viewing him today—as it was in his own time—is separating "David" from "Davy," the fact from the legend.

As with most every hero, his early life gave no indication of his future greatness. He was born in Tennessee on August 17, 1786, the fifth of nine children. Crockett related that his childhood was a mixture of hardship, poverty, travel, and adventure (Shackford & Folmsbee, 1973). Typical of most frontier children, he would have no formal education and purportedly ran away from home to avoid school, much to his family's dismay (Derr, 1993). Instead, the Tennessee wilderness educated him to be a skilled hunter and trapper. Marrying at age nineteen, David and his first wife Polly raised three

children. Her early death led to a second marriage to Elizabeth who bore him three more children.

David's determination to advance socially and politically was interrupted by the Creek War in 1813, which prompted him to join the Tennessee militia for a five-year stint and the beginning of his legend. "Affable, honest, and renowned as a skillful bear hunter" (Boylston & Wiener, 2009, p.14), his natural leadership abilities were honed and demonstrated as an Indian fighter. Little did David realize how powerful the legend of Davy would influence his future as he was discharged as a Lt. Colonel, a title he proudly held for the rest of his life. Conversely, however, his experience as an Indian fighter also led to a life-long empathy for Native Americans.

During this time, David had modestly begun his political career, first as a local magistrate, justice of the peace, and town commissioner. This eventually led to his election to the Tennessee State Legislature and three terms in the U.S. House of Representatives. Success fed his political ambitions, but it was clear from the beginning that David's reputation was built on fairness and honesty. What he lacked in formal education he more than made up for in common sense and street smarts. "A masterful campaigner among his frontier neighbors, an amusing jokester, storyteller, and speaker" (Boylston & Wiener, 2009, p.7), his homespun Will Rogers-type appeal helped him win elections through his usually exaggerated backwoods demeanor and a self-deprecating humor which were a refreshing change to the typical stuffed-shirt politician. But David proved to be a far more astute politician than he is historically given credit for (Lofaro, 1985). He understood the issues at hand, understood where his colleagues stood on them, but most importantly had the rare ability to effectively connect with and thoroughly understand the common frontiersman whom he unfailingly served. It was perhaps in no small part due to the fact that he was always one of them and never forgot from where he came.

He first burst onto the national scene in 1827 as Tennessee's newly-elected member to the U.S. House of Representatives. This was a golden age of statesmen and Crockett would serve with such luminaries as Webster, Clay, Calhoun, Benton, and Polk. Up to the task as a political veteran, he was not intimidated and got along very well with most of them by making an immediate impression as a "tall, robust man with a taste for alcohol, a fondness for gaming tables, and a solid reputation for independence in the service of his constituents" (Bolyston & Wiener, 2009, p.14). It also became readily apparent that David knew how to play the political game when he had to, but he was a staunch activist for his political agenda and firmly allied himself with those who shared his views (Boylston & Wiener, 2009). Though he could occasionally be "too outrageous and over-the-top" (Bolyston & Wiener, 2009, p.22), he consistently fought for the interests of his constituents.

The primary issue for David in both Tennessee and Washington was land ownership. He would spend his entire political career protecting the rights of "squatters" who basically claimed they had taken great risk in working and improving the land to which they admittedly had no legal title. The practice of recognizing their claim was tolerated in some areas, but growing national sectionalism and federal land policies brought the issue to a head. Land speculators who often represented the wealthy class further complicated the matter. Always supporting legislation that offered relief, support, and property tax reform to the poor and underprivileged, Crockett's stance was simple: give the land outright to poor established farmers who indeed lacked legal title but had worked the land, or give them a fair chance to reasonably purchase the land while at the same time protecting the rights of those who had legally obtained their land. Making good on his promise to protect and advance the cause for land ownership, Crockett would ultimately lose this fight due to the emerging larger national argument over public land use and dispersal. The issue would make him serious political enemies and force him to break ranks from his Democratic Party. Though he would never achieve his objective, his exhausting devotion to his constituents over his party speaks well of David as an advocate for the commoners whom he viewed as being unjustly and constantly pushed aside or ignored by wealthier and more influential interests (Boylston & Wiener, 2009).

Perhaps he "may have been naïve to think that he could survive in politics while remaining so fiercely independent" (Boylston & Wiener, 2009, p.36), but he believed he was simply acting on the desires of his constituents. The action would put him in direct opposition to Tennessee's other favorite son, Andrew Jackson, whose considerable forces would now take extraordinary measures to unseat the locally popular Crockett by branding him as disloyal. This was not always the case. Ironically, David always maintained that he was a "Jackson man" in principle and did not hesitate in using the Jacksonian philosophy as a springboard for his own political aspirations (Boylston & Wiener, 2009). The two adversaries were similar in many ways and though their political lives were intertwined, Jackson's higher economic status was the dividing wedge, but David would later correctly assert that Jackson betrayed his own philosophy (Jones, 2006).

Openly opposing President Jackson could be and frequently was political suicide, but to the dismay of the Jackson forces, the rise of Jackson coincided with the rise of Crockett. Despite concerted efforts to unseat him led by the ingenuous fellow-Tennessean James Polk, David's rising local popularity translated into voter confidence and he was easily re-elected to a second term. Jackson in turn used the land issue as a weapon to thwart his efforts and politically isolate Crockett. But perhaps fortunately for the volatile Jackson, David's turn to religion and the comfort it gave him allowed him to keep a cool head amidst the turmoil and his ensuing re-election encouraged him to continue his independent course without fear of Polk and the powerful Jackson machine (Boylston & Wiener, 2009). David's carefully crafted image as an honest and charming politician had certainly overcome his educational and social shortcomings, but he was becoming more aware of the "Davy" legend relating a "nearly superhuman backwoodsman" (Boylston & Wiener, 2009, p.51) of extraordinary exploits that was threatening to grow out of his control and border on embarrassment.

Besides finding himself politically isolated and more distrustful of Jackson, his failed objective of the land issue left him with little to show for his years in Congress, beyond his good intentions (Boylston & Wiener, 2009). Crockett would be narrowly defeated for a third term in 1831 but he would regain his seat in 1833. Embittered, he was realizing that he had lost the game of high-stakes politics to Jackson, but the two men were still to clash over two signature issues.

Long before his presidency, Jackson had been an outspoken proponent of removing Indians from the land. In 1830, he successfully rationalized and rammed through the Indian Removal Act that "was one of the most brutal and most disgraceful [policies] in U.S. history" (Boylston & Wiener, 2009, p.65). From our inception, America had a contradictory attitude toward Native Americans in terms of moving them off the land. There was a sentiment to civilize, convert, and assimilate them into mainstream culture, but the desire to unequivocally push them out of the way became too great during the Age of Jackson. Claiming to have their best interests at heart while simultaneously coercing them to cede their land and relocate west of the Mississippi, the draw of obtaining their land in this expansionist era proved to be the sole rationalization.

Because the issue involved land ownership by the claims of those who lived and worked on it without formal legal title, David's experience and familiarity with it made him a natural to oppose the measure. He vehemently did, proclaiming that relocation was strictly up to the Indians and not by a government mandate. His support of and empathy with Native Americans had long been engrained and for the only time, David would go against the prevailing attitude of his constituents. His action, he proudly maintained, was a matter of conscience which he would not betray. He boldly sided with the Cherokee Nation's attempt for justice via the Supreme Court, which ultimately ruled in its favor. But the decision proved to be unenforceable, thus beginning one of the darker episodes for the Native American. Openly expressing his outrage and disgust, David continued at great political peril to support Native claims of ownership as he did for his own constituents. Though it would be to no avail, his singularly and unpopular defense of Indians stands out in an era totally dominated by racism, greed, and injustice (Boylston & Wiener, 2009).

Going against Jackson's removal bill no doubt cost Crockett his re-election bid in 1831. Though he was narrowly defeated, the political tide had turned against him and he returned home to play farmer while contemplating a comeback. During this interim, theatrical plays and a biography of him that promoted the increasingly outrageous "Davy" image at least provided him a national platform to re-launch his career, but he underestimated the growing and unflattering caricature that was growing beyond his control. Utilizing his talent for hardball campaigning, he persevered as "David" to carefully address only the prevailing issues and downplayed "Davy." Regaining the trust of his constituents, he narrowly won the 1833 election despite the continuing onslaught of the Jackson machine. Feeling somewhat vindicated, he returned to Washington with celebrity status to voice his alarm over the last defining issue of Jackson's presidency. Still alienated by his party, Crockett entered a volatile political war in which he would actually play only a peripheral role but it would also validate his genuine fear of expanding executive power and threatening the Constitution.

Despite his considerable personal wealth, Jackson had always mistrusted banks and was now in a position to reform the banking system by consolidating power in the executive branch. In a harbinger of concern that would resurface in the first decades of both 20th and 21st century America, the issue revolved around the lack of a central banking system to regulate and capitalize state banks. Since 1816, the Second Bank of the United States (SBUS) independently acted as the repository/collection/disbursing agency for the government, and as the largest lending institution it powerfully controlled the nation's credit by expanding and contracting loans to all other banks. It was not perfect in operation, but it did provide a stable economy that was basically detrimental to institutions relying on credit as well as the small farmer and businessman. Jackson's major complaint was that the SBUS was a private corporate enterprise which had limited accountability to the federal government (Boylston & Wiener, 2009). The questionable constitutionality aside during its twenty-year charter, the SBUS had expanded its operations to become a financial and political power that tightly controlled the economy, brought in huge profits which it was required to share with the federal government, and had shrewdly garnered political protection by extending generous loans to influential politicians, including Crockett.

With the SBUS's charter coming up for renewal in 1836, Jackson antagonistically campaigned against the banking industry in general and the SBUS specifically by promoting a return to federally-regulated hard currency and no credit buying. The predictably ugly fight between the two factions destroyed any possibility of compromise and further enraged a determined Jackson to literally kill the SBUS. Public opinion was divided as the factions exchanged sometimes groundless charges concerning the soundness of currency, but when Congress voted to renew the SBUS's charter four years ahead of schedule, an incensed Jackson took it as a personal affront and promptly vetoed the measure in a purely political reaction.

In doing so, Jackson was toying with the limits of executive power and Crockett joined many who opposed the veto. But Jackson's popular image led to his stunning re-election which he perceived as a public mandate of approval to continue and further ended any hope of a veto override. Despite its limitations, the SBUS had served a useful purpose, but Jackson had no clear-cut alternative to replace it (Boylston & Wiener, 2009; Remini, 1967). Worse still was his hypocritical and poorly disguised attempt to portray himself as the understanding common man, yet the public conveniently forgot that he was a wealthy man. "He thought he was sincere when he spoke to the people, yet he never championed their cause. He merely encouraged them to champion his" (Remini, 1967, pp.32-33). Not content to savor his victory and let the charter expire, he took the unprecedented step of withdrawing federal funds from the SBUS and placed them in "pet" state banks solely of his choosing. The resultant shortage of available funds invariably set the stage for a crippling recession that would plague the nation shortly after Jackson left the presidency.

From the sidelines of his regained House seat, Crockett could only fume and join the protest. His outspoken opposition to Jackson intensified, along with a disdain for Jackson's heir-apparent, Martin Van Buren. Still a man without a party, David was courted by the newly-formed Whig Party and though he never officially joined it, he saw it as a vehicle to advance his continuing agenda. Though he was never reluctant to bask in the celebrity limelight, "Davy" was overtaking "David." Perhaps as a means of balancing the legend as well as advancing his high-profile causes, David was inspired at this point to pen his autobiography (Shackford & Folmsbee, 1973). The public loved the book but it did not help his tailspinning political career. The continuing gridlock and partisanship in Congress stalled or outright derailed his legislative hopes. He remained a popular national celebrity, but "Davy" had finally transcended "David."

His political hourglass was running out and there was scant little to show for his three terms, save his integrity. Still struggling as always to repay his debts and facing a much tougher re-election bid, David was further despaired by Van Buren's imminent election the following year. His vigorous campaign fell short in the face of the relentless attacks from the Jackson machine and he was narrowly defeated. His reaction was one of both bitterness and relief, for his term had been sheer torture and disappointment. David now prepared to make good on his promise to leave the country if Van Buren was elected and delivered a parting shot, perhaps out of frustration: "I told the people of my district that I would serve them as faithfully as I had done; but if not... you may all go to hell and I will go to Texas" (Boylston & Wiener, 2009, p.123). The new venue of Texas offered him a chance for recreation, recuperation, rehabilitation, and a badly needed respite from the taxing political environment in the United States (Boylston & Wiener, 2009). It was also a hotbed of activity. The opportunity to join the Texan quest for liberty was a further challenge that the forty-nine-year-old Crockett needed.

As he journeyed to Texas, "Davy" was vaingloriously in control and this time "David" did not resist. Together with a handful of his fellow-Tennesseans, Crockett arrived at the Alamo in late February of 1836 to join the 185-man garrison in halting the advance of a large Mexican army led by General Antonio Lopez de Santa Anna. Delaying Santa Anna's advance would buy precious time for General Sam Houston to train his volunteer army into a viable fighting force that would ultimately gain independence for Texas. Santa Anna initiated what would be a thirteen-day siege at the mission and as it progressed, it had to be apparent to the garrison's stellar figures of Crockett, William Travis, and Jim Bowie that no reinforcements would be forthcoming (Davis, 1998). It is unknown if Crockett may have had the opportunity to save his life by escaping before the end. If he had, "David" might have seriously entertained the notion, but "Davy" could not.

In a final pre-dawn attack that lasted about ninety minutes, the siege ended on March 6, 1836. Save for a few women and slaves, all of the defenders within the walls were killed and their bodies were summarily stacked and burned to ashes. Nearly a year later, the undisturbed ashes were retrieved and buried in a simple coffin with the names of Crockett, Travis, and Bowie on the lid. The burial spot was not marked but is probably near the Alamo (Crisp, 2005; Groneman, 1999).

While it is certain that Crockett died on March 6, stories began surfacing as to the circumstances of his actual demise. Some accounts had him killed very early in the battle, while others had him as the last to fall, using his empty rifle as a club (Groneman, 1999). Several enduring accounts that persist to this day assert that Crockett was one of a small group of defenders who surrendered and survived the battle (Crisp, 2005). An incensed Santa Anna then demanded the immediate execution of the survivors by the sword despite pleas from his own officers to spare their lives. But this is highly improbable for two reasons. First, such accounts were probably created to further demonize Santa Anna and spur Houston's army on to avenge the heroes of the Alamo. Second, and more likely, the Mexican army had explicit orders to give no quarter to the defenders and in the heat of battle would have had no inclination to spare the life of a Texan combatant.

Crockett's glorified demise at the Alamo in itself has secured his place as an American hero, but the man who sacrificed his life there was "Davy," which in many respects is an injustice to "David." The legend had overcome the fact and the "David" persona was relegated to oblivion. By the late 19th century, even "Davy" was virtually forgotten but would resurface in the early 20th century as an Indian-fighting hero in numerous films. The mid-20th century, however, brought a serious revival of the Crockett saga, first in the guise of a now-discredited 1955 publication that caused a sensation by asserting that among other things he did not die in battle; and second in the curiously timed 1955 Walt Disney television miniseries that introduced the baby-boomer generation to the coonskin hat image of the king of the wild frontier.

Certainly Crockett's heroic sacrifice for Texas liberty should not be forgotten or even discounted. But the true nature of David Crockett should be rightfully showcased in his political honesty, his tireless efforts to serve his poor and working-class constituents by putting their interests above his party, and his honorable defense of Native Americans whose unjust treatment was a national disgrace. In an age when public distrust of elected officials merits serious attention, David Crockett serves as a heroic model of the public servant our nation envisions.

DISCUSSION GUIDELINE QUESTIONS

1. What values are depicted in the story?
2. Where did Crockett learn his values?
3. What may have been his greatest character trait?
4. What was his greatest flaw?
5. Is there evidence that Crockett struggled with certain moral dilemmas? If so, what were the consequences?
6. Is there anyone currently on the scene who may be comparable to him?
7. Based on his values and character, why would it be difficult for Crockett to serve in Congress today?

REFERENCES

Bolyston, J. & Wiener, A. (2009). *David Crockett in Congress: The rise and fall of the poor man's friend.* Houston: Bright Sky Press.

Crisp, J. (2005). *Sleuthing the Alamo: Davy Crockett's last stand and other mysteries of the Texas revolution.* New York: Oxford University Press.

Davis, W. (1998). *Three roads to the Alamo: The lives and fortunes of Davy Crockett, James Bowie, and William Barret Travis.* New York: Harper Collins.

Derr, M. (1993). *The frontiersman: The real life and many legends of Davy Crockett.* Knoxville: University of Tennessee Press.

Groneman, B. (1999). *Death of a legend: The myth and mystery surrounding the death of Davy Crockett.* Plano, TX: Republic of Texas Press.

Jones, R. (2006). *In the footsteps of Davy Crockett.* Winston-Salem: John F. Blair.

Lofaro, M. (Ed.) (1985). *Davy Crockett: The man, the legend, the legacy.* New York: William Morrow and Company, Inc.

Remini, R. (1967). *Andrew Jackson and the bank war.* New York: W. W. Norton & Co.

Shackford, J. & Folmsbee, S. (Eds.) (1973). *A narrative of the life of David Crockett of the state of Tennessee.* Knoxville: University of Tennessee Press.

Chapter Nine

The Conductor: Harriet Tubman

Courage, perseverance, and faith are the cornerstone values of the American pantheon and grace the character of many of our heroes/heroines. But they may be best personified in the person of Harriet Tubman. Though she too frequently remains a somewhat mythical figure consigned to juvenile biographies read by elementary school students that only reveal her as a conductor on the Underground Railroad in the pre-Civil War era, the shrouded facts and misconceptions of her remarkable life make her more a symbol without substance instead of a heroine without peer (Larson, 2004)."Small in stature, neatly but often poorly dressed, with an understated modesty about her accomplishments, she seemed no different from anyone else. But she was different" (Larson, 2004, p.136).

Because she was illiterate, her narrative would be recorded by others, but it clearly revealed that she "demonstrated an unyielding and seemingly fearless resolve to secure liberty and equality for others" (Larson, 2004, p.xix). This "Moses" of her people was a woman of profound faith and a humanitarian passion, a slave who was a liberator and warrior, and a fighter for equality that symbolize a courage and determination that can still inspire 21st century Americans (Clinton, 2004; Humez, 2003).

Birth records in pre-20th century America were notoriously obscure, even for whites but especially for blacks. As a result, there may be a question of accuracy, but Harriet was born in Maryland between 1822 and 1825 in "a time and place gnarled by slavery's contradictions" (Clinton, 2004, p.4). Her given name was Araminta "Minty" Ross, "born somewhere in the middle a string of children, perhaps a dozen" (Clinton, 2004, p.5). Her undocumented childhood was "a series of tough seasonings" (Clinton, 2004, p.16) defined by family separations and displacements in a turbulent environment of abolitionists, kidnappers, slavecatchers, and fugitives (Franklin & Schweninger,

85

1999). As a slave child, she was a bartered commodity of labor. Slave sales via the auction block constantly threatened her family's stability and they often traveled great distances to toil for temporary masters. Daily survival was uncertain. Harriet would endure beatings, whippings, and general neglect at the hands of temporary masters, which marred her childhood and young adulthood by forever scarring her mind and body (Larson, 2004). Yet by adolescence she developed a remarkable stamina that rarely failed her (Clinton, 2004).

Her adolescence also featured two life-changing events. Religion played a key role in black culture, especially during the 19th century. Religious instruction—as it was with most every aspect of a slave's life—was strictly regulated by slaveholders, but Harriet learned a deep spirituality rooted in Methodist evangelical teachings that gave her strength and endurance for the rest of her life (Clinton, 2004; Larson, 2004). While there can be no doubt that Harriet's faith was deep and founded upon strong religious teachings, her spirituality would also be affected by another event. While a young teenager, Harriet was accidently struck in the head by a thrown iron weight. Nearly dying, the resultant skull injury (probably temporal lobe epilepsy and possible narcolepsy) plagued her for the rest of her life in the form of uncontrollable seizures and blackouts that evidently promoted "potent dreams and visions" (Larson, 2004, p.43) which she believed foretold her future. Such visions became central to her spirituality and firmly reinforced her religious beliefs.

At age 19, she married a free black, John Tubman, about whom little is known other than his free status. It was significant in that her slave statues made it an "informal arrangement or intermarriage" (Clinton, 2004, p.25) rather than recognized as a legal marriage. But the marriage would be childless which may have weakened John's commitment to Harriet. In any case, they moved in different emotional directions and, unlike him, her eyes were drawn to the freedom of the North.

The year 1849 brought the pivotal moment that revealed the courage and resourcefulness that would define the rest of her life. The death of her master led her to believe that she would be summarily sold on the auction block. This prompted her to take a more active role in God's plan, rather than letting others dictate her destiny (Clinton, 2004). The risks of escape were great and it further meant abandoning her parents, siblings, and husband. But her belief that freedom was something worth dying for outweighed the risk of becoming a fugitive slave. She boldly fled north, eventually working her way to the freedom of Philadelphia. To commemorate this new phase of her life, she adopted the name of her mother, Harriet.

A runaway slave's successful escape was often dependent upon the crucial assistance of sympathetic whites. Harriet's "web of assistance" was a complicated network and system of shelter, safeguards, codes, and silence known as the Underground Railroad (Still, 1970). The term first appeared in the 1830s but such freedom networks had existed long before Harriet's birth; in fact, as long as slavery itself and originally designed to maintain family and community ties among slaves seeking liberation to the North and Canada. As the anti-slavery movement gained momentum in the 1830s, many religious and civilian organizations committed to actively helping runaway slaves within the broader abolitionist movement (Larson, 2004; McLard, 1991). Such support allowed the networks to become better and more complexly organized in many Northern states. The Underground Railroad network was a vast tangle of interconnected systems and "a full-fledged grassroots resistance movement representing the true national goals of democracy and liberty" (Clinton, 2004, p.65). Participants in the network took such titles as agents, engineers, conductors, and station masters, which coincided with actual railroad positions. It was this system that would later make it possible for Harriet to become one of the rare individuals capable of executing successful and daring rescues repeatedly (Larson, 2004).

Harriet easily blended into Philadelphia's free black community and though she was nominally free in Philadelphia, she soon learned that freedom did not guarantee happiness (Larson, 2004). For one, slavecatchers and bounty hunters continually looked for fugitive runaways. But what set her apart from other runaways was her fierce determination and sheer willpower that not only allowed her to pursue her own path to freedom, but in doing so also led the way for others (Clinton, 2004). For another, her feelings of family deprivation prompted her to action. Her loyalty and love for her family totally dominated Harriet's life and she vowed to bring them all to freedom (Larson, 2004).

Such an endeavor, however, would require more than her considerable efforts and she joined the Underground Railroad network as the vehicle to achieve her goals. Inspired by her faith as an instrument of God, she quickly became familiar with the system, its "depots," and the risks of personally leading runaways to freedom. She would eventually become the only woman to achieve prominence and direct identification within the Underground Railroad, despite having to crucially maintain a secret identity outside of it.

Harriet's first rescue mission involved her niece. Disregarding danger, capture, re-enslavement, or even death, she immediately distinguished herself from other "conductors" by physically returning to a slave state to first "abduct" slaves and then personally "conduct" them to a free state. It was simply a reflection of her extraordinary courage. The success of this initial rescue emboldened her to continue, especially in regard to family members. Although she unhappily learned that her husband had remarried, her deep faith drove her on. The new Fugitive Slave Act (1850) made her freedom less safe, as she was still a fugitive runaway by law. It also made rescues more difficult, but she persevered in the belief that divine intervention would provide both protection and intuition. She "continued to plot and plan; members of her family remained enslaved and she could not rest until she brought them away, too" (Larson, 2004, p.92). Though she was not entirely successful in that regard, she never gave up her commitment to destroy the slave system.

Few "conductors" dared to venture into the South to extract slaves as she did and she gained anonymous notoriety among slaveholders since she brazenly and successfully executed mass escapes after the passage of the Fugitive Slave Act. This new phase of her life also brought her fame and recognition among anti-slavers throughout the network (Hine & Thompson, 1998; McLard, 1991). "Her seizures continued throughout this time, and the religious visions accompanying them often comforted her" (Larson, 2004, p.102) and bolstered her faith and trust in God's protection. Over an 11-year period, Harriet would make at least thirteen trips into slave states and the number of slaves she brought north was remarkably high (Larson, 2004). She "would never allow more to join her than she could properly care for though she often gave others directions by which they succeeded in escaping" (Larson, 2004, p.100).

Harriet was not of course personally responsible for the liberation of all of the successful runaway slaves, but her bold method of operation inspired many to action (Franklin & Schweninger, 1999; Still, 1970). Her rescue missions were always pre-planned and meticulously organized, using established safe routes and station masters with whom she was well acquainted. She preferred to execute her missions on winter nights, though she was confident enough to do so at other times (her only summer rescue involved saving her parents and conducting them to Canada and later New York). Utilizing her considerable skills of disguise and deception, she guided her groups using gospel music and spirituals as coded messages. But she also required total commitment and obedience from her charges, carrying a pistol "as added encouragement" (Larson, 2004, p. 101; Clinton, 2004). As a result, "she never lost a passenger" (Larson, 2004, p.137).

Her rescue missions inspired respect and awe from both blacks and whites, and while her reputation as the Moses of her people was taking shape, she continually grappled to secure funds to finance her operations by working at odd jobs (Larson, 2004). This restricted her from executing more than one or two missions annually. By the late 1850s, missions were increasingly becoming too risky even for her and she began channeling more of her efforts into relief activities amidst rising racial tensions and abolitionist threats that were driving the nation to an inevitable showdown. Harriet was now openly advocating women's rights and racial equality through various humanitarian efforts.

One of the more mysterious episodes in Harriet's life also occurred during this time. In an unexplainable contradiction to her usual actions, she allegedly "abducted" 8-year-old Margaret Stewart from the girl's mother and brought her to the safety of Lincoln's future Secretary of State and sympathetic abolitionist William Seward. Seward had recently befriended Harriet and offered a New York home as a haven. Harriet adopted Margaret and their close bond fueled speculation that Margaret may have been either her niece or possibly her daughter (Clinton, 2004; Larson, 2004). There was never, however, a satisfactory explanation concerning Margaret's true identity and status, and their relationship was considered both mysterious and complicated (Clinton, 2004).

It was perhaps inevitable that Harriet's work in the abolitionist network led to contact with the radical abolitionist John Brown. She claimed to have had dramatically vivid visions of John Brown long before she ever met him (Larson, 2004). They impressed each other immediately, sharing a personal crusade to destroy slavery. "To Brown, Tubman was a doer; acting on her convictions and risking her life like few others, she stood apart from most men Brown knew" (Clinton, 2004, p.158). Brown, however, was maniacally obsessed with the abolition of slavery by any means necessary and was committed to a plan of violent recourse and armed resistance. Harriet did not advocate violence, but she actively supported and encouraged his plan for a slave uprising as a recruiter and guide, providing him with practical information and her expertise in clandestine communication networking. Her respect for him knew no bounds and at great personal risk she solicited as much support for him as she could.

Brown had hoped that Harriet would be at his side when he raided Harper's Ferry, but perhaps her instincts or divine guidance told her that his plan would fail and thus she opted not to directly participate. Indeed, poorly conceived and executed, Brown's plan was doomed from the outset. Though it failed, it served the purpose of hastening the ever-growing showdown over slavery. Brown's hanging was symbolic as well as sacrificial, making him a martyr in many quarters. Harriet deeply mourned him, believing that his death was a sign of final reckoning and vowed to continue his legacy (Larson, 2004).

Though she was still considered a fugitive slave without rights as per the disastrous Dred Scott Decision (1857), Harriet believed firmly in the ideas set forth in the Declaration of Independence and the Constitution, cherishing her own liberty and seeking to extend it to all blacks (Clinton, 2004). To this there could be no compromise and the outbreak of the Civil War in 1861 brought both optimism and yet another new role. Her personal civil war had certainly begun long before, "but it was Tubman's battles to claim liberty for scores of friends and relatives that marked the beginning of a strategic, political, and even military consciousness that eventually prepared her for a role on the battlefields" (Larson, 2004, p.203). Infuriated at Lincoln for not immediately emancipating all slaves, she nevertheless enthusiastically offered her leadership skills, passion and commitment to aid the Union war effort by not only continuing to conduct runaway slaves but also act as a nurse, cook, and scout. She fearlessly journeyed at great peril to Union outposts in enemy territory to tend to the wounded and other special projects (Clinton, 2004). Her apparent skill at curing stricken soldiers was well known (Larson, 2004).

Adept at quickly adjusting to changing and unexpected environments, the Union gave Harriet "broad powers and freedom of movement" (Larson, 2004, p.212) which was unprecedented for a woman and a black. She was also determined to serve militarily. As a spy, scout, and advisor, she became the first woman to plan and successfully execute an armed expedition during the Civil War in June 1863 that ultimately liberated many slaves under her personal guidance (Larson, 2004). The resultant press coverage of that event solidified her image as the "heroine of the day" (Larson, 2004, p.216).

Yet throughout all of her considerable service and sacrifice during the war, Harriet received no salary or compensation and sadly struggled to support herself and her aged parents through odd jobs. Her disappointment over lack of payment eventually prompted her to return home to Auburn, New York, to earn money to pay her mounting debts. The struggle to find adequate work dominated her post-war life and she returned to the lecture circuit to raise funds as she had before the war. This was in like contrast to another black female abolitionist of the time, Sojourner Truth. Harriet's legendary exploits reflected a very personal yet collective experience of resistance and liberation that resonated for both white and African-American women and her storytelling skills were captivating for both of these female crusaders (Larson, 2004). Their mutually profound religious devotion allowed them to attain respectability and authority with white audiences. But unlike Truth, Harriet's lectures were of the private nature to protect her identity, yet her larger-than-life persona catapulted her into the public eye.

During the war, Harriet had held Lincoln in low regard, even after the Emancipation Proclamation, which she believed did not go far enough by liberating all enslaved people. But her stance toward him softened into admiration with the passage of the 13th Amendment that forever abolished slavery. She would genuinely mourn his assassination. But the war's end signaled new challenges for her and the nation. The struggles of African-Americans were just beginning and she would dedicate the rest of her life to helping alleviate the backlash of Reconstruction; namely, its prejudice and discrimination that dominated the era and hindered the fight for black and women's suffrage and the basic rights of citizenship. The struggle for these issues prompted her to focus her energies on fund-raising and relief efforts, many of which were quite successful.

Her stamina and commitment to her people never wavered in spite of her personal setbacks. These would be bittersweet times for her. She endured the personal indignity of non-compensation for her unparalleled war service and was yet again forced to do odd jobs and take in boarders in her home to make ends meet. Harriet predictably fell on hard financial times but she astonishingly created "a refuge for the forgotten and abandoned" (Clinton, 2004, p.191). Her charitable endeavors were symbolic of the work still necessary for African-Americans and women's suffrage, yet she lived impoverished without complaint. A racial discrimination episode in which she was serious-ly injured by allegedly being thrown from a train became another symbol of the plight faced by a newly-freed people (Larson, 2004).

Harriet persistently made claims for compensation to the government, but they fell on deaf ears. Sinking further into debt, she became dependent upon donations to continue. In hopes of securing funds for her humanitarian work as well as to support herself and her family, an early biography of her intro-duced another phase in her life (Clinton, 2004; Larson, 2004). Besides pro-viding desperately needed funds to repay many of her debts, it more impor-tantly increased public awareness of the African-American plight while im-mortalizing her public identity as a true American heroine in her own time. Despite the fact that it was imperfectly and poorly written, it at least chal-lenged "conventional stereotypes of black womanhood while allowing her to continue her tireless work toward justice and equality" (Larson, 2004).

In addition to surrounding herself with family members as well as strang-ers who needed her support, Harriet's personal happiness increased in 1869 when she married (officially, this time) Nelson Davis, who was one of her boarders and about half her age. It was a happy union lasting nineteen years and with their adoption of daughter Gertie, Harriet completed her dream of family, motherhood, and home (Clinton, 2004).

Her philanthropic endeavors continued, but so did her financial woes and she fell victim to several scam artists and opportunists taking advantage of her fame and lack of savvy. A second biography of her appeared in the 1880s which reformulated her legendary image to better suit a nation now more disposed to conciliatory stories of slavery, the war, and its aftermath (Larson, 2004). This muted version again eased some of her financial strain but also kept her in the public eye as she continued to promote women's suffrage. Her frequent speeches to advance the cause gained her further national recogni-tion.

Harriet's health became precarious but she relied as always on her faith to see her through every crisis. Considerably more aged and worn, she could no longer endure the blinding headaches and seizures from her childhood injury and she underwent delicate brain surgery to alleviate them but it was limited in its success. She was also struggling against the changing of the generation-al guard and the continuing racism that hindered racial equality. Financial setbacks and the pain of family deaths plagued her and she turned repeatedly to the spiritual sanctuary of her church which helped her to forge strong networks to support racial, gender, economic, and educational advancement (Larson, 2004). But she was not yet done.

Her persistence in making government claims finally paid off in 1899 when Congress appropriated $20 monthly for her wartime service and wid-ow's pension. While it provided a small measure of security, it prompted Harriet to take action on her dream of establishing a charitable home for sick and aged African-Americans. To that end, she successfully bid on a 25-acre lot to be paid for through contributions and fund-raising. The financial burden of the project, however, became too much for her and she eventually transferred the property to a church. The Harriet Tubman Home would indeed be established five years later, but ironically she disagreed with its administration and left the project.

Harriet's health rapidly declined by 1910 and she was confined first to a wheelchair and finally to bed. She continued to offer advice and inspiration but was confident that God would raise up others to take care of the future (Clinton, 2004). In perhaps a final irony, she entered the Harriet Tubman Home during her last year before dying of pneumonia on March 10, 1913. She was buried with military honors.

The true story of Harriet's life fell into literary obscurity that was confined to children's books until the mid-20th century when a renewed interest in the Underground Railroad naturally prompted the just revival of her life that reveals her for the flesh-and-blood heroine that she is. Many thousands of African-Americans can trace the freedom of their forefathers to her heroics of courage and persistence based on an immovable faith in being an instrument of God. It is unfortunate that the obscurity of her life that has "remained until now is a deeply troubling reflection of the racial, class, and gender dynamics of our nation" (Larson, 2004, p.295), for that reflection serves as a complete antithesis of her life's work. As 21st century America contemplates inevitable challenges, her life creed is as relevant as it ever was: "If you are tired, keep going; if you are scared, keep going; if you are hungry, keep going; if you want to taste freedom, keep going" (Clinton, 2004, p.221). Harriet's light will never dim, for the truth of her life is the essence of heroism.

DISCUSSION GUIDELINE QUESTIONS

1. What values are depicted in the story?
2. Where did Harriet learn her values?
3. What might be her greatest character trait?
4. What might be her greatest flaw?
5. Is there evidence that she struggled with certain value dilemmas? If so, what were the consequences?
6. Are her values still important today?
7. Is there anyone currently on the American scene who is comparable to her? Why or why not?

Chapter 9

REFERENCES

Clinton, C. (2004). *Harriet Tubman: The road to freedom.* New York: Little, Brown and Company.

Franklin, J. & Schweninger, L. (1999). *Runaway slaves: Rebels on the plantation.* New York: Oxford University Press.

Hine, D. & Thompson, K. (1998). *A shining thread of hope: The history of black women in America.* New York: Broadway Books.

Humez, J. (2003). *Harriet Tubman: The life and the life stories.* Madison: University of Wisconsin Press.

Larson, K. (2004). *Bound for the promised land.* New York: Ballantine Books.

McLard, M. (1991). *Harriet Tubman and the Underground Railroad.* Englewood Cliffs, NJ: Silver Burdette Press.

Still, W. (1970). *The underground railroad.* Chicago: Johnson Publishing Company, Inc.

Chapter Ten

The Hidden Man: Abraham Lincoln

He is arguably the most written about and most famous American. He is also often hailed as our greatest president, even though he is the only Chief Executive whose presidency can be defined by a single event: the Civil War (DiClerico, 2000). However, the true nature of Abraham Lincoln is in many respects a mystery in that the myth and legend surrounding him only initially serve to make it easier for us to understand him today (Freedman, 1987). In his own time, he was roundly scorned and denounced, for in essence he was a proven and repeated political loser. Yet no one may have been better suited to the challenge of the nation's most horrific moment. The real Lincoln was an enigma: "Of all the paradoxes of Lincoln's life, none is more powerful than the fact that the man who would come to be known throughout the world was deeply mysterious to the people who knew him best" (Shenk, 2005, p.216).

Lincoln's fairly obscure life is focused upon the actions of his last four years. His conduct during the most harrowing time in our history is pre-eminent in the annals of leadership. To save his country from dismemberment and to give it new direction by freeing it from the evil of slavery required a magnitude of perseverance and courage that few today can even understand, let alone emulate. He redefined presidential power and used it both constitutionally and unconstitutionally with great humility and stead-fastness for the common good, his eloquent words always reflecting the strength of his conviction that he was simply doing the right thing based upon the biblical principles he so deeply believed in. As the most photo-graphed man of his time, his disintegrating images further reflect the price he willingly paid for the mission. Indeed, his life, words, and images make him one of the few Americans whose character bridges time (White, 2009).

But to understand the full scope of this hidden man, it is necessary to separate legend from fact. In truth he was indeed born of humble and poor beginnings in a Kentucky wilderness log cabin with a dirt floor and a single window on February 12, 1809. His father Thomas was a hardworking farmer but little is known of his mother, Nancy Hanks who died when Lincoln (along with his older sister Sarah) was nine years old. Moving to Indiana, his father remarried to another Sarah, of whom Lincoln was exceedingly fond, later saying "All I am, or hope to be, I owe to my angel mother" (Lorant, 1954, p.13). But from a young age, Lincoln began exhibiting a chronic depression—perhaps inherited from his parents—that would plague him throughout his life (Shenk, 2005). This depression would touch every aspect of his life as his unfathomable face could rarely hide the sadness and melan-

choly that "dripped from him as he walked" (Lorant, 1954, p.118). He would struggle his entire life trying to hide this condition, sometimes succeeding and sometimes failing.

It is also true that he basically educated himself by reading all of the books he could lay his hands on, but his lack of a formal education was yet another aspect that haunted him (White, 2009). His self-education was a life-long process that may have also caused a permanent estrangement from his father as the family moved to Illinois in his late teens. In his early 20s, the exceedingly tall (6' 4"), thin, raw-boned youth with an unruly shock of black hair was demonstrating the moral integrity that would survive beyond him, earning the name "Honest Abe" for responsibly paying off large debts. Also present from the beginning was his unbridled ambition to do something of significance. Yet his endeavors in this regard ended in failure. During these years he was a failed store clerk, served very briefly and unspectacularly in the army during the Black Hawk War, and sidelined as a railsplitter, which would later mythically establish him as a common man.

His first political position was local postmaster, but it was the law that drew Lincoln's attention and would later serve him in his quest for political success. Passing the bar at age 28, the man without a formal education established himself as a very capable Springfield law partner and built a name for himself through his extraordinary speaking ability. Balancing law and politics, the ambitious Lincoln would serve four terms in the Illinois state legislature. By age 29, he "was living proof that in Illinois a young man could begin with nothing and through hard work rise to statewide influence" (White, 2009, p.88) with a growing reputation for political intelligence, judgment, and honesty. Though never an abolitionist in the literal sense, Lincoln openly declared his opposition to the spread of slavery at this time, an issue that would soon beg a national showdown.

Serving in the state legislature further fueled his relentless ambition. His political horizons widened, learning that politics was an art of give and take, knowing his constituents, and understanding their problems. His future greatness would be built upon this foundation. He was also dealing with his depression. Sensitive, emotionally reserved, and undemonstrative, Lincoln tended to keep people at a distance with his belief "that his suffering... was his lot to bear" (Shenk, 2005, p.113). He bore it therapeutically through reading, poetry, and especially a self-deprecating humorous nature. Laughter was crucial to him and "gave Lincoln some protection from his mental storms. It distracted him and gave him relief and pleasure" (Shenk, 2005, p.116), allowing him to connect with people in the process while masking the moodiness and melancholy of a man "tormented by long and frequent bouts of depression" (Freedman, 1987, p.4). Ironically, the mental suffering he endured "lent him clarity, discipline, and faith in hard times" (Shenk, 2005, p.126).

Lincoln's political misadventures were underscored by three women who would change his life in various ways. He lost his legendary first love, Ann Rutledge, to an early death before they could be married. Emotionally shattered, he became involved with the more mature and imposing Mary Owen, a very spirited and witty woman who did not tolerate his depression (White, 2009). Their 2-year relationship was rocky at best and his deep insecurity and moodiness drove her to flatly reject his marriage proposal. He then met his future: Mary Todd, who was nine years his junior, vivacious, temperamental, and attractive. Educated and wealthy, she had a strong-willed determination in getting her way with "temper and tongue" (White, 2009, p.108). It was a case of opposites attracting, but Mary genuinely admired his sincerity and honesty in spite of his moodiness. She attracted many suitors, including Stephen Douglas, who was destined to be Lincoln's political nemesis on several occasions, but she spurned them all in favor of Lincoln. Their on-again, off-again 3-year courtship was sheer torture for both, but oddly matched that they were, they were soulmates in their passion for politics. Whatever political insecurities Lincoln may have had—and he had many—Mary's ambition for his success more than offset them.

Her ambition for him soon paid off with his first success in national politics but it disastrously appeared to be his last before it virtually started. Finally elected to the U.S. House of Representatives, Lincoln immediately assaulted President Polk on the issue of the Mexican War. Lincoln interpreted the war as an attempt to ultimately expand slavery, but his actions were construed by his Illinois constituents as unpatriotic in the face of war. Severely criticized and humiliated, his single term ended in abject failure and he returned home in 1849 to focus on law and his self-education.

Lincoln's 5-year hiatus from political pursuits ended abruptly with the national debate over the Kansas-Nebraska Act in 1854. Roused by the issue of expanding slavery, he re-emerged with a stronger disposition into the political arena and on a collision course with the rising figure of Senator Stephen Douglas, the "Little Giant." It is uncertain if Lincoln's political ambition had been quietly continuous or reborn in 1854, but he was more than ever determined to oppose the spread of slavery whose restriction would then, he believed, make it extinct. Naïve as that may have been, Lincoln's growing disillusionment with his Whig Party led him to join the new Republican Party which more closely matched his political philosophy. In a bold move, he challenged Douglas for the Senate, a position that he prized above all others. Their famous series of seven debates in 1858 gave Lincoln national prominence, but again he went home a loser.

As 1860 approached, Lincoln was cautiously ambivalent and at a low point in his depression, fueled by his lack of political experience and formal education. But his gift of eloquent public speaking enhanced his reputation and gave him a platform to refine and redefine his emerging vision of a new

America, one without sectionalism (which he viewed as the root of slavery) and one that would not compromise on the extension of slavery (White, 2009). His words were now being taken seriously by the Republican Party as it sought a presidential nominee from a field of ten candidates. Lincoln's nomination was largely unexpected and surprising, but his timing was perfect. "Put plainly, Lincoln was a politician, building a public life on points that could be sustained by popular opinion" (Shenk, 2005, p.129). That opinion was the preservation of the Union to be sustained without interfering with slavery where it already existed, but there could be no compromise on its extension.

The Election of 1860 was arguably the most critical in our history and a tense, 4-horse race of sectional candidates, which included his old nemesis, Stephen Douglas, who was at the peak of his power and influence. But this time, Lincoln emerged victorious, though his victory was by a minority of 40% of the popular vote in the highest voter turnout in history (White, 2009). Besides being the tallest, he also became the first bearded President solely due to the suggestion of 11-year-old Grace Bedell, who wrote to him to suggest that a beard might balance his thin and homely face.

Lincoln had a habit of embroiling himself in fights where the odds were overwhelmingly against him and he immediately faced what was undoubtedly the greatest of political challenges (Shenk, 2005). "Lincoln came to the presidency lacking executive experience, and his first weeks in office did little to inspire confidence that he could launch and run a new administration" (White, 2009, p.397). His stated governing motto was justice and fairness for all, and he made no distinction between North and South in that regard, but he "did not fully understand the very real possibilities for secession and war" (White, 2009, p.349) by underestimating the Southern mindset. His vow to not interfere with existing slavery quickly fell on deaf ears and seven Southern states seceded by his inauguration.

The shelling of Fort Sumter on April 12, 1861 dashed any hope of compromise and a divided nation prepared to fight over the principle of secession and the preservation of the Union. The new President stood poised to "grasp the awful work of his future" (Shenk, 2005, p.172). Never had conditions been so severe and never had a leader appeared so ill-prepared for them. Lincoln's innate cautiousness prompted a brief period of indecisiveness, which immediately brought loud and continual criticism both publicly and politically. But he was a quick learner. Free of the usual personal animosity in political appointments (he never let personal feelings deter him from selecting the right person for the job), Lincoln assembled an able group of advisors but made it very clear that he was in charge. He was about to take the role of Commander-in-Chief in a new, dynamic, and very controversial direction through unprecedented actions (White, 2009).

His growing list of troubles was lengthy and it is impossible to express in words his daily anguish and grief in finding the right commanding general (it would take three years and over seven appointments before finally finding Grant), diplomatic difficulties with foreign powers who threatened to intervene, increasing problems with Republican radicals, irregularities within his cabinet, and public discontent. There would be no relief as he immersed himself in military theory and strategy, insisting that as president he would be the first and last authority in setting military policy (White, 2009). "No president, before or after, ever spent nearly as much time in the day-to-day, hour-by-hour command of the armed forces of the nation" (White, 2009, p.540). Critics constantly railed against his unprecedented expansion of war powers as he suspended the writ of habeas corpus and power became a daily juggling act.

Inevitably, the pressure of nonstop work took a tremendous toll on him but in 1862 personal tragedies added to his woes. His favorite son, 12-year-old Willie, died after a short illness. The Lincolns had four sons and Willie was their second loss (Edward had died at age 3 and his brother Tad would later die at age 18; only their oldest, Robert, lived to adulthood and an old age). In many respects, he never got over Willie's death, but grieved as he was he was rightfully more worried about Mary. She had many difficulties as First Lady, not the least of which was her exclusion from Washington society due to her family's loyalty to the South. She had always been a loving wife and mother, but she was humorless, strongly opinionated, and overly sensitive to anything she perceived as a slight (Baker, 1987). Perhaps out of needless jealousy of her husband who no longer considered her his chief advisor, she felt entitled to spend huge sums on clothes—especially white gloves to self-consciously hide her hands—which put Lincoln in financial straits (Donald, 1995). But Willie's death pushed her over the edge and she remained inconsolable. Her grief knew no end and Lincoln feared for her mental health (in point of fact, her son Robert would have to commit her to an asylum after Lincoln's assassination).

At the outset of the war, Lincoln's solitary goal was to preserve the Union. But in 1863 he boldly moved to change the war's purpose and promote a new vision for America (Striner, 2006). The Emancipation Proclamation "was a political weapon, wrought of danger" (Lorant, 1954, p.176). It could have provoked the crucial slave-holding border states to bolt and further antagonize Congress to not support it if it became the war's primary goal. Lincoln himself had entertained the idea of relocating freed slaves to Central America even as the conflict entered its second year (White, 2009). Now, however, his new vision called for emancipation and equality of opportunity. There were two problems with such a move. First, it would theoretically free slaves only in areas where the federal government currently had no authority. Thus, it would solely be a symbolic act. "The proclamation was not so much a fact accomplished as a promise to be realized" (White, 2009, p.540). Second, if it was to change the war's goal and promote a new national vision, it would crucially require timing so as not to appear to be an act of desperation; namely, it would have to be preceded by a major Northern military victory, which was difficult to come by.

The Battle of Antietam provided Lincoln with the opportunity to officially sign the Proclamation. "I never, in my life, felt more certain that I was doing the right thing, than I do in signing this paper" (White, 2009, p.535). Using his war powers to issue the decree, Lincoln masterfully used newspaper editorials to garner public support for this initially very unpopular idea which infused a new moral grounding to the conflict. Bringing the expected diversity of political and public reaction/criticism, Lincoln's steadfast perseverance to defend it gradually swayed opinion to his side as he was virtually wrestled with the soul of America itself (White, 2009).

The Battle of Gettysburg shifted the war's momentum, but in late 1863 "Lincoln understood more than ever that his task was to convince more than half of a wearing Northern public that this terrible war was worth fighting" (White, 2009, p.589). To that end, his carefully revised 3-minute Gettysburg Address initially met with great public disappointment and by Lincoln himself. Only gradually was it appreciated for its message promoting the continuance of the conflict and a new America (Donald, 1995).

The great turning point came in 1864: Grant was now commanding the army and he would bring the conflict to a bloody end within a year. This election year also saw Lincoln continuing to battle forces within his own party which questioned his electability. The public appeared to be torn. Many scorned and criticized him while many recognized that this kind and gentle man with no false modesty was a leader that could be trusted. Military victories helped bolster his popularity and though he entered the election with shaky confidence, he was the first president in 32 years to be re-elected to a second term. His troops—who respectfully referred to him as Father Abraham—admired him greatly in the midst of the political turmoil and their votes helped put him over the top (Striner, 2006). It was personal vindication for a man whose confidence had been severely tested.

But there was serious trouble on the horizon as he prepared for a second term. As the war wound down in early 1865, Lincoln was newly assailed by his political enemies for seemingly making little effort to negotiate a peace. The Radical Republicans were already preparing to nullify his plans for amnesty and reconstruction to reconcile the seceded states. But Lincoln was prepared to hold his ground. He had always considered himself a human instrument doing God's work (Donald, 1995). Though he was never officially a member of any church, he was a religious man who loved the Bible, knew it intimately, and lived by its principles (White, 2009). He had demonstrated a spiritual growth from the fatalism of his youth to the providence of his leadership years. It was a growth that provided a solid inspiration for him and his determination to lead America into a new era.

It was, of course, not to be. Fresh on the heels of a victorious end to America's most tragic conflict and the beginning of a new vision, Lincoln's assassination on April 14, 1865 proved to be the ultimate sacrifice: as virtually the last casualty, he died for the cause and even his former enemies now catapulted him to hero status, too late realizing what the nation had lost. He had fought for an America that would be "an ecology of political, social, and economic life that could nourish the common person's opportunity to pursue their dreams, unrestricted by artificial obstacles" (White, 2009, p.426). This was the America of our forefathers and he believed that his generation's mission was to transmit those values (Harris, 2007). That mission required the character of an individual who could preserve the Union, free it from the long-standing evil of slavery, and set a new course for the future. Lincoln was that individual who further understood the price of power and was willing to pay it; and it consumed him in the process.

One can only speculate what might have been had Lincoln lived to lead us through the early years of the post-Civil War era. What he was preparing to prevent would indeed happen: a vengeful reconstruction policy and ensuing backlash that basically kept the nation divided, and the shamefully inadequate provision for freed slaves that would last long into the 20th century (Shenk, 2005). Would his strength of character have been enough to prevent it? His successor, Andrew Johnson, could not fill his shoes in the firestorm that resulted; perhaps no one could have. For current and future generations, however, it is Abraham Lincoln's moral/emotional/intellectual connection to us that makes it worth revisiting him: the model of his character can change who we are for what we can become as the 21st century unfolds before us.

DISCUSSION GUIDELINE QUESTIONS

1. What values are depicted in the story?
2. Where did he learn his values?
3. What was his greatest character trait?
4. What was his greatest character flaw?
5. What evidence is there that he struggled with certain moral issues?
6. Did he make any wrong moral/value choices? If so, what were the consequences?
7. Are there any individuals currently on the scene who are comparable to him? Why or why not?
8. Could Lincoln be elected today based upon his character, values, and experience?

REFERENCES

Baker, J. (1987). *Mary Todd Lincoln: A biography.* New York: W.W. Norton and Company.
DiClerico, R. (2000). *The American president.* Upper Saddle River, NJ: Prentice-Hall.
Donald, D. (1995). *Lincoln.* New York: Simon & Schuster.
Freedman, R. (1987). *Lincoln: A photobiography.* New York: Clarion Books.
Harris, W. (1987). *Lincoln's rise to the presidency.* Lawrence: University of Kansas Press.
Lorant, S. (1954). *The life of Abraham Lincoln.* New York: New American Library.
Shenk, J. (2005). *Lincoln's melancholy.* New York: Houghton-Mifflin Company.
Striner, R. (2006). *Father Abraham: Lincoln's relentless struggle to end slavery.* New York: Oxford University Press.
White, R. (2009). *A. Lincoln.* New York: Random House.

Chapter Eleven

The Free Man: Frederick Douglass

The mission of America has in many ways been a cultural laboratory for the sustaining values of a higher civilization. Uniquely personal and remarkable contributions by heroic individuals have continuously served as the vehicle in that mission. Their moral and ethical worth serve to inspire us if we are willing and prepared to follow their examples of character. In that regard, much can be gleaned from the courageous and intellectual character of Frederick Douglass, a self-made man who began life as a slave but heroically attained acclaim as one of America's celebrated social reformers, influential writer and orator, intellectual, and statesman. His life is a testament of honorable attainment and greatness through perseverance and education that refused to be restrained by the racial boundaries and prejudices of his time.

He never knew the exact date or year of his birth in Maryland, but he believed it to be in 1817 or 1818, eventually choosing February 14 as the date. Lack of specific records for such was of course common for slaves. Frederick's mother, from whom he was separated as an infant, was a slave but he never knew the identity of his father who was rumored to be her master (Douglass, 2003). One of the many cruelties of the slave system often separated mothers from their children and his first recollections were of his grandparents who raised him during his early years. Despite rarely seeing her, his mother's death when he was seven was a grief that he never quite got over. He would only remember her as dignified, a trait he certainly inherited. Later, he would find out she could read, which was extraordinary for a slave, and he would further attribute his genius and love of education to her.

Typical of the slave system, young Frederick was periodically hired out to various masters, but his early life experiences were centered in the Baltimore area. Basically robbed of his childhood, he made the best of his environment, learning much by socializing with the numerous slave and white children.

Respect for elders was an early lesson and it would later help him to develop into a gentleman. But mostly he learned the cruelties of slavery. By age nine, he "was well aware of the unjust, unnatural, and murderous character of slavery" (Douglass, 2003, p.45). Yet he also deduced that the cruel nature of slavery was in the system itself and not necessarily the person: "Nature never intended that men and women should be either slaves or slaveholders, and nothing but rigid training long persisted in can perfect the character of the one or the other" (Douglass, 2003, p.51). He innately questioned the nature of slavery, realizing that not all Blacks were slaves nor all Whites masters.

Religion served to comfort him, though he would periodically grapple with it as an adult. As a child, however, Frederick's spirit was enlightened through a personal relationship with God and constantly prayed that in God's good time he would be delivered from his bondage (Huggins & Handlin, 1980). The successful escape of other slaves also prompted him to contemplate his own and by age eight he already possessed the spirit and purpose of a fugitive from slavery (Douglass, 2003).

Sent to labor for the Auld family in Baltimore for seven years provided a fortuitous turning point in his life. Auld's wife Sophia took a liking to Frederick and not only treated him as one human ought to treat another, but took the highly unprecedented- and illegal- step of teaching him to read and write from the Bible for religious instruction. It served to increase his resolve for freedom. Eventually, however, the master/slave system divested Mrs. Auld of her humane qualities toward him and she ceased teaching him, becoming nearly violent in her opposition to his further education. With his intellectual appetite whetted, Frederick continued secretly to educate himself through his White playmates and reading what he could gather, understanding that "knowledge is the pathway from slavery to freedom" (Jacobs & Appiah, 2004, p.xiii). At age thirteen, he saw no end to his bondage, but education had opened his eyes to understanding the system he would battle.

Pride, power, and avarice, he concluded, were the root of the system. That revelation led him to view everything through the eyes of liberty and the pain of evil. By reading published speeches, young Frederick learned the words of oratory, especially when they denounced slavery. The words of abolitionists and their shuddering effects on slaveholders gave him hope that he was not alone in condemning slavery's inhumanity. Still, he was chattel and life became a matter of self-preservation. Forced to drink "the bitterest dregs of slavery" (Douglass, 2003, p.82) as an adolescent, starvation and the lash nearly broke him but also gave him further resolve. Desperate to escape, the solace of his spirituality underwent a severe shock as well, although he briefly taught a Sabbath-school to other slaves which momentarily restored him.

A major turning point came at age sixteen when for the first time he bravely stood up and physically resisted flogging from an unusually cruel master. Such punishment would not happen again and it rekindled Frederick's self-respect and confidence. No longer afraid of death, the youth was now a man, but a marked man, for he was educated with a burning indignation that would symbolize his future writings and speeches. Two failed attempts at escape did not abate his restlessness and discontent, and he began to secretly accumulating some of his wages earned from a shipyard apprenticeship supervised by his master who in turn was collecting most of the money.

A romantic relationship with a free Black named Anne Murray strengthened his hope to escape after nearly three years of plotting and waiting for the right opportunity. In a moment of high anxiety and timing, Frederick boldly executed a train escape using a free Black's identification papers on September 3, 1838, the date that began his eventful free life. Taking refuge in New York City, Anne joined him and they were soon married. New York was not, however, the safe haven he envisioned and with the help of the Underground Railroad the couple relocated in Massachusetts where Frederick officially took the surname of Douglass. Working various jobs proved quite satisfactory and as he quickly learned Northern culture he immediately saw that the superiority of an educated mind was the key to his future (Douglass, 2003).

The anti-slavery movement was on the rise and Frederick was introduced to William Lloyd Garrison's religious-based abolitionist journal, *The Liberator*, and a subsequently historic introduction to Garrison himself. Attending abolitionist conventions in 1841, he was unexpectedly invited to tell his story in public and it was immediately apparent that he was an electrifying anti-slavery speaker. Frederick thus entered a new life with an enthusiastic spirit as a touring lecturer. In less than four years, he became renowned as an awe-inspiring public speaker and writer sponsored by the influential Garrison. So dynamic were his written and spoken words that many Whites openly questioned if such could emanate from a man of color, a charge that continually amused him. Fortunately, he had the ability to see the humorous side of things, which enabled him to laugh at follies that others would resent (Douglass, 2003). Yet all the while Frederick lived under the apprehensive shadow of recapture.

Perhaps for his own protection, Frederick's abolitionist friends encouraged him to tour England and Ireland for what would be a two-year visit. His humane and equal treatment by Europeans taught him much about civility and justice, and he was transformed by their kindness and deference (Schama, 2006). He noted that "they measure and esteem men according to their moral and intellectual worth, and not according to the color of his skin" (Douglass, 2003, p.174). Further perfecting his considerable oratory skills through many lectures, public support was overwhelming as he advocated an international crusade against slavery and he was given funds to start his own abolitionist publications as a testimonial to disprove racial inferiority.

Returning home to an increasingly hostile environment, however, proved to be disheartening. There was basic opposition to his *North Star* publication because it both interfered with his lecturing success and competed with Garrison's paper. A break between the two men was imminent, but the deal-breaker came with Frederick's shift of opinion over the interpretation of the

U.S. Constitution. Reversing his earlier agreement with Garrison that it was a pro-slavery document, Frederick now viewed it as a literal warrant for the abolition of slavery in every state in the Union and as an anti-slavery instrument that would not necessitate the division of the country (Douglass, 2003). The ensuing rift between the two men was permanent.

Conscious of his dignified and powerful oratory tempered with a sharp wit, Frederick diversified his mission in the late 1840s and 1850s. As the only African-American to attend the first women's rights convention at Seneca Falls, he eloquently asserted that the right to vote must be extended to all Americans regardless of race or gender. Understanding the crucial importance of education in his own life prompted his strong advocacy for desegregating schools, even going so far as to state that an equal and proper education as the key to improvement was a more pressing need than suffrage (Douglass, 2003).

The anti-slavery movement was inevitably intensifying politically, culturally, and legally, laying the foundation for open conflict. Frederick first met the radical abolitionist John Brown over a decade before the latter's failed raid on Harper's Ferry. He greatly admired Brown's fierce and bitter denouncement of slavery and would consider him a great American hero. Brown, on the other hand, admired Frederick who fulfilled his need for a man of color as a confidant. But he strongly disapproved of Brown's ultimate plan for an insurrection and when it failed, Frederick so feared arrest as a co-conspirator that he was forced to flee the country for six months, returning only after Brown's execution led to his martyrdom.

The effects of Harriet Beecher Stowe's *Uncle Tom's Cabin* touched the American soul, even if it did ignite further agitation. Frederick noted that "nothing could have better suited the moral and humane requirements of the hour" (Douglass, 2003, p.202). Upon meeting, the two became partners-in-arms for a common cause, later contemplating the creation of an industrial college for vocational education aimed at elevating Blacks, though it did not come to fruition.

But the country was on a collision course over the slavery issue which "omitted no occasion for inviting disgust by seeking approval and admiration" (Douglass, 2003, p.209) and only served to provoke the abolitionist movement. The shameful decision in the Dred Scott Case and the failed Harper's Ferry raid merely hastened the inevitable showdown. Frederick did his considerable best by pen and oratory to fan the flames of ensuing agitation and by 1860 it was clear that a peaceful solution would not be found.

He used his great fame to wholeheartedly support Lincoln for the presidency, even though Lincoln believed that the resultant Civil War's aim was to preserve the Union. Frederick believed from the beginning that the war's true aim was to end slavery and to that end stressed that Blacks had the right to fight for the North (which in his mind should also give them the right to vote). He would work tirelessly to impress this conviction upon Lincoln who in turn was disappointingly cautious to alter the Northern mindset which was still influenced by prevailing prejudice. The Emancipation Proclamation would officially change the war's aim to Frederick's way of thinking, but it was two years down the road. Nevertheless, he fervently campaigned for Black military recruitment and later fought for fair treatment of Black soldiers. A face-to-face meeting with Lincoln, however, changed Frederick's previously unfavorable opinion of him, leading Frederick to view Lincoln as a man whose character he could honor and trust. The two would become close friends.

His life mission invariably led to a political perspective and he became an ardent conservative Republican based on that party's stated willingness to do more for his race; to not only promote their equality but to leave them alone to grow and prosper through opportunity (Levine, 1997). He also clearly understood that the right of the ballot would be crucial in the mission and that meant citizenship. Lincoln's re-election gave him further incentive to press that issue on the presupposition that he had the most powerful political ally upon whom he could rely (Oakes, 2007). Lincoln's assassination, unfortunately, changed the entire outlook and Frederick deeply mourned his death, no doubt aware that he would be fighting the crusade single-handedly.

With the war ended, President Johnson and Congress would buttress the previously initiated 13th Amendment by additionally overseeing the 14th and 15th Amendments, all of which would legally abolish slavery, provide for citizenship and equal protection, and guarantee voting rights. It was not the renaissance that it should have been, as the government pursued more detrimental plans that quickly led to racial backlash in the Reconstruction South and set back the mission of equality for decades. In the midst of the upcoming battle for racial equality, Frederick also found himself temporarily estranged from the women's movement due to his support of the 15th Amendment which excluded women from the vote. He would return to that issue in due time, but his mission was clear as he again took to the lecture circuit in that although slavery was abolished, the wrongs against his people had not ended (Douglass, 2003). Blacks were not totally free, still slaves to a society bent on ignoring the laws that were now paradoxically on their side.

It would take federal power to secure and protect civil rights. To influence that end, Frederick chose to become more politically involved but was wise enough not to seek public office. Instead, he accepted several political appointments to positions spanning the ensuing years that included the presidency of the Freedmen's Bank, Ambassador to Haiti, Recorder of Deed, and U.S. Marshall of Washington, D.C. For various reasons outside of his control, Frederick was not as successful in these endeavors as he had hoped and often came under harsh public criticism. To his great credit, however, he maintained his dignity throughout every ordeal and persevered for the bigger picture of equality. He put the ghost of slavery beneath him, though its lingering memory followed him everywhere, but stood tall in the power of his intellect and self-worth as an outspoken champion of equality for all.

He continued to work within the political system by supporting Republican candidates but he was becoming impatient and disillusioned with the lack of progress toward equality, especially as the post-war South stubbornly and boldly enforced disfranchisement and segregation, a situation that would sadly endure deep into the 20th century. What frustrated him most was the national failure to follow through on the real meaning of the Civil War: the abolition of slavery liberated Whites as well as Blacks and the potential for kindness, brotherhood, and justice were before us to be cultivated. But the disease of racism lurked and prevailed.

For his part, Frederick demonstrated a forgiving nature that other former slaves would find difficult. He took the step of reconciling with his old master, Thomas Auld, as the old man lay dying. In his mind, they were both victims of a dreaded system. "Our courses had been determined for us, not by us. We had both been flung, by powers that did not ask our consent, upon a mighty current of life, which we could neither resist nor control" (Douglass, 2003, p.321). It was a humane endeavor typical of him and provided an example that both races could learn from.

Frederick also never forgot those who helped him advance his mission throughout his life. "Gratitude to benefactors is a well recognized virtue, and to express it in some form or other, however imperfectly, is a duty to ourselves as well as to those who have helped us" (Douglass, 2003, p.340). He always acknowledged that he was not the sole architect of his success, though he could proudly claim much credit for his extraordinary courage in overcoming adversities. As a result of his own perseverance, others believed in him, encouraged him, and through them he was brought to the attention of the world in addition to the American people (Douglass, 2003). He continued to be especially supportive of women's rights, "for the cause of the slave has been peculiarly woman's cause" (Douglass, 2003, p.342), which gave further motive to his mission of equality for all. For him, the logic was irrefutable in that the united strength of all Americans as a whole could accomplish much more than a part.

His private life was a different matter. Anna had been his wife for forty-four years and mother to their five children. She was ever the loyal supporter of his long public mission but severe strains on their marriage were evident. Frederick's force of character that she loved so much may have been without peer, but he apparently had affairs with two women with whom he worked professionally, resulting in recurring speculation bordering on scandal (Huggins & Handlin, 1980). Neither publicly spoke of the effects, but Anna's death in 1882 was nevertheless a severe loss and left him depressed for a time. Within two years, he took what was unsurprisingly considered in

American society a most controversial step by marrying Helen Pitts, a White feminist who was twenty years his junior. Frederick was indifferent to the expected storm of public criticism from both races, but he had to painfully endure the wrath of his children who felt the marriage was a betrayal to their mother.

As he entered the last decade of his life, Frederick had for some time been one of the pre-eminent men and intellectuals in America. Among the remaining kudos he garnered was the distinction of receiving a vote for the presidential nomination at the Republican National Convention in 1888, the first African-American so honored. Still fighting for the equality of all, his writings and oratory continued to be energizing by his belief that on his side he always had the invisible forces representing the moral government of the universe (Douglass, 2003).

On February 20, 1895, Frederick spoke at a national women's meeting in Washington, D.C., where had resided for many years. He received what was to be his last ovation. Returning home, he died of a massive heart attack or stroke. Earlier, he had expressed no regrets for his life, stating that "… my day has been a pleasant one. My joys have far exceeded my sorrows and my friends have brought me far more than my enemies have taken from me" (Douglass, 2003, p.349). He had always been fearless in risking personal battle to achieve the goals of liberty, citizenship, equality, and brotherhood, though he understood that the civil rights issue that encompassed them all was a national issue requiring national effort. It was all fueled by a simple principle: "No man can put a chain about the ankle of his fellow-man, without at last finding the other end of it about his own neck" (Douglass, 2003, p.400); that a wrong to one is simply a wrong to all. Towards the end of his life, he reluctantly accepted that Whites were still not quite reconciled to the issue of Black equality. Though he could not understand the lack of progress toward brotherhood as based upon the biblical perspective, he accepted that it would take patience and understanding. Equality "was yet far down the steps of time" (Douglass, 2003, p.380) and others- such as Martin Luther King- would have to take up the fight.

Never had there been a stronger model of and advocate for the sheer power of education and was the living example of his self-proclaimed creed that the attainment of an education is the primary pillar of hope for any race striving to succeed and live free; that one must improve oneself first before the world can be improved (Douglass, 2003). Frederick fervently encouraged the pursuit of knowledge which in turn spawned self-reliance, self-respect, perseverance, and industry (Douglass, 2003). His life demonstrated that intelligence is the great leveler in the mission of equality and he continually found "that the higher the gradation in intelligence, the farther removed are all artificial distinctions and restraints of mere caste and color" (Douglass, 2003, p.331).

The epitome of the self-made man, he could claim several lives: from slave, to fugitive, to free man, to crusader. But in the end, it was a life faithfully devoted to his race. Improving their condition was his life's mission and he set the example by fighting the degradation of slavery and overcoming its brutality and ignorance through sheer force of perseverance, courage, and education. Frederick would no doubt be pleased at the great progress in civil rights made during the last century, yet its ultimate solution is still to be realized. While it yet remains an American task, the values of his life are proof that it can be achieved.

DISCUSSION GUIDELINE QUESTIONS

1. What values are depicted in the story?
2. Where did Douglass learn his values?
3. What may have been his greatest character trait?
4. What was his greatest flaw?
5. Can a person today become "self-made" as he did? Why or why not?
6. Are there any current issues on the American scene that require a Frederick Douglass?
7. Is there anyone currently on the scene who is comparable to him? Why or why not?

REFERENCES

Douglass, F. (2003). *The life and times of Frederick Douglass.* Mineola, NY: Dover Publications.

Huggins, N. & Handlin, O. (1980). *Slave and citizen: The life of Frederick Douglass.* Boston: Little, Brown.

Jacobs, H. & Appiah, K. (2004). *Narrative of the life of Frederick Douglass, an American slave & incidents in the life of a slave girl.* New York: Mass Marketing Paperbacks.

Levine, R. (1997). *Martin Delaney, Frederick Douglass, and the politics of representative identity.* Chapel Hill: University of North Carolina Press.

Oakes, J. (2007). *The radical and the republican: Frederick Douglass, Abraham Lincoln, and the triumph of antislavery politics.* New York: W.W. Norton & Company, Inc.

Schama, S. (2006). *Rough crossing: Britain, the slaves, and the American Revolution.* New York: HarperCollins.

Chapter Twelve

Comforter of the Afflicted: Clara Barton

The Civil War provided the defining moment for more than a few American heroes, both famous and unsung. The classic example of the former is Abraham Lincoln, whose entire presidency was defined within its parameters. But perhaps equally heroic to Lincoln during this harrowing moment in our history are the understated exploits of Clara Barton, whose name is singularly associated with the Red Cross. That, however, was a later phase of her heroism. Rather, it was her Civil War achievements at a relatively late age that would earn her status as an American heroine. Her story reflects 19th century values that were unique for a woman, but 21st century America still has need of them.

She was born Clarissa Harlow Barton in Massachusetts on Christmas Day 1821, the youngest of five children. Her sad childhood presented a contradiction. On the one hand, her family ties would mean everything to her, including her extended family which played an important emotional role for her as an adult (Pryor, 1987). She idolized her affectionate father and loved her siblings who provided a need and reason to live; and the significant other that she would never have. But Clara's ferociously tempered mother neglected her upbringing and she was basically raised by her military father and siblings (Ross, 1956; Barton, 1922). As to her childhood, she remembered "nothing but fear" (Oates, 1995, p.25) and grew up frightened and insecure. It also brought a recurring depression with which she would battle long into adulthood. Growing up with the hurt of her parents' contentious marriage may have significantly contributed to the reason Clara never married, though she had many suitors and proposals. But no man ever permanently held her heart.

Clara was "small, slender, and striking: only five feet tall with silky brown hair parted in the middle and combed into a bun in the back of her head; she had a round face, a wide, expressive mouth, and exquisite, dark brown eyes" (Oates, 1995, p.3). Physically strong, she was a vegetarian who maintained a remarkable health and vigor. Her father had tutored her to be a skilled rider and sharpshooter. Clara was also a superb conversationalist and

when in the company of those she liked, she exuded warmth and a disarming informality about her (Oates, 1995; Pryor, 1987). Always acting as a proper lady, she intensely disliked authoritarian people, especially women. She was unmarried by choice and rejected marriage, which she associated with death, and thus turned her back on the idea of marriage and motherhood as the female ideal (Oates, 1995).

As an adult, Clara grew increasingly dissatisfied with her life. Though she was a former schoolteacher who established the first public school in New Jersey, she railed against the socially imposed restrictions of gender and yearned for an opportunity to demonstrate the power of a woman outside of the expected domestic role (Pryor, 1987). Clearly, this was a woman who longed for independence, meaningful and fulfilling work, and responsibility over her own life (Oates, 1995). But by age thirty-nine—which was considered late middle age by the day's standards—her only solace was that she was a relatively successful single working woman in the Washington, D.C. Patent Office and one of the very few female federal employees. It was not enough: her fierce will and go-ahead spirit demanded a challenge.

The outbreak of the Civil War in 1861 would provide her the opportunity as a woman to seize control of her own destiny (Oates, 1995). It would be the defining event of her generation and would shape who she was and what she was to become. The war's outbreak signaled that history was going to be written in blood and Clara desperately wanted to protect her beloved Union by serving in the army as a soldier, which was obviously impossible. Waiting impatiently for any chance to serve, she immediately began nursing duties following an April 1861 riot in nearby Baltimore. Camps were being quickly established with the onslaught of military operations whose most immediate need was for stores and medicine. The critical lack of same provided the opportunity for her to at last do something for the Union cause and she became "a one-woman relief agency" (Oates, 1995, p.17). She longed, however, to serve at the front. But propriety demanded that she could visit front-line camps only with government permission and a male escort, lest she be branded as a camp-follower prostitute.

The Union disaster at Bull Run was not just a military defeat. It also revealed the disorganized and shamefully inadequate medical treatment of wounded soldiers. These conditions consumed her with anger and frustration, as she was firmly convinced that the battlefield and its pressing needs was where she needed to be (Oates, 1995). Yet astonishingly, female nurses were not allowed to accompany armies into battle (Hall, 1993; Massey, 1966). Despite pressure on the government to immediately improve the medical service, it would remain a mismanaged disgrace for much of the war. None of this deterred Clara, who was still limited to sending supplies with the cooperation of a full-fledged women's organization. She made up her mind that if her countrymen were suffering, then her place would be with them

(Oates, 1995). While continuing to work in the Patent Office for income, she began by visiting the wounded in hospitals, especially regiments from her home state, and she quickly earned respect from "her boys." The final push that Clara needed came from her dying father who supported her desire "to seek and comfort the afflicted everywhere" (Oates, 1995, p.41). Fiercely determined to challenge any obstacle to go anywhere soldiers were fighting, her frustration was compounded by initial failure to receive the necessary government and military approval. She wanted to be in the war.

A temporary hospital transport service manned by female volunteers gave her some hope of participation, but Clara was far too independent and too much of a loner to enlist (Oates, 1995). It was a trait that would both help and hinder her life mission. Tragically working to her benefit, the intensifying battles increased casualties and suffering. This allowed her to finally break through the barriers set up by the male military bureaucracy and she received permission to take supply stores to the front in mid-1862 (Oates, 1995). Working to some purpose, she engaged assistants to help her successfully distribute vital supplies which signaled the beginning of an extraordinary mission. Because knowledge of infectious diseases was basically non-existent, they quickly became the war's leading killer. Dysentery, malaria, and typhoid were treated with the war's "wonder drug": quinine. In turn, its bitterness was often washed down with the war's "all-purpose medicine": whiskey. The overall devastation and suffering offered Clara the opportunity she was seeking. Finding conditions aghast, she "rolled up her sleeves and went to work" (Oates, 1995, p.61) against the "second" enemy of infection, disease, and ignorance.

With the conflict entering a more vindictive and horrific stage, she was on her way, relatively free from constraint, and more exhilarated than ever. Clara was determined to show the government and the army that her supplies, her skills and her energy could make a positive difference in the battle-front hospitals. Only momentarily did she question her nerve, but she was ashamed that she had allowed the prevailing social mores and her accursed sense of propriety keep her from the field for over a year (Oates, 1995). Receiving a leave of absence from the Patent Office, Clara henceforth devoted her energies to the battlefields of damaged humanity.

Clara soon learned that the horrors of the field hospital service were too great and too consuming to handle by herself, but her take-charge approach led to some semblance of sanitized conditions. More importantly, it led to the admiration of many who thought that "if heaven sent out a homely angel, she must be one, her assistance was so timely" (Oates, 1995, p.63). During the battles of Second Bull Run, Antietam, and Fredericksburg, she learned on the job the functions of the independent battlefield nurse, treating the wounded with loving care, and realizing that whatever she did was not enough. Risking capture and death under fire, she persevered, often alone and often the only female, calmly, methodically, and tenderly nursing the wounded with a single-minded intensity. Clara was the only Northern female nurse and relief worker who served on the battlefield itself, tending to troops while under fire, and demonstrated a different kind of heroism that brought love and compassion amidst the rage and hatred of battle (Oates, 1995). She was not only an angel of the battlefield but also from her Washington warehouse command post where she relentlessly prepared for future campaigns and readied her crew for service at a moment's notice (Pryor, 1987; Ross, 1956).

A bout with typhoid fever forced a lengthy convalescence, but she eagerly returned without skipping a beat. By 1863, a new, more efficient field hospital system had at last been implemented and she was confident that her services as an independent field nurse would still be needed. She identified so strongly with common soldiers that she considered herself one of them. They also considered her as one of them in that Clara shared their experiences while always maintaining her womanly dignity, and she won both the affection and respect of many hardened veterans. Nursing the wounded gave her a sense of control and power she had not known was possible, as well as the responsibility she had sought through the deeply personal satisfaction of completeness and fulfillment (Oates, 1995). She also heartily approved of Lincoln's Emancipation Proclamation which changed the war's aims and bolstered her belief that she "saw the hand of God shaping events to suit His own designs" (Oates, 1995, p.95). It would also directly affect her personal philosophy of the war.

Clara was driven as never before and never flinched in her nursing duties. She could not be deterred by relentless gun and cannon fire, nor by the spattering of "blood, brain matter, and fragments of bone, muscle, and skin" (Oates, 1995, p.112). She often heard the phrase "you saved my life," but she couldn't save them all. Her personal Civil War was waged against death in the battlefield hospitals and dressing stations. But when death did come, she kept meticulous record of the dead. No soldier was going to end up in an unknown grave and forever lost to his grieving family if she could help it (Oates, 1995).

Her battlefield service had been nothing less than heroic and by the war's midway point she had become a beloved celebrity and symbol. Clara's open dedication to justice, mercy, patriotism, and God were widely respected. Soldiers would salute her as she walked the streets of Washington and visited hospitals. Her motherly instincts had found the proper outlet in tending the wounded: they were her family and she always found the strength to carry on for their sake.

The fact that she had found her true vocation and purpose spurred her on. Before 1863, Clara had relied almost exclusively on women's aid societies to solicit supplies. She now boldly requested the War Department to designate her as an unofficial relief worker which would give her the power to tap other supply sources and dispense them while retaining her independent status. Facing formidable competition from other relief workers and official government units, the move further put into question the actual need for independent nurses. Though she could be easily hurt and was extraordinarily sensitive over the possibility of rejection, Clara unashamedly used her newly acquired political influence to get her brother commissioned as Quartermaster (Oates, 1995). The appointment not only satisfied her request but also provided her with the official escort she would need to new theaters of war.

Clara's next battlefield assignment took her to the southern campaign in South Carolina. There she directly observed the brutal effects of slavery on the black population which would prove to be a life-changing experience that affected her future work. Her charm, youthful appearance, and single status obviously created quite a commotion among the single officers and men, but as always she had no time or inclination for dalliances (Oates, 1995). That changed when she met courtly Lt. Colonel John Elwell, a married man who greatly intrigued her. Clara found herself irresistibly attracted to this physician/lawyer/professor/officer who was serving as the local quartermaster for her upcoming service. Elwell was bedridden with a broken leg and yellow fever, prompting her to tenderly nurse him back to health. Their relationship quickly blossomed into an intensely passionate love affair. However, "they accepted boundaries to their relationship. She made no effort to win him from his wife, nor did he offer to leave her for Clara" (Oates, 1995, p.151).

Despite her alleged love for Elwell, battlefield service was her top priority but it was not happening as planned in this theater. Their briefly idyllic life wore thin as she impatiently waited for battlefield action. Action finally did come and it helped alleviate her increasing guilt over both the affair and inactivity. Significantly for Clara, the stated action included the famous attack by the all-black 54th Massachusetts in a battle that she personally witnessed. She would also proudly understand the historical importance of the 54th's magnificent effort for the cause of freedom.

Clara was also displaying her shallow side. Fiercely and singularly independent to a fault, she would never allow a female assistant to stand with her on the battlefield, but only after a battle and only in the field hospital (Pryor, 1987). As ambitious as she was altruistic, Clara did not want to share her position with anyone else, especially younger women who were potential rivals (Oates, 1995). She was also never afraid to use her supply dispensing power to force authoritarian officers into line. Perhaps for these reasons, it caught up with her. Incredulously, she was summarily ordered to leave the southern operation, a move that left her embittered, humiliated, and depressed. Suddenly entering a period of "enforced leisure," she predictably felt guilty about not being in the field. Her days drifted without purpose and her depression deepened. Astonishingly, even the hospitals were off-limits to her due to the vindictive edict of a government unit with which she had previously clashed.

She found it most difficult to endure this change of events. A female friend would help draw her out of her depression and gave her new direction by converting her to the cause of women's suffrage and basic equality. Clara also became more racially conscious of the African-American's plight and vowed to assist that cause. But because she was no longer in the field, her paid leave of absence from the Patent Office was terminated under petty circumstances and left her with no income. Though her position would later be restored, the bitterness of the ordeal stayed with her.

The fact of the matter is that Clara desperately needed the rest and a change in venue. Reluctant as she was to leave the southern operation, she was rundown and could not hide the physical toll that was taken on her appearance. Returning to Washington with mixed emotions to an uncertain future in late 1863, she resumed her unsatisfying position of replenishing stores to be sent to the front. She was now a female "temp" rehired in the Patent Office and looking for any method, plan, or opportunity to return to battlefield service. Her prospects were dim. "It was a painful irony that Clara had cleared the way for other women to serve in Virginia field hospitals, only to find that she was excluded from them now" (Oates, 1995, p.213). Feeling unjustly cut-off, she again battled her depression on a daily basis and refused to give into it.

Clara's fortunes would dramatically change with General Grant's appointment to command in 1864. Grant's reputation for intense fighting and massive casualties inspired her to action. She had been temporarily visiting the camps of nearby Massachusetts divisions whose continuing admiration for her offered hope. In yet another bold move, Clara directly appealed to the Secretary of War for permission to yet again return to the front to nurse the wounded and she put her faith in God's will (Oates, 1995). The opportunity came after three long months with the medical emergency of the Battle of the Wilderness. Suddenly and easily obtaining permission, Clara was again on her way to serve in the field as an independent nurse.

The carnage was as always horrifying and the number of wounded overwhelming, but a revitalized Clara tirelessly toiled in the midst of misery with the help of her sisterhood of female volunteers to ease the strain. She openly fumed over the improved but still inadequate medical service and lack of supplies. Clara continued to work effectively as an independent with little or no bureaucratic restraint, yet "there were times, she confessed, when she could not bear the killing and mangling of so many young men… but believed that God had His own designs in letting it continue" (Oates, 1995, p.275). "Daily exposure to twisted bodies, splintered bones, raw flesh, burning fevers, and fetid air" (Oates, 1995, p.256) could not demoralize her, for she was back in her element. Her special brand of care rallied many from the brink of death. Her patients—her family—were tenderly nursed, especially black soldiers for whom she gave extra care.

Clara constantly pushed the need for more nurses, but objected if they were not under her personal supervision. She still felt jealous of younger women who might gain attention and threaten her position of power as a volunteer matron. But her insecurities were basically unfounded: the admiration she earned from field doctors netted her a hard-won authority over nurses and kitchen operations, and her reputation by this time knew no limit of respect.

With the war ending in April, 1865, Clara returned again to Washington due to administrative changes and the need for rest after over six months of continuous, grueling service. Now nationally reputed as "the soldier's friend," she set her sights on a new role and challenge that would require government approval and military assistance. She accurately surmised that a major cause of the post-Civil War anguish would be the large number of unidentified dead soldiers and those missing in action. With her trademark commitment, she set about the task of devoting herself to locating these men. Government approval had come in the form of a support letter from President Lincoln shortly before his assassination. Military assistance, however, would prove to be another matter.

Thousands of inquiries about the dead and missing began pouring into Clara's office of operations and she realized that the task was too large for one individual to handle. Hiring a staff out of her own funds, she simultaneously used her political connections to directly appeal to Congress for additional appropriations. Forging ahead in what would be her final war-related mission, Clara's search inevitably led her to investigating Confederate prison camps.

Assisted by a surviving prisoner of war, Clara was led to investigate the most infamous of Confederate prisons: Andersonville. Beginning an episode of complexity and intrigue, the surviving prisoner possessed a registry of over 12,000 Union soldiers who had died there and buried in mass graves. In an ensuing military expedition to Andersonville, Clara experienced unnecessary humiliation and disrespect from her military escorts who proceeded to undermine her efforts. Finding herself in the field again, however, she thrived on the hardship of properly identifying the dead and burying them in what would be commemorated as a national cemetery. To her great despair, she did not win over her disrespectful escorts who in turn cut her out of their final report. Clara, however, recorded her findings in her own report which further cited the inhumane treatment and miserable environment of Union prisoners. Her report was so significant that it became part of the evidence in the trial and conviction of Andersonville's commandant, Henry Wirz.

But Clara sought vindication and proper recognition for the expedition and eventually found it in the press. In a stunning turn of events, Clara convinced the influential editor Horace Greeley to publish the registry and the factual story of her role in the venture. The resultant publicity not only brought her vindication, but virtually assured her of receiving desperately needed funds to continue her missing-soldiers work and earn a living. By doing so, Congress went a step further by nobly acknowledging the country's gratitude to a true heroine. Clara reopened her operations which would continue for over two years and successfully identify over 22,000 soldiers. Only after being satisfied that she had done all that was humanly possible did she close the operation in 1868, thus bringing to an end her Civil War career.

Now in her late 40s and basically out of work, Clara accepted an invitation to lecture on her war experiences. Prospects were bleak and she looked upon it as an opportunity to provide some income. But she would surprise herself by becoming an enthralling and gifted speaker; so good, in fact, that she received the same fee on the lecture circuit as such eminent men as Ralph Waldo Emerson. People thronged to see this small, slender, and very feminine woman, dressed usually in her light blue traveling dress, and still looking younger than she actually was (Oates, 1995). Clara spoke candidly about the gender restrictions that initially kept her from the battlefield, her fierce determination to get there, the unspeakable horrors she experienced, and the unfinished work that remained as long as there were widows and orphans in need.

Clara lavished praise on the doctors she worked with and the other women who similarly served. She now ironically felt a binding sisterhood with them, though she still would not admit that she absolutely hated sharing her patients and hospital, which were her power and glory, with other women (Oates, 1995). She spoke as a war veteran, and rightfully so, for she had won the undying respect, gratitude, and love of countless thousands of veterans who always turned out to cheer her and thank her. As perhaps the most famous woman of the era, she broke the restraints of gender and brought about new opportunities for women in the field of nursing and medicine. More importantly, she inspired her generation with a new sense of worth by proclaiming that "her great service to the Union cause was an act of momentuous self-discovery and self-empowerment" (Oates, 1995, p.383) made all the more remarkable by independent attainment without compromising her respectability as a lady. Had she been the battlefield soldier she wanted to be, her heroic exploits would have earned her the Congressional Medal of Honor. Instead, she was hailed as the role model for the battlefield nurse and led the way for other women to serve in battlefield hospitals. Clara was compared to the legendary Florence Nightingale but would decidedly outshine her in that Nightingale never worked on the battlefield itself under fire as Clara bravely had.

Many veterans named their daughters after her in tribute and in these younger women who bore her name, the very spirit of Clara lived on (Oates,

1995). Having found her calling and purpose, Clara's humanitarian efforts and sense of duty took her abroad to the battlefields of foreign wars where she continued to serve with distinction. She would later go on to found and become the first president of the American Association of the Red Cross, the organization with which she is historically linked. But even that was no desk job, as she was still serving in the field at age seventy-seven during the Spanish-American War. Upon her death at age ninety in 1912, Clara's legacy continued to inspire ensuing generations of nurses. Her values and character continue to endure a century later and still inspire us to greatness.

DISCUSSION GUIDELINE QUESTIONS

1. What values are depicted in the story?
2. Where did Clara learn her values?
3. What may have been her greatest character trait?
4. What was her greatest flaw?
5. Is there evidence that she struggled with certain moral dilemmas? If so, what were the consequences?
6. Why are her values still relevant today?
7. Is there anyone currently on the scene who is comparable to her? Why or why not?

REFERENCES

Barton, W. (1922). *The life of Clara Barton, founder of the American Red Cross.* Boston: Houghton Mifflin Company.

Hall, R. (1993). *Patriots in disguise: Women warriors of the Civil War.* New York: Paragon House.

Massey, M. (1966). *Bonnet brigades: American women and the Civil War.* New York: Alfred A. Knopf.

Oates, S. (1995). *A woman of valor: Clara Barton and the Civil War.* New York: The Free Press.

Pryor, E. (1987). *Clara Barton, professional angel.* Philadelphia: University of Pennsylvania Press.

Ross, I. (1956). *Angel of the battlefield: The life of Clara Barton.* New York: Harper & Brothers.

Chapter Thirteen

The Cantankerous Hero: Thomas Edison

The American character as we know it today has been historically defined by a cadre of values exemplified by our heroes/heroines. Two of the more formidable values certainly include ingenuity and work ethic, which have not only advanced our culture but also contributed to our world standing in the technological arena and social realm of success. But the individual who may best represent those values is also one of our more misperceived heroes: Thomas Alva Edison. Most of us have grown up with a standard image of worship for this great inventor who is credited with an astonishing 1093 patents spanning a career of over sixty years. Legendary among those inventions is the electric light bulb which brought the nation out of darkness and into the light of the industrial age. Yet the true story of Edison is laced with contradiction, sadness, and misperception, for he proved to be a cantankerous hero who could not overcome the heroic public image that he himself had crafted.

He was born in Milan, Ohio, in 1847, the last of seven children. Known as "Al," he soon proved that formal schooling was not for him. Labeled as "addled," the rambunctious youth left public school to be home-schooled by his mother (Baldwin, 2001). The experience left him contemptuous of book learning and formal education (though he did voraciously read) and he would rely on his instincts and common sense (Stross, 2007; Clark, 1977). Edison was hearing-impaired from an early age, though its cause was never actually attributed to a single reason. As it worsened into adulthood, however, it would have predictably detrimental effects on his interactions with others. But he would never allow his lack of education and deafness to be obstacles.

When he was seven, the Edison family moved to Michigan where he spent his adolescence and, influenced by his father, began a series of entre-

preneurial ventures that included selling candy and vegetables, and printing his own newspaper aboard trains. He also experimented as a novice chemist, which cost him his train-based ventures when he started a fire (Israel, 2000). While still an adolescent, Edison became a telegraph operator as a reward for saving a small boy's life in the train yard. His amazing and highly regarded proficiency at the key led to his first paid position but also set the stage for his inventing passion. Edison's early inventions were directly related to telegraphy and electricity. These included a stock ticker and his first patent for the electric vote recorder, which at age twenty-two propelled him into full-time inventing (Stross, 2007).

It was risky to start such a career without capital, but "Edison [would never] lack for self-confidence and held fast to the conviction that he could remove any technical obstacle that impeded his progress, no matter what field of invention he explored" (Stross, 2007, p.3). That stance would lead to many planned and accidental successes, as well as some dead-ends. But it was Edison's utter fearlessness that would place him above all other meritorious inventors of the Industrial Age. Whitney, Fulton, McCormick, Morse, Bell, Goodyear, and Ford would all alter the face of the American economy and the way citizens lived, but Edison would outshine them all. Ironically, however, he was the only one who would not be able to comfortably deal with fame and larger-than-life hero status.

Edison's early goals were modest: his own shop to work on his own projects with enough profit to continue. Throughout his life, such autonomy was critical to him, even though he would often be dependent on financial partners to secure the necessary capital as he hopped from one project to the next. His goals also had indirect effects on his personal life. At age twenty-four, he married one of his shop employees, sixteen-year-old Mary, whom he had known for only two months. She would bear him a daughter and two sons, but he was so utterly indifferent to them that they may as well have not existed. Edison would never be accused of being a devoted family man, for his work always came first.

His real ascent to fame began with the major innovation of his first industrial research laboratory in Menlo Park, New Jersey. Though he worked there only five years before moving to other labs in New Jersey, New York, and Florida, he would be forever associated with Menlo Park where his celebrity was created. Established in 1876, Menlo Park's relative isolation provided an atmosphere of limitless creative freedom, focusing on creating technological innovation and then controlling its application (Stross, 2007). The lab employed twelve workers who were "directed by a disheveled figure of medium height... [and] grimy hands... [penetrating gray eyes]... a collarless shirt and a seedy black jacket, and his hair was uncombed" (Stross, 2007, p.22). Fame would come early and suddenly during the Menlo Park years and as he struggled with becoming a world-famous celebrity/inventor, he fought to forge his own public image to use for his own ends. He had been totally indifferent of his image as a youth, but as an adult he cared very much yet ironically he would not quite be able to control it as he intended.

Edison's first big financial success was the quadruplex telegraph and it solidified his growing reputation. The mass-marketing of this and subsequent inventions fueled his ambitions for business success because it meant total control, but it also signaled the beginning of constant disappointment: the man who would be acclaimed as the world's greatest inventor was no astute businessman. The basic problem was his inherent stubbornness: he simply was not receptive to anyone's guidance, be it technical, strategic, or business (Stross, 2007). Though he would accrue a measure of wealth, huge profits would elude him.

In a manner of speaking, Edison "peaked early" with the invention that propelled him to international prominence in 1877. The phonograph was actually an unexpected by-product of his technical pursuit of a practical telephone. Bell, of course, would ultimately gain that patent, but the two were in tight competition to complete it (Stross, 2007). The idea of voice recording, however, led Edison in a different direction that ushered in the era of a new home entertainment industry. Its successful debut superseded Bell's acclaim for the telephone and basically galled the latter who himself was close to perfecting Edison's "toy." The phonograph would emerge as Edison's greatest personal accomplishment and was his "baby," but he did not initially appreciate its significance or future as an industry. He would continually tinker with it after it was introduced in an effort to "get the bugs out of it" (Stross, 2007, p.43) and alter its operation. But the fact of the matter is that he could not or would not focus enough to complete its development, leaving the details as he frequently did to his staff. His short-sightedness of its business potential led him to syndicate its production to other inventors in exchange for short-term royalties and maintenance funds.

The phonograph also gave Edison an opportunity that he never had again. Its renown allowed him to move forward unimpeded in an open field without competitors (Stross, 2007). But he could not effectively cope with the acclaim it brought and his fame would distract him from properly reading the market as he customarily flitted from project to project.

Part of his acclaim lay with his legendary work ethic which few could match. Rarely able to relax, the laboratory was his life and eighteen-hour-days frequently seven days weekly were his norm. He unfortunately expected the same devotion from his employees and drove them relentlessly; and frequently drove them away. Edison's mythical ability to function without sleep was also a misnomer, for he sustained himself with regular "catnaps" that were his privilege alone. But fame and expectation was a double-edged sword that increasingly irritated and distracted him. Trying to remain ambivalent about it all, he nevertheless readily accepted the attention and privately basked in it, but shunned public invitations to speak by using his deafness as an excuse. His ego spurred him on and he was genuinely amused by such press statements as "Edison has not invented anything since breakfast. The doctor has been called" (Stross, 2007, p.67). Lack of Edison ideas would never be a problem.

In the late 1870s, Edison began work on the invention with which he is most famously associated in the public consciousness. When he began "inventing" the electric light in 1878, European inventors had already been working on it for seventy years (Jonnes, 2003). A bright light was relatively easy to invent but the problem was moderating and sustaining its intensity in a bulb. Reliable bulbs were on the market but they were limited to street lighting. A soft incandescent light bulb that would be commercially practical for the home required a filament that would brightly glow without melting. That challenge had been tried and failed by at least twenty inventors before Edison entered the contest (Stross, 2007). Knowing that success would bring him further acclaim, he egotistically did not believe it was a tough problem and relished the idea of triumphing over so many who had failed. This time he was wrong.

Perhaps poetically, his optimism waned with repeated failures. His claims and promises of success were premature and he grew increasingly uncomfortable with not being able to deliver; delay was hurting his reputation. Setback after setback infuriated him but he pressed on, if anything but to gain revenge against the existing gas company monopoly which he believed had personally mistreated him. Needing capital to continue, Edison and his investors formed the Edison Electric Light Company in 1878, a move that bought him more time. But the move was also misleading, as commercial introduction and production of the incandescent light bulb was still three long years away. It would take thousands of failed experiments and the constant threat of competition before he found success with a carbonized bamboo filament that would change the world.

The pressure was on him from all quarters and he did not handle it well. "Edison was reminded daily that as the world-famous inventor, he had to defend himself daily against attacks that his counterparts in obscurity could never imagine" (Stross, 2007, p.105). As always, this was especially true with the commercial aspect and he reluctantly became involved in marketing wars with competing power companies. Playing the role of glad-hander and PR man was loathing to him, for it took time away from the lab which he was forced to move to New York. His system would ultimately work well, but profit-wise it was disappointing and he predictably turned the operation over to others.

In his late thirties, he longed for new challenges while ignoring the one that inevitably caught up to him. Mary's mental health had been steadily slipping but he had shown only distant concern for her and his children, instead immersing himself in work. Edison prided himself on his wizardry for inventing, but he now had to painfully face the fact that he could not invent something to cure Mary. Unable to cope with her illness, which may have been a brain tumor, he watched her die at age twenty-nine in 1884.

For the first time he was deeply shaken and could not find solace. Spiritual comfort was beyond him, for while he was not an atheist, his professed deism merely allowed him to acknowledge a Supreme Intelligence who was uninvolved and unconcerned with human existence (Israel, 2000). This was typical of Edison because it gave him the continued control that he believed he had over all matters. The death of a spouse sometimes brings the survivor closer to his children, but this would be only partially true for Edison. He responded by taking his daughter Marion closely under his wing, home-schooled her, and virtually made her his constant companion for a while. But he continued to ignore his two sons who did not know him.

Professionally, he entered a brief period of drifting, not quite sure what to do with himself but longing for some grand project to pursue. Paradoxically, what he was really looking for was "a wifely helpmate" (Stross, 2007, p.147). Two years after Mary's death, thirty-nine-year-old Edison married nineteen-year-old Mina, who totally devoted herself to helping him. At the outset, he actually brainstormed with her, but shortly after she turned instead to managing the household and bearing him a new family of two sons and a daughter. Even with this second chance, however, Edison did not learn his lesson and his work would always take precedent over his family.

Re-energized and eager to pursue new projects, Edison built his new "dream laboratory" in West Orange, New Jersey. But the "old" would linger. He briefly returned to tinkering with the phonograph and struggled with its commercial potential. By default, he would increasingly become concerned with an invention's utility and sales by letting the market dictate his professional direction. He was also relying more heavily on his superb staff but did not hesitate taking full credit for their work.

By the early 20th century, he was heroically established as the world's greatest inventor but remained its worst businessman. Edison was wealthy but most of his assets remained tied up in what would eventually amount to nearly fourteen of his companies. When his frustration level inevitably led him to either "cash-out" or simply but stubbornly relinquish control, those who took over the operations profited immensely from his work. The most profound example was General Electric, which "took off" only after Edison yielded control. One of his more celebrated commercial battles in this regard was his electricity distribution "war" with his adversaries Tesla and Westinghouse concerning the latters' promotion of AC current over Edison's DC current. As usual, it was an endeavor which Edison miscalculated, mishandled, and withdrew (Jonnes, 2003).

Then came an unusual turn of events. Ignoring for the only time in his public life what he perceived was expected of him, Edison set off on a five-year venture in a field totally foreign to him: developing an efficient system to mine ore. It took him away from his family—though that was never a major concern to him—and while the entire project ultimately failed, it offered him a measure of fun that he previously had only experienced in his lab. But unlike his successful avoidance of his first family—and, to a great degree, his second—he surprisingly and tenderly missed Mina. Their ensuing correspondence by letter revealed Edison's belief that unhappiness could be eliminated by sheer force of will (Stross, 2007). Astonishingly, the correspondence held the marriage together but did not bring him closer to his children.

There were other subtle changes. He was still losing a fortune through his business ineptness and "distracted in the pursuit of his own fancies, was slow to observe the limitless business opportunities made possible by the commercialization" (Stross, 2007, p.194) of his inventions. But now he appeared to care less and returned to inventing. Emerging on the scene was his patent for the first commercially available fluoroscope for x-ray radiographs. Edison then turned his attention to another media invention.

Edison's early success had been based on learning the basics of electricity. With the same firm grounding in electromechanical design that allowed him to produce the phonograph, he now pursued optical development in the form of the Kinetoscope, or motion-picture camera, which was first publicly exhibited in 1891. Some immediately saw its commercial potential, but not Edison, who considered it an interesting novelty. His "Black Maria" lab studio produced motion pictures and promoted their future, but he was too slow to realize it and ended up fighting a twenty-year legal battle to protect the patent. It resulted in what may have been his single biggest financial blunder. That is, he failed to realize that the "peep-hole" images that were commercially available for a mere nickel needed to be projected from the camera to a larger screen that would accommodate crowds of viewers. Others did, and he lost out on a projection system and a veritable fortune while occupying himself with other projects. It was ironic that he was still willing to lend his name to that system but did not profit by it.

Edison's early 20th century fame eclipsed that of any other inventor and his name associated with any invention practically guaranteed public approval. It also spurred him to push harder, even into his eighties. It was of great personal importance to him to protect "the public image of 'Thomas Edison,' omnipresent and omniscient, the Wizard with a magical touch" (Stross, 2007, p.230). Living up to that image was not problematic as long as he was making the decisions, regardless of consequence. His fame was built on his work which in turn increased his eagerness to be the hardest-working and longest-working inventor. Besides, he could not imagine doing anything else: every minute of work was paradise.

Friendship was not his forte and few called him friend. Perhaps the sole exception was Henry Ford. Edison first met the unknown Ford in 1896 when the latter sought advice on his gas-powered Quadricycle, the forerunner of his automobile. It would take Ford three more years to commercialize his design but Edison greatly encouraged him at the outset. Edison had an inherently solitary nature that forbade closeness, but he was somewhat taken with Ford who in turn idolized the Wizard. After Ford attained acclaim, the two formed a non-competitive friendship of equals that became business as well as personal. In point of fact, Edison had invented an electric car ahead of Ford, but its severe limitations left it a novelty. Later, Edison worked on an electrical battery system for Ford's Model T, but it proved not to be viable. Nevertheless, the two became business partners on the strength of their common hatred of Wall Street and their anti-Semitism, though Ford was publicly vocal about his prejudice while Edison—ever concerned with his public image—kept his private.

Family gatherings at their Florida homes became frequent and Edison dared to let his guard down during these respites, although they rarely socialized outside of these (Albion, 2008). The vacations eventually evolved into their famous annual summer camping trips, which would later include the wives, Harvey Firestone, the naturalist John Burroughs, and on one occasion President Warren Harding. The party's cumulative fame, however, rarely allowed privacy and the trips would cease after a few years.

The Edison-Ford friendship was mutually benefitting, but mostly to Edison in the form of frequent Ford loans for work purposes. To Ford, Edison was and would always be an American hero but even he eventually realized that Edison had little business savvy and would in essence forgive his monetary debts to him (Stross, 2007). Yet there were never any ill feelings between them and they maintained a mutual respect.

Never willing to step back from work or step down from gripping control, Edison began resenting "being treated like a statue" (Stross, 2007, p.259); that is, in the past tense. His legend was enhanced by mistaken associations with competitors' products in addition to his own, but he arrogantly clung to the notion that whatever he worked on would be of benefit to the entire world (Stross, 2007). His celebrity had echoed that notion so many times in the past that he firmly believed it would go on indefinitely. But professionally he took a series of hits that personally and deeply undercut him. The federal government had sought his advice on weaponry during World War I and despite producing forty-five patents, none were adopted.

Edison's selfish and cantankerous nature worsened in his old age. He was not one for serious philanthropy, always seeking isolation, and never feeling any civic obligation to offer community service as others of fame had done. Always self-absorbed, he remained convinced that only he knew best how to manage his affairs even after a veritable lifetime of evidence to the contrary. At the lab, he continued to demand at least a twelve-hour day from his workers, but paid scant attention to them and their contributions. Only at home would he unsurprisingly yield authority, where Mina kept control of the family that he neglected.

During the last decade of his life, Edison's profound work ethic still drew admiration and challenged him to attempt industrial botany and rubber research, as well as a venture into radio production. Neither was successful. Deafness—which had plagued him most of his life—along with diabetes and stomach problems (probably from radiation exposure in his lab) was taking their toll and he began resting more and working less. While celebrating the fiftieth-anniversary of his incandescent light bulb in early 1931, he applied for the last of his 1093 patents. Most of them in reality were directly related to two of his inventions: 400 of them toward the incandescent bulb and another 200 for the phonograph. Despite this, his list of achievements was justifiably impressive.

Though he remained remarkably active right up to the end, health issues consumed him. In his last few years Edison had been influenced by and firmly believed in the restorative powers of a milk diet and it was purportedly the only liquid he consumed (Baldwin, 2001). But not even the Wizard could stave off the inevitable. Failing kidneys and diabetes prompted his collapse in August of 1931 and he drifted in and out of comas until expiring at age eighty-four on October 18th. A state funeral and a national dimming of lights were an appropriate tribute to an American hero. For nearly sixty years, Edison had carefully crafted his public image of a genius performing miracles which ensured eulogies of praise as the man who "was given credit for not only bestowing light upon benighted humanity, but also for making life worth living" (Stross, 2007, p.284). Ironically, he had never truly enjoyed his fame.

Edison's $12 million estate was certainly not a small one in the Depression-era or any other one, yet it was trivial compared to the credit given him for the industries he created but not the resultant wealth he could have and should have accrued had he not been so stubborn and short-sighted in his business dealings. His fame has justifiably endured because his genius fortuitously shaped technological advancement; namely, through the phonograph and motion-picture camera for public entertainment and of course the incandescent light bulb and related electrical conveniences associated with his name. His work was his life and no one before or since demonstrated the essence of the American work ethic as he did. For this alone, Edison merits heroic acclaim. It was the defining characteristic of his image, an image passionately and tirelessly devoted to inventing. But he paid a huge price, never truly able to embrace his heroic fame because "he was a prickly person who was used to getting his way, insufferably opinionated, and a carrier of the hateful prejudices of his day" (Stross, 2007, p.290). Seriously flawed as the great inventor was, he might merit some contemporary sympathy, for he could never escape the unrealistically high personal expectations he put on himself which hindered him from separating Edison the Image from Edison the Man.

DISCUSSION GUIDELINE QUESTIONS

1. What values are depicted in the story?
2. Where did Edison learn his values?
3. What was his greatest character trait?
4. What was his greatest flaw?
5. What were the consequences of his flawed character?
6. In terms of his ingenuity, who might be comparable to him within the past fifty years?
7. Why did have so much difficulty dealing with his acclaimed heroism?
8. Why might there never be another like him?

REFERENCES

Albion, M. (2008). *The Florida life of Thomas Edison.* Gainesville: University Press of Florida.

Baldwin, N. (2001). *Edison: Inventing the century.* Chicago: University of Chicago Press.

Clark, R. (1977). *Edison: The man who made the future.* London: MacDonald & Jane's.

Israel, P. (2000). *Edison: A life of invention.* New York: John Wiley & Sons.

Jonnes, J. (2003). *Empires of light: Edison, Tesla, Westinghouse, and the race to electrify the world.* New York: Random House.

Stross, R. (2007). *The wizard of Menlo Park: How Thomas Alva Edison invented the modern world.* New York: Random House.

Chapter Fourteen

The Birdmen:
Wilbur and Orville Wright

The essence of America is built on the values demonstrated by its heroes, both faceless and personal, to renowned and shared. Their values have sustained us through times of disparity and prosperity, perpetually advancing the noble ideal of our republic. They go beyond mere abstraction and speculation by embodying a continual reaffirmation of attainable greatness with a humility that endures through the restraints of historical time to nurture our individual dreams of what we can be and do. Though varying in combination and intensity, heroic values define the essential qualities that we can agree are profoundly and uniquely "American" in such a way as to inspire us to follow the lead. Such can be the only proper homage to their deeds.

With few exceptions, our heroes/heroines are individual entities, but on rare occasion comes along an exception of duality worth examining. Among the most acclaimed in this category are Wilbur and Orville Wright, brothers whose near-mythical heroism went beyond genius and reflected the highly esteemed American values of strength of will, dedication to principle, and the strength of family (Crouch, 2003). Their early 20th century endeavors ushered in a new technological age that transformed America and the world. The invention and demonstration of the world's first successfully mechanized, sustained, and controlled flight in an airplane of their own design was even then made comparable to the discovery of America. No one could have possibly predicted the outcome of such a discovery and "in a like manner these two brothers [had] probably not even a faint glimpse of what their discovery [would] bring to the 'children of men' "(Freedmen, 1991, p.2).

They were born four years apart during America's second Industrial Revolution, Wilbur in 1867 and Orville in 1871, and were the two youngest sons of seven children born to Milton—a bishop—and Susan Wright. Both of the

boys had blue-gray eyes but shared few other physical traits, as they were a stark contrast to each other in most every other way (Howard, 1998). Wilbur was lean and balding, very serious, self-assured, and a gifted communicator. He was also the visionary and thinker of the pair, though rather humorously indifferent to his appearance which his younger sister Katherine had to periodically inspect (Crouch, 2003; Jakab, 1997; Freedman, 1991). Orville was the impulsive and excitable one, the enthusiast who provided the drive to Wilbur's ideas. Mustached even in high school, he enjoyed pranks and was very particular about his appearance, even bleaching his face with lemon juice to proudly pale his complexion (Crouch, 2003). As the more handsome of the pair, he was "dapper and tidy... by far the more clothes conscious of the two" (Freedman, 1991, p.16), always immaculately dressed yet very withdrawn among strangers. Neither of the brothers smoked, drank, or married.

Different as they were, the secret of their future success was their reliance on each other's strengths which compensated for their respective weaknesses. This was in large measure due to their Christian upbringing, which they lived as well as believed. Milton and Susan departed to their children a great sense of family, faith, and good character. The boys would live their entire lives on these principles and from the time they were children were inseparable. Their demonstrated ability to function as a team was nothing short of extraordinary, and they lived, worked, and thought as one in a relationship that was more binding than most marriages (Crouch, 2003; Howard, 1998; Freedman, 1991). Neither, astonishingly, finished high school but both had a proverbial knack for tools and problem-solving that boded well for their destiny. Their true genius would be their extraordinary ability to observe and understand fundamental principles of physical and mechanical images that had yet to be constructed (Crouch, 2003; Howard, 1998).

The boys always credited their mother for their mechanical aptitude, though an inspirational moment in their childhood was Milton's gift to them of a toy helicopter which may have been a sort of baptism to their future (Howard, 1998). But it was the Wrights' close and affectionate family environment that was the formidable factor. Orville would relate that they were lucky enough to grow up in an environment where there was always much encouragement to the children to pursue intellectual interests and to investigate whatever aroused one's curiosity (Crouch, 2003). Despite Susan's premature death, their iron-willed father continued to encourage their talents with resolve and determination. The Wright family unit would be the enduring factor as youngest child and only daughter Katherine rose to both supervise the household and play a pivotal future role as her brothers' ally and confidant (Crouch, 2003; Freedman, 1991). Susan's early death was a turning point for them all, as Milton became quite possessive of the three offspring and the four of them were bound for life.

The three siblings had in fact bonded as a team, "bound by an unspoken agreement to remain together and to let no one come between them" (Crouch, 2003, p.117). None had any interest in marriage. "Will" feared that romance would interfere with his interests, while "Orv" was simply too shy. Katherine's attitude was far more complex in that her strong will kept her from pursuing any serious relationship until very late in her life, a circumstance that would cause a serious rift with Orv. She was instead content to be both a schoolteacher but more importantly the house manager who took care of her brothers and father. A sustaining warm and stable household was the result.

Will and Orv's first endeavor was a printing shop where they published a local newspaper which stressed their firm belief in honesty and personal morality. But the business was not all they hoped for, especially financially, and they turned to another pursuit with renewed confidence in a partnership bolstered by their mutual sense of humor and the ability to effectively argue through solutions to problems (Crouch, 2003). As the 1890s progressed, an apparent revolution in transportation was there to cultivate. The boys opted to pursue the bicycle business to take advantage of the national craze and quickly became proficient at selling, repairing, and even manufacturing their own brand. Within four years and a succession of shops in their home base of Dayton, Ohio, they had attained financial security. But their attention was already being redirected with the emergence of the automobile and the dream of a flying machine.

The quest to conquer the skies was hardly a new one, dating as far back as mythology and as recent as da Vinci's time. Aeronautical experimentation began with kites and then manned gliders, but the ultimate challenge was a manned, power-driven aircraft. The dream was initially Will's, who "was the leader from the beginning to the end" (Tobin, 2004, p.92) and it gave the boys a newly directed sense of purpose in life. In 1899, the boys began seriously studying the groundwork laid by such glider pioneers as da Vinci, Cayley, Lilienthal, Chanute, and Samuel Langley, the latter emerging as the early American leader in building a powered flying machine (Anderson, 2004; Tobin, 2004; Jakab, 1997). Though all of them had fallen short of success, the boys were convinced that aerodynamic success had to begin with gliders. They also learned that a flying machine had three basic requirements to be mastered: first, wings to lift it into the air; second, a power source or engine for propulsion; and third, the means to control and steer it horizontally and vertically inflight.

The glider pioneers had basically solved the first two issues yet seemed to overly concentrate on them while basically ignoring the control problem. Will had correctly asserted that the problem of equilibrium was the problem of flight itself and thus the control issue became their primary focus (Crouch, 2003). In their bicycle workshop they began building kites to be adapted into full-sized gliders. Since they were in unexplored territory in learning the virtually unknown science of aerodynamics, their genius for visualizing mechanical solutions to theoretical problems with precision and confidence would be tested to the extreme over the next four years of endless experimentation.

In 1900 they were ready to test their glider but needed a proper testing site "where there were strong, steady winds day in and day out" (Crouch, 2003, p.181), secluded hills, and soft sands. Doing his usual thorough investigating, Will settled on the relatively perfect place: Kitty Hawk, North Carolina. Late in that year the boys set up camp and began testing kites and unmanned gliders before ending the season with Will successfully flying the manned model. It gave them great encouragement as they returned home to Dayton for more testing with plans to return the following year. Little did they realize that they would be returning to Kitty Hawk for several years.

Those ensuing years proved to be a period of pure intellectual excitement and their confidence soared despite highs and lows. But after more than two years of extensive testing, their increasingly larger gliders were not performing as expected. Balance and control continued to be problematic with the rigid wings. Will suddenly deduced that " a spiral twist running along an aircraft's wings would make it possible to tilt one wing up and the other down" (Freedman, 1991, p.31) as a bird does to roll its body right or left. Through tedious and repetitive experimenting, implementing this "wing-warping" system was showing positive results. All doubt vanished and confidence soared as patient testing with their biggest glider yet resulted in only minor mishaps. But it still wasn't perfect. It was Orv who discovered that the problem was the tail, which would have to be movable like a ship's rudder or a bird's tail (Anderson, 2004; Howard, 1998; Freedman, 1991). After hundreds of controlled glides with the new tail, the final obstacle was removed.

As they neared the final phase, their expenditures for the Wright Flyer were significantly less than one thousand dollars. This was in stark contrast to the more than fifty thousand dollars of government money given to their only serious competitor, Samuel Langley, who was nearing completion of his power-driven aircraft (Tobin, 2004). The boys had not sought external funding for fear of unwanted obligations and interference. Neither did they want annoying publicity which could threaten the safety of the project. After three seasons of testing at Kitty Hawk, they were fully confident that they could design, build, and fly the world's first controllable aircraft and they now focused on a means of propulsion (Freedman, 1991).

The engine for their 1903 Flyer faced three challenges: first, it had to be light but powerful; second, propellers would have to produce the necessary thrust; and third, the aircraft's body had to be sturdy enough to sustain the added weight and withstand vibration (Freedman, 1991). Settling on a breakthrough system of two propellers, they turned to their shop mechanic, Charlie

Taylor, to build the engine under their supervision, a feat he accomplished in six weeks.

Despite lacking a patent on their work, they confidently returned to Kitty Hawk in late 1903 with their largest design yet, determined that this would not be just another experimental season but rather with the goal of mechanized, sustained, and controlled flight. Initial trials did not go well in the unfavorable weather conditions as Will and Orv alternated as pilots. A potential obstacle was cleared on December 8th when word came that Langley's last machine had failed to fly, thus ending his twenty-year quest for the airplane and removing any pressure on the Wrights. Resolved to return home by Christmas, the boys stepped up their efforts. On December 17th with Orv at the controls, the plane lifted off and flew 120 feet for twelve seconds before safely landing. It may not have been much, but "for the first time in history, an airplane had taken off, moved forward under its own power, and landed at a point at least as high as that from which it started—all under the complete control of the pilot" (Crouch, 2003, p.268). Longer, further flights followed before the day was over, but a man had flown. A mere five people witnessed the historic event, but one of them had fortuitously photographed the initial flight. The age of aviation had begun.

Shortly after their return home, the boys followed up a press release issued initially by Milton with their own statement, but amazingly the press paid little heed to the accomplishment and gave it very short shrift (Mortimer, 2009). Orv reasoned that "it was mainly due to the fact that human flight was generally looked upon as an impossibility, and that scarcely anyone believed it until he saw it with his own eyes" (Freedman, 1991, p.87); and indeed, local newspapermen admitted years later that "frankly, none of us believed it" (Tobin, 2004, p.201).

The only immediate drawback to the lack of news coverage was the basic disbelief of their feat in Washington, DC and Europe, but the boys were complicit with it because they were rightfully fearful of competitors taking advantage of their lack of a patent. Moreover, this was a time of important decisions since mechanized flight was no longer a mere hobby and obtaining a patent was crucial. On the other hand, the brothers realized that since there were still problems to be solved toward their goal of a "practical" flying machine, continuing their work in relative obscurity was an advantage. Plus, for the moment, there were no serious competitors, a circumstance that would shortly change.

In a financially risky move, the boys abandoned their lucrative bicycle business to devote themselves to the design and manufacturing of a practical flyer, a goal they achieved within the next two years. The public was slowly becoming more aware of the world-changing technology but the boys decided that the airplane was not their gift to the world, but a product to be sold (Crouch, 2003). Its ultimate value was in the knowledge it required to build and it would prove difficult to patent it. Though they would finally obtain one, the problem they would encounter was in the analogy of inventing the wheel but only patenting its axle. But at this point, however, they vowed that until a contract had been procured, there would be no public flight demonstrations. To that end, they would not fly for nearly three years while attempting to persuade governments to purchase their machine.

Rather incredulously, selling their machine was challenging. One problem was their first choice of buyers, the U.S. War Department. Its previous and significant funding of Langley's failures prompted the government's hesitancy to pursue a purchase, especially in light of the Wrights' refusal to publicly demonstrate their airplane. A more serious problem was that the Wrights proved to be almost as bad at business as they were good at inventing (Crouch, 2003). This was perhaps because everything had to be strictly on their terms and they were insulted not to be taken at their word for their accomplishment. In any case, the military rejected their offer and the boys instead turned their attention to a foreign deal in Europe, especially in France which would show prolonged interest but also expected public demonstrations.

By 1908, aviation technology was no longer the brothers' sole domain as European machines began appearing, all of them influenced in some way by the Wrights; and all of them basically infringing on their patent. These inferior machines flew but were not as controllable as the Wright Flyer which remained the standard. Still holding out for a deal with the U.S. Army, the boys reluctantly realized that procuring any contract would be dependent upon successful public flight demonstrations. To this end, they decided to divide their efforts: Orv would fly for the Army, while the more tactful Will would fly in France. By this time there were many other fliers to compete against but the brothers did not feel threatened in the slightest.

Will's successful public flights in France in 1908 virtually captivated the world, bringing the Wrights overnight international fame by deftly proving their claim of flight and setting many initial aviation records in the process. To less acclaim, Orv flew for the Army, though he was seriously injured in a crash that killed his passenger. Requiring Katherine's devoted services as a nurse, Orv never fully recovered and the effects of his injuries plagued him for the rest of his life. Nevertheless, the Army finally extended a contract as did the French.

Joining their brother in France in 1909, the three Wrights basked in countless accolades and the brothers were accorded the title of the Birdmen (Freedman, 1991). The three siblings totally impressed Europeans through their straightforward honesty, poise, wit, and common sense (Crouch, 2003). They became the first great heroes of the 20th century as they prepared to return to America to even more acclaim, but above all, this became Katherine's time to shine. As their social manager, she handled all of her brothers' business and social contacts and was instrumental in helping negotiate the Army contract (Kelly, 2002). Her considerable charm, educated manner, and gregariousness triumphed through their many public obligations.

Backed by investors, the brothers formed the Wright Company in late 1909 for financial and production security. In ten years—from their first kite experiments to the establishment of their airplane factory—Will and Orv had single-handedly ushered in the age of aviation. They now aspired to a simple return to research and experimentation but it was not to be. The boys saw little reason to compete with the now-many competitors that filled the skies, especially when they considered most of them as patent infringers. They only wanted to establish their rightful claim as inventors of the airplane and defend themselves against those who wrongfully tried to profit at their expense (Crouch, 2003). Thus ensued decades of patent battles, especially against their main American rival, Glenn Curtiss. It would be a continuous struggle on the domestic and foreign fronts, consuming most of their time, costing them many friendships, and tarnishing their previously bright public image.

The seemingly endless legal issues crushed their hope of returning to research and hindered their efforts to work on new designs. Worse was the personal toll it took. As he always had done concerning issues involving the family, Will took the lead in dealing with the patent wars and over a two-year period it plainly wore him out. With exhaustion and stress contributing to his condition, he took seriously ill with typhoid fever attributable to food poisoning in early May of 1912. After a four-week struggle, he died on May 30th at age forty-five. His premature death naturally devastated Orv and Katherine. Part of them died with Will and the two siblings drew even closer.

After Will's death, Orv assumed the company presidency but it was apparent that he "had almost none of his brother's restless ambition nor the energy and drive to succeed that came with it" (Crouch, 2003, p.455). The company began to founder due to his lack of vision and leadership, despite the courts finally upholding the Wright patent against Curtiss two years later. No doubt feeling vindicated, Orv sold the company and his interests in it shortly after and simply walked away from it all. In an ironic twist of fate, the Wright Company and the Curtiss Company later merged (in 1929) and still produce aeronautical components today.

Opening a small research laboratory which allowed him to spend most of his time tinkering on whatever interested him, Orv retained a mythical fame as the living symbol of the American tradition of heroic invention that stretched back to the beginning of the Republic (Crouch, 2003). Though he remained a painfully shy man who desired privacy, he steadfastly represented Will as the elder statesmen of aviation and other members of the Wright family with great dignity. Family, as it always had been, was his shelter, but that too was changing. Milton died in 1917, leaving only the faithful Katherine in the immediate household. But she too would leave, finally marrying at age fifty-two. Orv bitterly broke from her as if betrayed and stubbornly turned his back on her. Three years later he would reconcile with her on her deathbed, but she had betrayed his faith in the inviolability of the family ties that provided his delicate emotional security (Crouch, 2003). All that remained for him was protecting the Wright legacy that he and his brother had forged.

That also was a struggle as he became embroiled in a thirty-year battle with the Smithsonian Institute over who would be recognized as actually being the first to have been capable of mechanized flight, an honor rightfully belonging to the Wrights but instead was incredulously bestowed upon Samuel Langley. The controversy bordered on the ludicrous and in point of fact no conclusive evidence supported Langley. The argument still raged in 1948 as Orv died on January 30th after his second heart attack at age seventy-seven. He had lived long enough to fully witness how their invention had transformed the world with the dawn of the jet age. On December 17th of that year—exactly forty-five years after the triumph at Kitty Hawk—the Smithsonian Institute ceremoniously and officially recognized Wilbur and Orville Wright as the first to power, sustain, and control a manned airplane.

For the past century, the Wright Brothers have possessed a mythical stature "whose success seemed compounded of hard work, perseverance, and commonsense, with a liberal dollop of Yankee ingenuity- raised to the level of genius" (Crouch, 2003, p.504). They are the ultimate proof that the "old-fashioned" values of the early 20th century are still relevant in 21st century America. Perhaps the most fitting tribute to their deeds came on July 20, 1969 when astronaut Neil Armstrong stepped onto the lunar surface carrying a piece of the original cotton wing from the Wright Flyer of that historic December day in 1903.

DISCUSSION GUIDELINE QUESTIONS

1. What values are depicted in the story?
2. Where did Wilbur and Orville learn their values?
3. What may have been their greatest character trait?
4. What may have been their greatest flaw?
5. Why are some inventors considered heroes?
6. Are their values too "old-fashioned" for contemporary Americans? Why or why not?
7. Is there anyone currently on the scene who is comparable to them?

REFERENCES

Anderson, J. (2004). *Inventing flight: The Wright brothers and their predecessors.* Baltimore, MD: Johns Hopkins University Press.

Crouch, T. (2003). *The bishop's boys: A life of Wilbur and Orville Wright.* W.W. Norton & Company.

Freedman, R. (1991). *The Wright brothers.* New York: Holiday House.

Howard, F. (1998). *Wilbur and Orville: A biography of the Wright brothers.* Mineola, NY: Dover Publications.

Jakab, P. (1997). *Visions of a flying machine: The Wright brothers and the process of invention.* Smithsonian History of Aviation and Spaceflight Series. Washington, DC: Smithsonian.

Kelly, F. (ed.) (2002). *Miracle at Kitty Hawk: The letters of Wilbur & Orville Wright.* New York: Da Capo Press.

Mortimer, G. (2009). *Chasing Icarus: The seventeen days in 1910 that forever changed American aviation.* New York: Walker.

Tobin, J. (2004). *To conquer the air: The Wright brothers and the great race for flight.* New York: Simon & Schuster.

Chapter Fifteen

Cultivating the Human Spirit: Jane Addams

In any era by any American standard, Jane Addams was a most remarkable individual. She is best remembered today as the co-founder of Hull House in Chicago, though contemporary America needs to be reminded of its purpose in order to better understand her. But she was also the first American woman (and second woman overall) to win the Nobel Peace Prize, a staunch advocate for women's suffrage, a supporter of civil rights and cultural respect, a political activist who lobbied for unionism and against child labor, served with the NAACP and ACLU, advised eight presidents, and for twenty-five years led the Women's International League for Peace and Freedom.

As a pragmatic visionary and social reformer, Jane's prodigious achievements were based on a life philosophy that would be pertinent for 21st century America: promoting conditions that nurture the potential of humanity (Knight, 2010). America's changing political environment in the early 21st century is a cry for social justice and a return to Progressivism based in part on promoting new sources of human energy in order to imagine new possibilities to bridge the desirable with the possible. In this regard, Jane's sense of civic responsibility is alive and relative to us today as a model of potential. Though some might question her political leanings—as they did in her own time—she fiercely lived her values on her own terms to promote her vision of the highest level of citizenship; that is, a new humanitarian ethic which was to be "inclusive, affectionate, and nurturing" (Knight, 2010, p.139).

She was born in 1860, one of five children in a wealthy family which was a circumstance that would advance and hinder her life course. The loss of her mother when Jane was 2 ½ left an emotional scar that she would never be able to heal. Death would in fact be a continuing and haunting presence in her life as she powerlessly endured the passing of family and friends. Yet it

also gave her a strengthening ability to control her destiny by choice as well as fate and by opportunities she either seized or created in the aftermath of unavoidable tragedies. Jane would never shirk from the realities of death and suffering in her mission to redeem life's purpose (Addams, 1961). She understood physical and psychological suffering from the outset, as she struggled

with a misshaped back from spinal tuberculosis. A painful and difficult operation would cure the condition when she was twenty, but her sensitivity and
self-consciousness would help set the stage for a life of self-sacrifice.

Books were her life's passion. They never failed to feed her soul with
beauty and meaning, and cultivated her moral ambition. But it was Jane's
father who initially shaped her ambition. His industrial ventures made the
family wealthy and he dabbled in politics, giving Jane a crucial foreboding of
the power of money and politics. He also raised her as a Christian to believe
in repentance and inner truth. Jane's spiritual beliefs would undergo periodic
shifts to fit her changing philosophies but the concept of Christian sacrifice
would be a mainstay in her life. Her Christian faith would be unorthodox in
that she relied on her conscience more than religious dogma, leading her to
be viewed as a Christian without formal religion (Davis, 1973; Elshtain,
2002; Knight, 2010).

But perhaps her father's greatest legacy to her was conveying "a sense of
the genuine relationship which may exist between men who share large
hopes and desires, even though they differ in nationality, language, and
creed" (Addams, 1961, p.23). Jane would later reject much of her father's
philosophy, but it was this lesson that led her to believe that choosing one's
hopes but being realistic about achieving them leads to spiritual action and
great results (Knight, 2010). This was indeed how she would live her life.

The mores of 19th century America dictated that family duty took priority
over personal ambition (Knight, 2010). For females there was no encouragement for self-development outside of marriage and motherhood. Of marriage
she would have no interest, believing that only platonic love would allow her
to freely pursue her dreams. As for those dreams, Jane had "an early urge to
fix the world" (Knight, 2010, p.17) through social reform as a self-sacrificing
doctor to the poor. But her father and stepmother thwarted her desire to
attend medical school at prestigious Smith College, forcing her to instead
attend a girls' seminary. This did not dampen her ambition and she developed a talent for oratory which she would use to maximum benefit in the
future.

The sudden death of her father when she was twenty and the mental
breakdown of her brother took her in a different and darker direction. She
would briefly attend medical school as she had initially planned, but a ner-
vous collapse forced her withdrawal. She blamed the collapse on manifesta-
tions of moral failure: she had gone against social mores by not denying her
freedom for family and "failing to do so was selfish and [led] to illness"
(Knight, 2010, p.41). Jane feared a lifetime of failure as a result and tried to
redeem herself as a kindly spirit selflessly caring for her ailing stepmother.

The specter of failure continued to plague her in the process and she
boldly decided that the only way to rid herself of it was the first of two trips
to Europe. It would prove to be the pivotal moment in her ambition to help

the destitute. In London, she witnessed the reality of abject poverty and it left her reeling. She vowed to act and became obsessed with the suffering of the poor (Knight, 2010). They too appeared to be carrying her similar pain from death, failure, and illness. Though she could not directly identify with their poverty due to her wealth, the experience completely changed her. Among other revelations, it gave her a new insight on Christian sacrifice and she drew closer to converting to the religion from which she had previously abandoned. Medicine was no longer the focus of her mission, but rather serving humanity through the gentleness of nonresistance.

Jane was "emotionally cool, self-contained, [and] steady" (Knight, 2010, p.59) as she immersed herself in the plight of the poor. Closely investigating a new European concept, she chose the experimental and philanthropic idea of a settlement house that would serve humanity and put the idea of universal and democratic fellowship into action (Knight, 2010). Partnered with her good friend Ellen Starr, Jane saw the settlement house as a way she could live among the poor that was Christian in motive but would not require her to abandon either her gracious living or her love of culture (Knight, 2010). Yet it would offer the fellowship she yearned to experience. She was, however, naïve on at least two counts: first, the experiment would inevitably affect her wealthy status, and, second, she underestimated the problem of a woman being able to exert the necessary social power in the public realm (Knight, 2010).

The two emboldened women chose Chicago as the site for their settlement house. Moving there in 1889, they purchased Hull House, a structure in need of extensive renovation but typical for the crowded, impoverished, and industrial neighborhood. It would be the first settlement house in America and the largest of its kind for decades. Curiosity and necessity began drawing people in to this initially planned coeducational facility which had two purposes: first, to provide people "with a way to live up to the highest ideals they had been taught" (Knight, 2010, p.67), and, second, to somehow reduce the obvious economic gap between rich and poor due to the onslaught of massive immigration. Jane's wealth and purposeful idealism would at least in the short run subsidize the venture, but she was over her head and quickly realized that a political agenda would be central to Hull House's success. This in turn was complicated by women lacking the vote, an issue that would soon consume her energies. Hull House was about the human spirit as Jane intended via its various programs of education, daycare, culture, and support, but this new world was a shocking eye-opener to this wealthy woman. She was becoming increasingly anti-materialistic by continuous donation and her wealth was fast dissipating. Yet she clearly saw that money could not eliminate inner misery and poverty was debilitating to the soul.

Perhaps more importantly, Jane learned that it was a political issue. Poor working conditions inevitably led to unionism during this second Industrial

Revolution and while still committed to her creed of peaceful nonresistance, she became an advocate for arbitration to settle labor disputes. Political influence, she reluctantly concluded, was crucial and she cautiously plunged into the realm of lobbying on the realization that politics was not just about the vote but rather working for those citizens whose political voice was weak or unheard. It was a basic lesson in democracy that started her down the path that would lead to her becoming one of the nation's most effective and influential political activists (Knight, 2010). Jane had always believed it dangerous to cling to old ideas when free and vigorous thinking could lead to viable solutions. As she contemplated the deplorable social conditions around her, her intellectual broadmindedness and independent thinking now led her to consider the possibilities of Marxist/socialist philosophy, which was fashionable during this tumultuous time. She was not a convert at this point, but she kept it in the back of her mind for future reference.

Several pivotal events in 1893 profoundly affected Jane and her future course. The Chicago World's Fair brought her and Hull House national acclaim. After four years, Hull House represented the most distinctive example of the thriving settlement house concept in America. On a personal level, her close friendship with Ellen ended and she entered a more enduring one with Mary Rozet Smith, who would become for all intent and purpose Jane's life partner. A serious economic depression would significantly alter her feelings about herself (Knight, 2010). Material comfort now embarrassed her and she perceived that poverty was not always an individual's fault, but it did not have to detrimentally affect the human spirit. Concluding that local government should take responsibility for protecting citizens from economic collapse, "she toyed with embracing Marxist socialism as her new creed" (Knight, 2010, p.87). Her steadfast belief in nonresistance kept her from deftly accepting Marxism, but she was about to witness and experience an event that convinced her that workers were totally at the mercy of the system; and it would radically change her.

The Pullman Strike and its resultant effect on the working class shook her beliefs to the foundation. It prompted her to clearly see the effects of sharp social division, but her immediate response was to remain impartial, a stance that initially made her enemies. She used her now considerable influence to promote arbitration of the dispute while continuing to cling to the hope of promoting social understanding and sympathy across class lines. At this point, Jane was ignorant of the forces of economic power, but that situation would soon change. Her social conscience now led her to a social reform stance through the dual roles of an interpreter across divisions of understanding and as a visionary of future possibilities (Knight, 2010).

Her interpretation of the Pullman Strike completely changed her world. As a social reformer, moral leader, and political activist, Jane evolved into a full-fledged advocate of social justice. She abandoned her belief in the ethic

of benevolence and instead devoted herself to the political goals of redistrib-
uting political power and wealth based upon Marxist overtones. She immersed herself in a political world that she was clearly seeing for the first
time. The issue of women's suffrage would by necessity take priority as a
means to this end and moral absolutes that formerly affected her would no
longer guide her.

Yet one thing would not change: the growth of human potential and of
personal ethical growth (Davis, 1973; Elshtain, 2002; Knight, 2005; 2010).
Behind every political action Jane took in the future and behind every argument she would make for political action in the years to come, this remained
the foundation (Knight, 2010). The ethic of social justice would be her key to
promoting personal and economic prosperity. To that end, Jane took up the
workers' reform agenda to create a democratic state that would protect the
vulnerable through unionism and a government responsible to the needs and
demands of the people (Knight, 2010). The Progressive Era would further
that opportunity.

As the 20th century approached, Jane's fame and ambition to make a
significant social difference intensified. Her former stance on benevolence
had posed a danger to her new view of democracy and she launched into a
political agenda to further her aims. She began writing books with a moral
philosophy which "sought to undermine the social side of the class system by
persuading people to change their lives in ways that would change their
ethics" (Knight, 2010, p.107). New challenges and causes emerged as well.
The Spanish-American War and its perceived imperialistic overtones increased her fervor for peace and international humanitarianism. She also
began to focus on racial injustice and the fair enforcement of the law, even if
it meant openly supporting political dissidents. As both an inspiring assem-
bler and disseminator of the persuasive argument, Jane brought serious attention to promoting child labor laws and protection for working women. To
that end, she began lending her name and talents to national organizations,
such as the Women's Trade Union League, which embodied her belief that
the prosperous class must cooperate with the working class to achieve fairness and gender solidarity (Addams, 1961).

Jane began pressing a new social/political vision based on the end of
militarism, which she saw everywhere. Only its end could allow a government to then embrace the ideals of the common worker and the fusing together of cultures. The resultant patriotism would in her view foster international
peace. But all of this would again require political resolutions set in motion
by states' rights and the power of the people on a national level. The organized nature of the Progressive Movement highly appealed to her in its quest
to make the federal government more powerful on behalf of the people to
accomplish these goals. She viewed its stance on racism and women's suffrage as vehicles for dramatic social change.

Her involvements and official titles increased in the name of Progressive reform. People were drawn to her powerful vision of a generously spirited, all-inclusive, more socially conscious and politically democratic United States which she effectively promoted through her compelling presence and interpretive argument that directly appealed to the heart (Knight, 2010). It was a humble blend of statesmanship and sainthood that may have been an effort to counterbalance her personal interactions. Jane's lifelines were always simple and platonic human affection through constant companionship, but too much experience with death and the early absence of tenderness severely limited the intimacy she was capable of and/or willing to give. She thus tended to withhold deep personal feelings from others and buried herself in her life's work.

For the first time—but not unexpectedly—she became a partisan political activist by fervently supporting Theodore Roosevelt's bid for the presidency as the Progressive Party's nominee in 1912. She lauded the party's platform for its morally responsible and democratic spirit, especially in its support of suffrage. However, she nearly broke from the party due to its disappointing failure to address racial equality but she nevertheless stuck it out due to her personal regard for Roosevelt and future hope. Though he lost, he had at least spurred Jane's hopes, but they too would be lost: Woodrow Wilson's progressivism was of a different sort and she would shortly disassociate herself from national party politics.

World War I and America's inevitable entry into the conflict further adjusted her attitude: a government at war harmed its own citizens and blocked the "right" democratic path that could only be attained through peaceful collective action (Elshtain, 2002; Knight, 2005). Wilson contradicted this by viewing himself as the moral force for change through war. In a bold move that drew her sharp criticism as a dissenter, Jane openly went against the prevailing patriotic majority view by promoting a peace initiative of organized spirit and collective moral energy in hopes of staving off America's entry. But she failed miserably and the ensuing negative publicity shook her deeply. Her continuing anti-war stance prompted repeated persecution and the war years would be lonely ones for her.

Jane had always believed in the need to respond to emerging issues and to remain connected with one's times and even with advancing age, Jane persisted as a cutting edge reformer as the war ended by assisting with the post-war recovery in Europe (Knight, 2010). At home, stopping the oppression of free speech—even if it meant supporting Socialists and Communists—during the infamous Red Scare garnered her further unpopularity. Not even the passage of the suffrage amendment for which she had long fought eased a nation's seeming hostility toward her; and it battered her humanitarian heart.

In the 1920s, Jane focused her attention on global peace and more freedom for women, endeavors that required her to travel extensively. During this round of her world travels and pilgrimages, she found a hero in Gandhi, whose ideas were similar to her own. They both believed in the moral power of all human beings. They also thought that spirited values should permeate every action, and understood their lives were the best means they had to teach such values (Knight, 2010). But his destiny would be different from hers.

Health issues inevitably affected her as she returned home to Hull House for her last six years. A mastectomy and a heart ailment dramatically slowed her down as she turned seventy and Hull House turned forty. She now had to consider "passing the torch" to a younger generation of women whose morality of sexual expression she seriously questioned even if the flourishing of the human spirit was their mutual motive. Hull House represented a remarkable achievement that gave people a clearer understanding of the world by teaching them what living a democratic life actually meant (Knight, 2010). It also represented Jane's philosophy of leadership in action, and her influence and spirit spread beyond it.

But Hull House had changed with the times, or perhaps was a victim of changing times. Jane's causes, though not forgotten, went the way of the defunct Progressive Movement and only peace remained as her focal issue as the Great Depression ushered in a new and darker era. But one last triumph was to come. Jane had previously been nominated for the Nobel Peace Prize four times and in 1931 she would finally be recognized for her achievements. The award would underlie her humanitarian creed, which was inferred from her last book: "Achieving moral excellence was the path to living eternally. Moral excellence, for Addams, was finding the right balance among individual, family, and social morality and being sure that the social was not slighted and the individual and family not overemphasized" (Knight, 2010, p.259). Jane's morality was about widening one's affections for those outside of family and friends, which in turn cultivated one's personal potential and led to new conduct both personally and globally. This was her perception of patriotism for one's nation and a Christian stance without a formal religion.

In 1932, Franklin Roosevelt—the eighth president Jane had occasion to meet and advise—publicly stated that Jane understood more about the real people of the United States than anybody else did (Knight, 2010). Perhaps she did. In her last two years, steadily declining health forced her to move out of her beloved Hull House. Her remaining passions either stalled or struggled against the global rise of dictatorial powers and their potential would be derailed by another world conflict that she would not live to see.

Jane died from cancer in May 1935 at age seventy-four. Praise and mourning were universal. Though hers was a chapter that had ended, it was part of a longer American book where many chapters were yet to be written. Her passion to simply make things better is the spirit that symbolizes and outlives her. Many of the conditions she fought to change still exist in many quarters and on many levels, waiting for a new leader to take up the cause. The 21st century has seen a renewed interest in Jane with the rise of women's studies and liberal politics, and her ideas of civic responsibility merit revisiting in the current American environment. The question is whether or not 21st century America can harness patriotic virtue and humanitarianism to shape the peaceful world she envisioned.

DISCUSSION GUIDELINE QUESTIONS

1. What values are depicted in the story?
2. Where did Jane learn her values?
3. What was her greatest character trait?
4. What was her greatest flaw?
5. Did she make any wrong moral/value choices? If so, what were the consequences?
6. What evidence is there that she may have struggled with certain moral issues?
7. How might her values be relevant today?
8. Are there any individuals currently on the scene who are comparable to her? Why or why not?

REFERENCES

Addams, J. (1961). *Twenty years at Hull House.* New York: New American Library Signet Classic.

Davis, A. (1973). *American heroine: The life and legend of Jane Addams.* New York: Oxford University Press.

Elshtain, J. (2002). *Jane Addams and the dream of American democracy.* New York: Basic Books.

Knight, L. (2005). *Citizen: Jane Addams and the struggle for democracy.* Chicago: University of Chicago Press.

Knight, L. (2010). *Jane Addams: Spirit in action.* New York: W.W. Norton and Company.

Chapter Sixteen

Breaking the Barrier: Jackie Robinson

The American mystique surrounding the athlete as hero is arguably a 20th century phenomenon. However, a convincing case can be made that an athlete is merely a media-based celebrity whose prowess serves the purpose of entertainment in that he/she displays skills that the admirer or fan does not and often cannot possess. Only on the rarest of occasions does there exist that athlete whose achievements transcend the parameters of the playing field and into the social fabric of the nation to promote heroic values of true character with which the commoner can identify. Such an individual was baseball's Jackie Robinson, whose heroic exploits on and off the field played a crucial role in changing the American conscience and making him "a hero of the struggle to make American democracy a genuine reality for every American" (Rampersad, 1997, p.6).

As the first African-American in six decades to play major league baseball in the 20th century (several blacks briefly played professional baseball in the late 19th century), Jack was not the greatest player in the game (Loewen, 1995). Nor was he arguably the best athletic choice to merit being chosen as the century's first African-American player, an honor some claimed rightfully belonged to the legendary Satchel Paige, Josh Gibson, or Monte Irvin (Paige & Lipman, 1993). Rather, Jack's talent—considerable that it was in its own right—was in many respects secondary to what he additionally had to be as a person: possessing a fiery courage and deep faith, his perseverance reflected his dual role of influencing the course of America during one of its most tumultuous periods. His exploits not only tested him as an athlete but more importantly as a human being and he emerged triumphant as few others could. Breaking baseball's segregated color barrier through his athletic success had a coordinated impact in the struggle for civil rights and his efforts were crucial in promoting all Americans to respect and appreciate the individual's values.

He was born Jack Roosevelt Robinson on January 31, 1919 in southern Georgia, one of five children born to Jerry and Mallie Robinson, who named him in honor of Theodore Roosevelt for his outspoken opposition to racism. It was certainly a harbinger of Jack's future, fueled by the racially hostile environment established by the separatist Jim Crow laws that prevailed espe-

cially in the South. The Robinson's marriage, unfortunately, was doomed to failure and Mallie used the occasion to relocate her children to Pasadena, California. Just as unfortunate, however, was the presence of Jim Crow there as well. But her family would survive because Mallie worked hard to instill in them the key values she herself had learned growing up: the importance of family, getting an education, optimism, self-discipline, and, above all, faith in God (Rampersad, 1997). It would be those values that formed the un-shakeable foundation of Jack's life.

Though Jim Crow pervaded his upbringing, Jack persevered as a mischie-vous charmer and his "precociousness as an athlete undoubtedly helped him to negotiate the traps of racism early in his life" (Rampersad, 1997, p.27). Finding the equality he demanded only on the playing field, he gained a reputation as an individual star who was also a team player, but sports alone could not shield his perilous adolescence from economic distress and racial prejudice. Mostly, he suffered from lack of a father figure and his mother's moral heroism was strained to outbalance his growing shame. He joined a local gang and though it wasn't of the vicious nature of current urban gangs, it did border on the delinquent. Fortunately, his continuing excellence on the playing field basically kept him out of serious trouble.

Even as Jack successfully moved on to junior college and UCLA, Jim Crow hung over his life. To such injustice he refused to back down and an ensuing but overblown "talking back" incident with local police netted him a police record. Only on the playing field was he experiencing the acceptance and success that sustained him.

During this time Jack also experienced a pivotal moment in his young life in the person of Karl Downs, a pastor whose intervention changed the course of Jack's life. Downs taught him the true significance of faith and served as a "conduit through which Mallie's message of religion and hope finally flowed into Jack's consciousness and was fully accepted there" (Rampersad, 1997, p.53). It did not diminish his fiery competitiveness, but it did complement it by giving him an emotional and spiritual poise that would later inspire him to influence and shape young lives as his had been (Santella, 1996). It would indeed be this trademark competitiveness that "nurtured his greatness and encouraged him to rise to challenges and advance where others might retreat" (Tygiel, 2008, p.63) and was a major part of his future legacy.

He was gaining wide adulation in several sports as a college athlete, especially in football, but baseball was increasingly becoming his signature sport to the point where he could have been and should have been actively pursued by the major leagues. But the existing color barrier effectively slammed the door in his face. As a result, he was growing more frustrated and sensitive to prejudice. College provided him with another life-changing event in the guise of Rachel, who was destined to become a major pillar in his life as his future wife. Beginning a five-year courtship, her confidence in him despite an uncertain future with World War II looming spurred him on.

Jack chose to leave college early for a job as an athletic director but the certainty of war service temporarily led him to a defense factory position, and like many others he was drafted into the army shortly after Pearl Harbor. To his increasing dismay, he learned that black soldiers had two enemies to fight: the Axis overseas and Jim Crow at home. Yet Jack distinguished himself enough to breech the military color barrier and into Officer's Training School where he was commissioned as a Second Lieutenant. But racial friction continually grated on him, culminating in a racially-motivated incident on a bus in which Jack refused to move from the "white" section and led to his military arrest and court martial on charges of disrespect and insubordination. He relied on his faith to keep him composed in the face of this humiliation and though he was acquitted by an all-white jury, the incident would add to his false reputation as a hot-tempered troublemaker. It may also have led to his failure to be assigned to combat duty. After three disappointing years of military service, Jack was honorably discharged due to a physical injury.

His bitter military experience could have easily destroyed a lesser person, but instead he emerged far more mature and deeply interested in a personal commitment to the ideal of social justice, especially for blacks (Rampersad, 1997). Yet as the war ended in 1945, Jack was drifting without an apparent vocation or profession in a nation still divided by race. His life, however, was about to drastically and historically change.

The post-war opportunity that finally presented itself was to play baseball in the Negro Leagues. Jack signed with the best—the Kansas City Monarchs—and he humbly took advantage of the chance. He was somewhat uncertain about his abilities, but trusting in God to guide him to his intended purpose, he learned, progressed, and began attracting attention. One who took notice was Pittsburgh journalist Wendell Smith, whose sports writing began publicly pressing the issue of major league integration (Bryant, 2002).

There had been several black ballplayers in the 1880s, but the prevailing racial prejudice against them was too overwhelming for any to sustain a successfully lengthy career. Jim Crow was the norm and institutional segregation forced black players to form the Negro Leagues in the 1920s (Tygiel, 2008). There was bluntly no acceptance of blacks in the major leagues. Though the Negro Leagues developed indisputably talented stars with a distinctive style of play that favorably compared to white players, there remained a question of whether they could successfully compete in the major leagues; if they were given the chance (Tygiel, 2008). In any case, social stigma forbade integration and the color barrier was subtly and hypocritically enforced.

Integration would have to await a new public conscience toward baseball's segregation policy. That conscience had been stirred by the spectacular success of boxing's Joe Louis and track's Jesse Owens in the 1930s. "The efforts of integration advocates notwithstanding, World War II, more than any other event, caused Americans to re-evaluate their racial attitudes" (Tygiel, 2008, p.37). Post-war America seemed primed for a change but was still hesitant. A crusader was necessary.

Major league owners and management had long resisted the notion of integration, but a lone voice of dissent came from the general manager of the Brooklyn Dodgers, Branch Rickey. A highly moral and religious man, Rickey had long experience with baseball's racism toward blacks and Latinos. During the early 1940s, he began seriously contemplating integration initially as a response to the wartime shortage of major league talent and to rebuild his Dodgers into winners while simultaneously rebuilding America's social conscience. In taking the initiative to integrate baseball, Rickey emerged from the isolated world of baseball and aspired to influence developments in the broader scope of society (Tygiel, 2008). He knew this bold experiment was a matter of timing: a premature move would be disastrous and he refused to be impulsive, for his plan would go far beyond sports-inspired profit and winning games.

Moving cautiously and secretly, Rickey enlisted his scouts to find the most promising prospect. It would be Wendell Smith who helped identify Jack to Rickey, who in turn had Jack scouted not only for his playing ability but also for his character. Rickey intended to dramatically change the entire major league landscape by signing several black ballplayers, but he knew that one would have to blaze the trail for the others and that would require an extraordinary individual who would have to appeal to the heart and soul of an America ready but albeit not eager to advance the cause of equality (Simon, 2002). For such a noble experiment, Rickey sought a man who was skilled but not necessarily the "best" black ballplayer. Rather, he had to be an athlete who could maintain his talents at a competitive peak while withstanding the worst sort of pressure and abuse, a man of superior self-control who could maintain his dignity (Tygiel, 2008). After a meticulous search, he knew Jack was his man.

Their historic first meeting took place in Brooklyn in August 1945 where Rickey personally sized up this man with "a sensitive, intelligent face with strong features, a high forehead, wide and somewhat brooding eyes, a full mouth and determined chin" (Tygiel, 2008, p.66). The two men formed an instant rapport—one that would last throughout their lives—and Rickey bluntly offered him a contract to play with the Dodgers' highest-level minor league team, the Montreal Royals, and the chance to advance to the major leagues if he was successful. But Rickey also made it clear that the challenge required more than Jacks' abilities; namely, did he have the courage to endure the inevitable physical, verbal, and psychological abuse? Jack knew that his hair-trigger disposition would be severely tested, but he was as close to the perfect candidate to break the color barrier as one could be (Simon, 2002; Robinson, 2004; Tygiel, 2008). Making it abundantly clear that he was looking for a ballplayer with the courage not to fight back, Rickey submitted Jack to a devastating two-hour verbal tirade of the racial abuse he was sure to encounter. Jack passed the initial test, convinced that Rickey's experiment could succeed only if he turned the proverbial other cheek. Promising to avoid confrontation for three years, he was instinctively trusting Rickey as much as he did his own mother.

Jack's official signing was simultaneously praised for its boldness but laced with uneasy anticipation for the twenty-seven-year-old rookie who suddenly became the most famous black baseball player in the world, though he had yet to take the field. About to marry as the 1946 spring training session began, Jack and Rachel prepared to face the upcoming uncertainty together. Having faith in his own abilities and Rickey's integrity, the two men believed that God would guide them both through the ordeal.

Despite an unspectacular spring performance which required him to swiftly learn how to play several new positions, Jack won a place on the Montreal roster and vindicated Rickey's confidence in him for the first part of the experiment. But it came at an expectedly high price: he and Rachel had to endure constant humiliation and indignities, marking only the beginning of the ordeal they would face. But they had a unique and growing sense of themselves as a united couple facing the challenges together (Rampersad, 1997). Their mutual support of each other would be a decisive factor, as they realized that the experiment wasn't about baseball itself but rather racial equality.

Though the Royals only had modest expectations as a whole, Jack's electrifying play and demeanor totally captivated Montreal fans—white and black—who came out in groves to see and support him (Linge, 2007). Accepted by some but not all of his teammates, Jack was deftly proving that a black player could successfully compete with white players. Black fans especially took notice and found it extremely difficult to restrain the pride and sense of achievement engendered by Jack's performance (Tygiel, 2008). Burdened with anxiety and stress, his play was still magnificent and figured perfectly into the next part of Rickey's experiment: promotion to the major leagues in 1947. But few could have realized let alone endured what he was experiencing: opposing pitchers regularly threw at him and baserunners tried to repeatedly spike him at his second base position, in addition to the Jim Crow-based hostility from many players and some fans. The experiment may have been progressing, but it was still a long way from success. With gritted determination, Jack maintained his calm and poise.

Promotion to the Dodgers and the major leagues would make him the first black player of the 20th century to officially break the color barrier but it would require Rickey's direct intervention (Eig, 2007). The other owners still opposed integration but Rickey forged ahead with his plan by announcing that other black players were being signed to the Dodger organization. In addition, Rickey plotted to fill the team's first base vacancy by announcing that Jack would move there from his customary second base position, a move he would make quite flawlessly. His Dodger teammates gave him a cold reception, but both Rickey and manager Leo Durocher helped pave the way for Jack by reminding the Dodgers about the business of baseball; that is, to win games, enough games to win the first-place pennant, and advance to and win the World Series. To that end, Durocher addressed the racial tension in the clubhouse yet another way: "I don't care if the guy is yellow or black, or if he has stripes like a… zebra. I'm the manager of this team and I say he plays. What's more, I say he can make us all rich" (Kirwin, 2005, p.198). With that, there were no serious efforts by Jack's white teammates to oust him even though tension still lingered among some of them.

As the drama continued to unfold, Jack outwardly faced the moment with confidence but inwardly with a sense of foreboding and bolstered himself with his faith (Rampersad, 1997). Tuesday, April 15, 1947 was a cold spring day at Brooklyn's Ebbets Field for the season opener, but when Number Forty-Two took his position at first base, the air was positively electrifying. Though Jack went hitless that game and did not directly figure in the Dodger victory, history was made with his appearance (Rampersad, 1997; Simon, 2002; Eig, 2007). Initial fan reaction the entire first week was very favorable but winning over his own teammates took longer; and he brooded over it, but not for long. "In Robinson, Rickey had uncovered not only an outstanding baseball player, but a figure of charisma and leadership" (Tygiel, 2008, p.208) that demanded respect. His poise and sharpness won over most every-one who came to see him play, eventually most who would play with him, and later most who played against him. He was a true major leaguer in every respect but it was his intense competitiveness that provided the crucial ingre-dient his Dodger teammates needed to follow his lead as he singlehandedly brought a new dimension to the game through his dynamic play that made the team a winner (Santella, 1996; Rampersad, 1997).

Opposing players in every visiting ballpark made a concerted effort to make his color an issue, but Jack remembered his agreement with Rickey and his unspoken deal with his people to do what was necessary to make the experiment work (Rampersad, 1997). His coolness under fire would rally his teammates to his side. The abuse heaped on Jack angered them and his tortuous ordeal served to unify them in support of him. Despite an inevitable batting slump that shook his confidence, his teammates' confidence in him did not waver: he was now a true member of the Dodgers and he drew further strength from Rickey's ultimate faith in him.

He would pass the most severe test of courage that historic season. Daily threats on his life, constant torment and baiting from opposing players, discrimination at the team hotel, and rumors of a player strike to keep him from playing against them simultaneously engulfed him. With the added pressures of being a national phenomenon and the biggest attraction in baseball since the great Babe Ruth, Jack's "charismatic personality inspired not merely sympathy and acceptance, but sincere adulation from both whites and blacks alike" (Tygiel, 2008, p.196). His caliber of play and mere presence instilled a vital sense of pride in black America and further led many whites to reassess their attitudes of acceptance. A pivotal moment that symbolized that attitude was a gesture by southerner and team captain Pee Wee Reese on the field of play: "at one point, in full view of the public, he dared to put his white hand on Robinson's black shoulder in a gesture of solidarity" (Rampersad, 1997, p.182). Hecklers fell silent.

By midseason, Rickey's experiment was influencing other owners who were realizing the value of signing black players themselves, but the ordeal was far from over. Jack's play was exemplary in hitting, running, defense, and overall value to his team. Due in large part to his contributions, the Dodgers won the coveted 1947 pennant and though they would lose the World Series, his first season became a heroic tale of courage and triumph over adversity. For his efforts, Jack was awarded the Rookie of the Year, but more importantly he had revolutionized the image of black Americans in the eyes of white America.

Jack had taken hope onto the playing field and succeeded beyond expectations with a heroism not seen before and signaled the beginning of the end of Jim Crow in major league baseball; and made it possible for white boys to idolize a black man. The Robinson legend was growing as the emotional impact of Rickey's experiment melded into our national perception of not only fair play but also social progress (Tygiel, 2008). But the experiment was still in its crucial early stages and would have to cautiously advance in tune with Jack's continuing response to the challenge, a challenge to which he would rise to the occasion for an incredible ten seasons.

Baseball became one of the most powerful vehicles promoting racial/social change through the turbulent civil rights era of the late 1940s through the 1960s. The mid-1950s witnessed an expected backlash of intimidation and violence, but the continuing integration of baseball was a major foundation of hope. Breaking the sport's Jim Crow barrier was but the first stage of Jack's self-appointed mission of social responsibility, especially in regard to helping the young, poor, and sick. To that end, he fearlessly spoke out against racial injustice by using his new fame and making something political of it (Rampersad, 1997). Throughout it all, Rachel understood and supported his mission. She and their three children made their home a haven to which he could retreat and ease the stress of his ordeal. In many respects, it would be his only sanctuary over the years.

Jack sometimes had difficulty separating his athletic image from his social image. But while he felt obligated as a crusader to both roles, he was careful never to use the integration of baseball as a political tool but rather as proof that races could co-exist and flourish on an equal basis (Tygiel, 2008). His continuing outspokenness on and off the field, however, began to alienate many, but his efforts promoted the growing acceptance and appreciation of black players, an effort that would ultimately take twelve years before every major league team had formally integrated.

As with many athletes, Jack's fame allowed him to obtain commercial endorsements for his considerable charity work, and additional income came his way from a movie of his life in which he starred. He understood very early in his career that baseball longevity would be brief (although his ten-year career was longer than the norm) and he would have to plan for post-baseball financial security. But of more immediate importance was Jack's obligation to Rickey's experiment. "Ardent, tempestuous, and controversial, he continually probed and expanded the boundaries of acceptance for those who followed" (Tygiel, 2008, p.320). Fully in the American spotlight, his excellence on the field not only reflected his ability to influence the outcome of any game, but further symbolized the fiery spirit of the pennant-winning Dodgers.

Jack was clearly the team leader and the Dodgers rose and fell according to his play, highlighted by his selection as the league's Most Valuable Player award in his third season. But by then he was a dramatically changed player: his three-year promise of restraint to Ricky was over and Jack aggressively and defiantly stood up against any and all perceived injustices, be they from opposing players or umpires. Jack proceeded to battle with umpires over matters not simply of judgment calls but of ethics due to his growing belief that white umpires were abusing their power in order to put him in his place (Rampersad, 1997). Opposing players suddenly learned that he would no longer take personal abuse. His quick temper sometimes got the better of him and he readily acknowledged that on occasion his actions undoubtedly exceeded the boundaries of accepted conduct for all athletes (Tygiel, 2008). It would lead to his growing reputation as a troublemaker and a rocky relationship with the press which had formerly supported him. Perhaps unfairly, sportswriters would occasionally take exception to his outspokenness and aggressive play by stating that "if there was one flaw in Jackie, it was... [his belief] that everything unpleasant that happened to him happened to him because of his blackness" (Falkner, 1995, p.213).

Beside the ever-dependable Rachel, one other source of support never wavered through his ordeal: Rickey. But in an internal power struggle with ownership, Rickey was suddenly forced to leave the Dodgers. Though the two men retained a father-son relationship, the move devastated Jack and for the first time he was in doubt about his future. He need not have been, as the post-Rickey Dodgers still needed Jack's play and fiery leadership.

At the same time, however, he was becoming more deeply involved off the field in the civil rights movement as well as the pursuit of business interests. He fervently promoted his own core values of religion, education, family, and faith to America's youth who were more actively seeking racial tolerance and social acceptance (Rampersad, 1997). As these involvements increased the sometimes overmagnified controversy and notoriety surrounding him, the Dodgers were beginning to view him as an organizational liability.

As the 1950s progressed, he was still an intense leader and a respected teammate, though he knew he could be abrasive in the heat of competition, and his sense of team play was reflected in the inevitable accommodations he selflessly made. To make room for promising rookies, Jack voluntarily changed positions several times and agreed to diminished playing time in an effort to prolong his contributions. At age thirty-six, he was still the spark-plug for what was arguably Brooklyn's best team in 1955, as the Dodgers captured their fifth pennant with Jack and then finally triumphed over the dreaded Yankees in the World Series. But it had been an infuriatingly mediocre season for him personally.

More distracted than ever by ongoing social issues that consumed more and more of his time and strength, 1956 would be his tenth and last season. The game he had given so much to had lost its charm for him and though the Dodgers took their sixth and last pennant with him, his season performance was depressingly unproductive. He brooded but could not deny his lack of sharpness and the entire season was a miserable experience. As a result, during the off-season he became the subject of serious trade rumors.

His departure from the game became increasingly a foregone conclusion and he was determined to transcend baseball and his profound influence on American society into a business role with the firm Chock Full 'o Nuts in an executive vice-presidency position. It was not a difficult decision after learning that the Dodgers had indeed traded him.

It was simply the way of all athletes. After the toll of ten seasons of intense and unrestrained effort, Jack's prowess had inevitably declined and his body was failing him. He could no longer run the bases with his trademark speed and agility. His bat speed had drastically diminished and his range in the field was a liability. During the last four seasons, he had played in progressively fewer games as a concession to age. He could still display flashes of his former brilliance but those moments had become decidedly few. What had not changed was his leadership status: he was still the acknowledged leader to whom his teammates looked for inspiration and in that regard he could still deliver on the field or from the bench. But if his heart was still full of fire, his body told him he was at the end of his playing effectiveness. The Dodgers also realized it and made the trade. Jack announced his retirement, which nullified the trade, and although he was showered with deserved acclaim, the ever-present controversies surrounding him led to a bittersweet exit. Controversy would continue to stalk him in his post-baseball life.

The initial shock of retirement quickly faded and he began the new phase of his life by rededicating himself to family and home. "Anchored in the black world but with strong ties to the white, Jack and Rachel moved with apparent ease as they lived out the misty dream of true racial integration in the 1950s" (Rampersad, 1997, p.313). But with racism still looming in the social shadows of America, he devoted himself to the cause of equality, using his respected name and reputation to speak out frankly, enthusiastically, and idealistically. His growing concern with the political nature of the civil rights movement led to his characteristically aggressive involvement in state and national elections without regard to personal risk, but his frustration over the lack of progress with the movement resulted in a disillusionment with political influence. Yet as with other matters, he refused to give up the fight and soon lent his support to active social protest with Martin Luther King as the 1960s approached.

Social issues were not his only concern. In 1957 he was diagnosed with diabetes as had his brothers. The illness was largely responsible for his deteriorating condition and he feared for a shortened life expectancy. Worse, perhaps, was the deteriorating situation with his eldest son, Jackie Jr. Unable to cope with living in his famous father's shadow, the youth was experiencing increasing identity problems that manifested themselves in various ways. Eventually, he plunged into drug addiction. Jack's helplessness led him to lament that he had far more effect on other people's children than his own son and with neither he nor Rachel seemingly able to reach their son, Jack lived with a self-imposed guilt.

Baseball had not forgotten Jack's contributions and in 1962 the sport accorded him its highest honor. In his very first year of eligibility, Jack became the first African-American player to be elected to the Hall of Fame and it proved to be a national event. Present at his dedication speech were the three people he credited for his success: Rachel, Mallie, and Branch Rickey. His encroaching health issues and Jackie Jr.'s problems could temporarily be put aside as both the sport and the nation honored him.

Jack's devotion to the civil rights struggle as a voice of reason underscored his growing anxiety about the direction of the country and his personal life, as both headed toward crisis in the late 1960s. The despondency among the nation's youth was leading to a violent backlash and he used his respected image in continual hope of promoting racial equality and understanding, but he feared that the nation would dissolve into savage divisiveness. Rickey had died in 1965 and Mallie passed away three years later. Yet a bright spot shone with Jackie Jr.'s apparent turnaround, to Jack's great relief. The army had straightened him out psychologically and he was recovering from wounds heroically sustained in Vietnam. Under the strain of these events and his own shaky health, Jack suffered a heart attack. Though he heeded the need for rest and recovery, he believed that God had more for him to do. Sustaining him in his belief as always was Rachel and together they took a new pride in the accomplishments of their three children.

By 1970, he was declining in every respect, including encroaching blindness. But even an ailing Jackie Robinson possessed more fire and energy than most other people and he was always ready to do battle if the cause was right (Rampersad, 1997). But it was only in spirit. By this time, Jack no longer had a public forum or the physical strength to express his opinions. The breaking point came with Jackie Jr.'s accidental death, which crushed Jack but nearly destroyed Rachel. Though his faith saw him through the tragedy, it created a tension between husband and wife that was not there before.

As his strength steadily ebbed, there was a final tribute: the Dodgers were ceremoniously retiring his uniform number, an action that all of major league baseball would later extend to every team. In tribute to Jack's historic contributions, no major league player will ever wear Number Forty-Two again. To mark the 25th anniversary of his debut, he was invited to throw out the first pitch at the 1972 World Series. In what would be his last public appearance, he expressed one final testimony of his life's mission by stating, "I'm going to be more pleased and more proud when I look at that third base coaching line one day and see a black face managing in baseball" (Rampersad, 1997, p.459). That event would come to pass just two years later, but he did not live to see it. His badly weakened body gave out and he died from a heart attack on October 24, 1972, at age fifty-three. A stunned and mourning nation momentarily stood still to pay a final tribute to an American hero who exemplified courage and perseverance on the playing field and in life.

Post-World War II America was a time of tumultuous and sometimes violent social upheaval in the name of racial equality. All aspects of our culture were necessarily affected by various forces that would lead us to social change. But in turn each of those aspects had its own catalyst that individually contributed to the collective change; each was a unique part of the whole. It was also a matter of timing: each catalyst had to appear at precisely the right moment.

Thus, World War II provided the catalyst to successfully integrate the armed forces, though this was not the military's first attempt to do so. But America was ready for such an endeavor and gradually accepted the change through an executive order in 1948. Likewise, in the realm of public education, the historic case of Brown v. Board of Education (1954) was the impetus for school integration, though it too would be slow and limited in its realization.

Individuals naturally played pivotal roles as social catalysts. In the field of entertainment, actor Sidney Poitier and singer Nat King Cole were the leading catalysts for the artistic and box-office rise and acceptance of African-American performers and recording artists in the 1950s and 1960s, especially through the former's provocative portrayals in lead roles played with dignity in integrated settings which contributed to a black renaissance of sorts through the 1970s. In a similar vein, Martin Luther King's historic involvement in the mid-century's civil rights movement was a decided catalyst that helped redefine America's social consciousness.

No less important to the social conscience in the mid-20th century was the nature of the athletic arena. It had begun with boxer Joe Louis and track star Jesse Owens in the 1930s, but it would be the integration of major league baseball that was the defining event promoting racial equality in America; and it required a most courageous catalyst. Jackie Robinson fulfilled that heroic role but went far beyond the playing field in his demonstration of values and character that not only influenced the sport but the entire social landscape to promote respect and appreciation of the individual.

DISCUSSION GUIDELINE QUESTIONS

1. What values are depicted in the story?
2. Where did Jack learn his values?
3. What may have been his greatest character trait?
4. What may have been his greatest flaw?
5. How did Jack specifically bridge his athletic role with his social responsibility?
6. Could he have succeeded without Branch Rickey's assistance?
7. Why was America reluctant to embrace integration in baseball and society in general?
8. Is there a current athlete who is comparable to Jack?

REFERENCES

Bryant, H. (2002). *Shutout: A story of race and baseball in Boston.* New York: Rutledge.
Eig, J. (2007). *Opening day: The story of Jackie Robinson's first season.* New York: Simon & Schuster.
Falkner, D. (1995). *Great time coming: The life of Jackie Robinson, from baseball to Birmingham.* New York: Simon & Schuster.
Kirwin, B. (2005). *Out of the shadows: African-American baseball from the Cuban Giants to Jackie Robinson.* Lincoln: University of Nebraska Press.
Linge, M. (2007). *Jackie Robinson: A biography.* Westport, CT: Greenwood Press.

Loewen, J. (1995). *Lies my teacher told me: Everything your American history textbook got wrong.* New York: Simon & Schuster.

Paige, S. & Lipman, D. (1993). *Maybe I'll pitch forever: A great baseball player tells the hilarious story behind the legend.* Lincoln: University of Nebraska Press.

Rampersad, A. (1997). *Jackie Robinson: A biography.* New York: Ballantine Books.

Robinson, S. (2004). *Promises to keep: How Jackie Robinson changed America.* New York: Simon & Schuster.

Santella, A. (1996). *Jackie Robinson breaks the color line.* New York: Children's Press.

Simon, S. (2002). *Jackie Robinson and the integration of baseball.* Hoboken: Wiley.

Tygiel, J. (2008). *Baseball's great experiment: Jackie Robinson and his legacy.* New York: Oxford University Press.

Chapter Seventeen

Always Do Right: Harry Truman

In many respects, Harry Truman was not a typical politician. He was a nineteenth-century man of character whose twentieth-century values were based upon his biblical faith and the steadfast principle of "say what you mean and mean what you say" (McCullough, 1992, p.55). The former was embodied more by action than in talking while the latter was the simple philosophy of his moral character from which contemporary politicians could learn much (McCullough, 1992). He may also be the last of his kind. In an examination of cultural context, Hall (1976) lamented how American morality had decidedly declined in the arena of twentieth-century foreign diplomacy with one notable exception: "Truman had a deep moral sense, a sense of continuity, and was deeply conversant with the presidency as an institution. He came out of a past age... [when] a man's word was his bond [and took responsibility for his actions]... Truman belonged to this tradition" (p.71) and was the only twentieth-century president to be regarded as such.

As with us all, his moral foundation was established early. Born in 1884 and raised in Independence, Missouri, this youth of celebrated poor eyesight was very studious, extremely well-read, and impressed by his willingness "to do the work, but to face whatever ridicule might come" (McCullough, 1992, p.61). This defining trait began with his devotion to piano but would equally apply to all facets of his life. Perhaps as a result, he retained the gift for getting along with just about everyone (McCullough, 1992). People simply liked this common young man.

Truman's road to fame was a varied one. He was "a little man from Missouri, a failed small-town haberdasher turned farmer turned county judge then sent up to Washington as Senator by famously corrupt Kansas City political boss Tom Pendergast" (Wallace, 2004, p.341).

He learned the sociability and excitement of politics from his father and was introduced early to the Democratic Party and the ensuing power of the Pendergast Machine. But it would take his military experience in World War I to give him the maturity and confidence to enter the political arena. He clearly saw how politics could seduce and corrupt, but he couldn't resist its

fascination and allowed the Machine to sponsor him. His association with the Machine was a stressful and constant battle, but Truman firmly kept his integrity through his quest of helping ordinary people as a politician.

The Machine advanced him as Senator in 1934 but he always presented himself for what he truly was: a country boy with common sense doing what was best for the common people as an ardent New Dealer (McCullough, 1992). He distinguished himself almost immediately and though his integrity kept him as one of the financially-poorest of congressmen, his standing in the Senate rapidly rose. The fall of the Pendergast Machine finally freed him from the shadow of any perceived control and he proved it by personally running his own successful re-election. As World War II consumed the nation, Truman's stature continued to rise and he remained unpresuming even as the powers-that-be took notice of him.

It was as if his political life had been preparing him for the Election of 1944. Unbeknownst to the general public, Franklin Roosevelt's rapidly declining health was the major concern for Democratic delegates who understood that in all likelihood they would be choosing two presidents. FDR did not actively endorse a running mate and the sixty-year-old Truman did not seek or want the nomination, but he would be chosen primarily because he was wise to politics and a relatively safe choice (McCullough, 1992). The two men could not have been more different: FDR was the larger-than-life, well-educated, wealthy patrician; Truman was the common, "undeniably middle American" (McCullough, 1992, p.324) who was "truly uncomplicated, open, and genuine" (McCullough, 1992, p.526). Not surprisingly, the two did not get along, but Providence had placed Harry Truman in the wings of the world's biggest political stage.

FDR's "sudden" death now propelled Truman to tackle the duties of a wartime president and to the public (and political) eye he initially "did not appear to be at all qualified to fill Roosevelt's shoes" (Wallace, 2004, p.342). Truman never flinched. In his first three months in office, he would be faced with more far-reaching decisions than any President before him. The first of those decisions would be the most crucial and most second-guessed of any President, but it would also showcase the character of a man determined to do the right thing (Sanchez, 2006).

Upon assuming the presidency in April 1945, Truman quickly realized that his inexperience was the least of his worries. FDR had kept him in the dark concerning many of the administration's war policies, including the most secret: the atomic bomb. Its existence would lead to the most difficult decision for which a president would be responsible (Rawls, 1995).

Victory over Nazi Germany finally came in May 1945. The war against Japan, however, raged on with no apparent end in sight. Japanese atrocities against the Allies were now being widely reported, prompting a war-weary American people to push for a quick end to this "other" war as well. During the summer of 1945, American fire bombings of Japanese cities were killing an estimated 100,000 daily. Yet the tenaciously stubborn Japanese Empire remained unwilling to accept Truman's demand for unconditional surrender. That summer the Japanese had secretly sent "feelers" to the Russians to mediate a formal surrender but with certain conditions. This was extremely important to a culture in which losing face was worse than death.

While Truman and the Allies adamantly continued to cling to the position of unconditional surrender, a massive land invasion of Japan was being planned despite estimates that the plan would prolong the war at least another year and could cost one million American casualties. But another incident occurred that would have to take center stage in any war decision.

On July 16, 1945, the top-secret Manhattan Project successfully tested the first atomic bomb explosion in the deserts of New Mexico. Headed by the brilliant physicist Robert Oppenheimer, the project had required the services of 100,000 individuals working under extremely high pressure, necessitated tremendous industrial and economic resources, and had cost $4 billion over a 3-year period. So secret was the project that few of the people involved actually knew what they were producing until a team cane together for the testing that summer. With this new super-weapon, Truman now felt a sense of confidence that the war could be concluded on his terms.

Yet any decision to use the bomb carried many considerations, chief among them being how best to use this weapon that so few individuals understood. No one was certain of its outcome. One of the Project's team members, Enrico Fermi, had even made a bet with his fellow- scientists that the July test would incinerate the entire state of New Mexico. There was also the consideration of the unknown physical and psychological effects on the enemy. But Truman knew that his responsibility as president was to end the war as quickly as possible with a minimum loss of American lives (Kagan, 1995). The vexing question was how best to do this? Because the Project was so top-secret, the public was completely unaware of it, so there was no public opinion to consider. Armed with the knowledge that we possessed the most devastating weapon in history, Truman and the Allies issued an ultimatum of surrender to Japan on July 26th. Truman (1955) noted that he "wanted to afford Japan a clear chance to end the fighting before we made use of this newly gained power" (p.417).

Adding to the complexity of Truman's decision was the apparent crisis of conscience for many of the scientists who had worked on the Project. The program had been suggested in 1939 to President Roosevelt by Albert Ein-stein in order to keep Hitler from first developing the bomb. Many of the scientists were so caught up in the technical challenge of developing the weapon that they did not think about the moral dilemma it created until faced with its actual use on Japan, which was not the original intent. Leading scientists could not accept its use against Japan and advised against this option.

At this point, Truman's military advisors suggested seven possible courses of action (Strada, 1999):

1. A naval blockade of Japan to gradually starve out the enemy.
2. The previously-mentioned land invasion.
3. Continuing daily fire-bombings of Japanese cities which would cost fewer American lives.
4. Dropping the atomic bomb on a Japanese military site.
5. Using the atomic bomb in a harmless demonstration on Japanese territory (such as a deserted island) to inform the enemy of what they were up against and why they should surrender.
6. Giving the Japanese a verbal warning about the bomb in order to induce surrender.
7. Wait the Japanese out, since Allied victory was inevitable.

Each suggestion had advantages and disadvantages. A naval blockade might lose few lives but would be time-consuming. A land invasion would cost many casualties but would bring favorable surrender terms. Continuing fire-bombings would cost time and great loss on Japanese lives and property but few American lives would be lost. Dropping the bomb on a military target would be fast and devastating but would raise moral questions and include unknown environmental and health effects. A harmless demonstration would not destroy lives but it might fail to push the Japanese into surrendering (plus we had only two more bombs in our arsenal). Issuing a verbal warning could save lives but it might not be taken seriously by the Japanese government. Finally, waiting out the enemy would save lives but would not be politically popular with Americans who wanted a quick end to the war.

Ultimately, it came down to one man's decision: while he could hope for a miracle, the daily tragedy of a bitter war crowded in on him (Truman, 1955). Some believed he had no real choice other than military use of the bomb:

> Very possibly there was no one, clear-cut moment when he made up his mind, or announced that he had. Most likely, he never seriously considered not using the bomb. Indeed, to have said no at this point and called everything off would have been so drastic a break with the whole history of the project, not to say the terrific momentum of events that summer, as to have been almost inconceivable (McCullough, 1992, p.437).

Perhaps weighing most heavily on his mind was that if he failed to use it, the parents of those soldiers who would die while invading Japan would hold him personally responsible. But Harry Truman knew what he had to do:

> It was their [military and scientific advisory committees] recommendation that the bomb be used against the enemy as soon as it could be done... I had realized, of course, that an atomic bomb explosion would inflict damage and casualties beyond imagination... [But] the final decision of where and when to use the atomic bomb was up to me. Let there be no mistake about it. I regarded the bomb as a military "weapon and never had any doubt that it should be used (Truman, 1955, p.419).

While continuing to demand unconditional surrender, President Truman ordered the dropping of the bomb without warning on August 6, 1945. The city of Hiroshima was effectively incinerated, resulting in 80,000 immediate deaths and over 40,000 long-term deaths from radiation burns and poisoning. When the Japanese still astonishingly failed to accept unconditional surrender, Truman ordered a second bomb dropped on Nagasaki three days later. This second demonstration of the atomic bomb's horrific power apparently threw the Japanese into a necessary panic, as the next morning brought the first indication that the Japanese empire was ready to unconditionally surrender (Truman, 1955). Four days later, the long nightmare was finally over.

The post-war era would usher in the Cold War and the new atomic age. Though he was cognizant of the latter's "awful responsibility which has come to us" (Truman, 1955, p.315), he would find the mission of peace to be difficult. Foreign and domestic problems engulfed him. On the foreign front, the Truman Doctrine fought the spread of communism through the Marshal Plan and he firmly held his ground against Stalin but never made serious progress with him. Domestically, he began being faulted for failing to adequately handle a growing number of labor strikes which he appeared powerless to influence with few exceptions. He was heavily criticized in all quarters and his popularity tumbled. Perhaps he spoke his mind too often or was too candid. Perhaps he too frequently appeared to be bewildered at the increasing Soviet expansion in Europe and that he did not make clear his long-range goals. He would attempt to play tough against them all, yet he never complained, never felt sorry for himself, and never blamed others (McCullough, 1992).

He was not yet beaten. Truman was still to experience two more episodes of glory and redemption. The Berlin Airlift in 1948 would bring us precariously close to war with the Soviets. The incident would be predicated on American resolve and patience and, for once, "Stalin seriously underestimated just how stubbornly patient [Truman] could be" (Wallace, 2004, p.350). It became one of the most profoundly successful achievements of the post-war era and perhaps his proudest decision as Stalin meekly backed down (McCullough, 1992).

It came none too soon. Despite the turmoil, Truman thoroughly enjoyed the power of the presidency despite its trappings and was determined to be elected in his own right (McCullough, 1992). The 1948 presidential election and his "miracle" victory over Dewey would be his last episode of redemption, but it was not, however, so miraculous. Truman was aided by a suddenly booming economy and the success of the Berlin Airlift. The voters demonstrated that he was still admired by the public and he came across for what he was: "a President who was friendly and undisguised.., who cared about the country and about them... [and was] doing his best... He was one of them" (McCullough, 1992, p.664).

Truman's character would not allow his ego to come between him and his duties, though he must have been severely tested during his officially sanctioned term by Mao's revolution, the H-bomb, the rise of McCarthyism, and his disastrous mishandling of a steel strike (which was subsequently declared unconstitutional). But it was the outbreak of the Korean War that would prove to be the most difficult event of his presidency and would completely overshadow his attempts for a successful term. His ultimate firing of the egotistical General MacArthur over the latter's blatant call to expand the conflict into Communist China and insubordinately excusing his own failures was politically expedient, but it precipitated a firestorm of public outcry against Truman. Truman is famously remembered for his desk plaque stating "the buck stops here." However, he more frequently referred to a framed motto of Mark Twain: "Always do right! This will gratify some people and astonish the rest" (Wallace, 2004, p.348). He lived this principle before his presidency and for seven years and nine months in the free world's most powerful position he continued to live it. He knew by faith that he had always done his best in office and was content to wait for history's final verdict to bear it out. Politician that he was, Truman not surprisingly always took full credit for his accomplishments and basked in them. But more importantly, and true to his character, he also took full responsibility for his failings and never shirked from the repercussions: "I don't pass the buck, nor do I alibi out of any decisions I make" (Truman, 1955, p.422).

Beginning a twenty-year retirement, Truman became a plain American citizen again and to his great credit he blatantly refused to accept any position or lend his name to any organization or transaction that exploited or commercialized the dignity of the presidency. His death in 1972 brought deservedly respectful eulogies, but perhaps chief among them was that he brought to the presidency the values of the common American people. In the final analysis, Harry Truman was not our greatest President, but he may very well symbolize the type of president the Founding Fathers had in mind, for he came directly from the common people and ..."remembering him reminds people what a man in that office ought to be like. It's character, just character" (McCullough, 1992, p.992).

DISCUSSION GUIDELINE QUESTIONS

1. What values can be identified in the story?
2. Where did Truman learn his values?
3. What was his greatest character trait?
4. What was his greatest character flaw?
5. Has the importance of his values remained the same since his time or has it diminished?
6. Are Truman's actions surprising for an American leader during his time or are they bound to that particular time with little or no relevance to 21st century America?
7. Does political leadership necessitate some sacrifice in values and character?
8. Are there any individuals on the American scene today who are comparable to Truman? Why or why not?

REFERENCES

Hall, E. (1976, July). How cultures collide. *Psychology Today, 2:* 69-75.

Kagan, D. (1995, September). Why America dropped the bomb. *Commentary,* 100(3): 17.

McCullough, D. (1992). *Truman.* New York: Simon & Schuster.

Rawls, J. (1995). Fifty years after Hiroshima. *Dissent,* 7(2): 15-18.

Sanchez, T. (2006). Harry Truman and the atomic bomb: An excursion into character education through storytelling. *American Secondary Education,* 35(1): 58-65.

Strada, M. (1999). *Through the global lens.* Upper Saddle River, NJ: Prentice-Hall.

Truman, H. (1955). *Memoirs, vol. 1: Year of decisions.* New York: Doubleday.

Wallace, C. (2004). *Character: Profiles in presidential courage.* New York: Rugged Land.

Chapter Eighteen

The Forgotten American: Dr. Tom Dooley

The American Experience is resplendent with stories that often focus upon a hero's singular achievement as well as those whose exploits span a length of years. Yet many noteworthy figures are consigned to obscurity or oblivion because their lives or achievements "fall between the cracks" of historical events overshadowed by the passage of time and societal perspective. Such is the case with Dr. Tom Dooley, whose name and exploits have never found their way onto the pages of the contemporary American history textbook. In some respects, Dooley was a paradox and unlikely hero, despite the fact that during the peak of the Cold War in the 1950s he was acclaimed as one of the most admired individuals in the world for his humanitarian efforts. Today he is unknown to those under the age of fifty and forgotten by most of the Baby Boomer Generation and its parents to whom he seemed to speak. But his story is worth revisiting as he represents a model of character from which much can be learned.

Dooley's story is a celebration of a charismatic and selfless but far from perfect physician who devoted his enormous energies to caring for the refugees of Indochina as the ensuing war against Communism escalated around him while battling personal demons that nearly consumed him. But this "jungle doctor" is forgotten now, save for the three books he wrote of his experiences. Though he was the 1950s embodiment of the American humanitarian who could in many ways be compared to the celebrated latter-day achievements of Mother Teresa, this forgotten American is also the story of values that embody the character of the American citizen that our nation strives to produce by reminding us of all that we can be.

Born in St. Louis in 1927 of a fairly affluent family, his Irish-American upbringing provided at least one foundation for his future: he was a devout

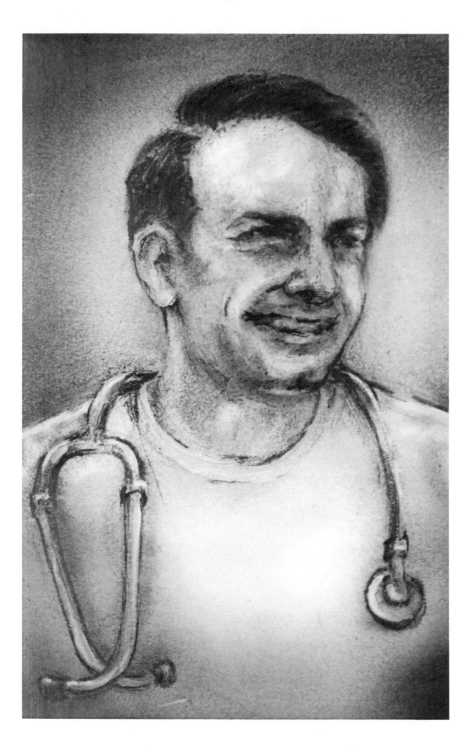

Catholic who would meticulously live by the doctrines of his faith. But the personal and historical events that defined the paradox of Tom Dooley went beyond affluence, religious belief, and patriotic service as a Navy doctor. The phenomenon who would be affectionately known as "Dr. America" for his humanitarian efforts would harbor the suppression of homosexuality, a fact that did not become public knowledge for almost three decades after his premature death and would have certainly had a detrimental effect on his life work as per the less-accepting societal perspectives of mid- 20th-century American mores (Fisher, 1997).

In many respects, Dooley was his own worst enemy long before he entered the international spotlight. Receiving his medical degree from Notre Dame before entering the Navy as a physician, he proved to be a compulsive yet charming nonconformist who demonstrated a brashness that did not endear him to the authoritarian figures he encountered and would be justifiably enraged by his frequent irresponsibility (Fisher, 1997). Throughout his abbreviated life he could be sensitive and compassionate one moment, then rudely arrogant and egotistically self-absorbed the next. But his life was about to change suddenly and drastically.

Dooley's life took a different course in 1954 when as a Navy doctor he was assigned to Southeast Asia and became part of the massive peacetime operation named Passage of Freedom. During this operation, the Navy was instrumental in evacuating over one million Tonkenese refugees to the perceived safety of Saigon. It was in overseeing refugee camps that he first saw humanity's sometimes sad song right before his eyes and it proved to be the pivotal moment of his life. As he treated the countless atrocity cases and rescued torture victims of the Red tide of Communism engulfing the region, he sensed an extraordinary opportunity that was beckoning him (Fisher, 1997).

He had in essence been nothing more than a spoiled playboy with plans to be a rich and successful orthopedic society doctor. But he quickly abandoned those now-frivolous plans to pursue a new role: a crusading servant of the sick, poor, and depressed of Southeast Asia (Monahan, 1961). His exploits soon earned him the Legion of Merit in 1955, the youngest medical officer to be so honored. Dooley's astonishing energy was legendary during his frantic service in Southeast Asia, bolstered by an enormously persuasive charm and charisma that occasionally worked against him (Fischer, 1997). He was determined to inform his fellow Americans of his experiences and as the first of his three books would reflect, he came to symbolize the American traditions of hope and compassion. The popularity of the book made his cause an international issue of helping the sick and depraved without regard to political and military interests, and for what it was worth, he was the most revered American in Asia. But he was about to take yet another course.

In 1956, Dooley resigned from the Navy and abandoned his military medical future to organize his own independent medical unit for a return to Southeast Asia. Though it was suppressed at the time, his resignation may have likely been the result of his paradoxical behavior over his sexual orientation. Due to the obvious religious and societal constraints of his orientation, Dooley suffered great mental anguish, but he was also apparently somewhat reckless in concealing it and thus may have been forced to resign (Fisher, 1997). His spiritual torment naturally affected his goals. He was certainly not the first devout Catholic to be homosexual, but he continually feared that he would not see the face of God because of his sin, so he struggled to be the best Catholic he could be by performing acts of kindness and obediently following the Church ideology (Fisher, 1997). As a result, Dooley's mission would be two-fold: first, and most importantly, to medically heal sick bodies; and second, to promote Christianity to spiritually heal souls. He would merit much credit in this regard, for the 1950s was a time when American Catholics were often denied the same legitimacy as American Protestants, a situation that would be altered by the election of John Kennedy as president in 1960. Dooley's dual role as primarily a jungle doctor and secondarily as a missionary would help transcend this theological battlefield (Fisher, 1997).

Dooley relentlessly pressed on in the face of adversity that few others would have undertaken. Armed only with love, faith, and pharmaceuticals which he procured through donations, he chose embattled Laos as the site for the building of his jungle hospital because, among other reasons, there was exactly one physician in the entire country of three million people (Fischer, 1997). During the next three tumultuous years, Dooley and his small but carefully selected and dedicated staff provided medical care and spiritual inspiration to Vietnamese refugees and Laotian villagers, making such an immediate and profound impact on Southeast Asia that Communist radio broadcasts frantically denounced him as an American spy and demanded his expulsion from the region (Fisher, 1997). During this time, no American played a larger role in heralding the arrival of South Vietnam as our new ally and decisively bound its future to that of America; and presaging a political and military situation that would eventually and disastrously involve the United States in a military conflict. By 1957, Dooley's second book of his accounts had put South Vietnam squarely on the map for millions of American readers who previously had no knowledge of its existence or problems (Monahan, 1961).

By the end of 1957, Dooley's pilot operation would be expanded through his creation of MEDICO (Medical International Cooperation Organization). A nonsectarian enterprise, its purpose was to build, stock, supply, and train staff for small hospitals to be located throughout Southeast Asia. Dooley believed that MEDICO would aid the sick and by that simple act win friendship for America (Dooley, 1960). It was based on the premise of understanding the responsibility of those who have towards those who have not and was quite naturally at the heart of his creed that we all possessed the realization that the only way one can truly achieve happiness is to strive for the happiness of others. It was a simple guide: "every man has a responsibility to every other man" (Dooley, 1961, p.276). The goal was to build and stock a hospital in a chosen site, train the local villagers to assist and run it on a single level, and then turn it over to the host government within four years. But little did Dooley realize that the entire operation would be totally dependent upon his sometimes overly brash and dramatic methods to gain public support and financing, a quest that would further require a seemingly endless trail of fundraising, shameless self-promotion, and speechmaking, which were tasks that regrettably and frequently took him from his jungle hospital.

As 1958 progressed, Dooley was characteristically tireless and relentless in his mission. "I do not believe in days off. My crew works every day, all day" (Dooley, 1960, p.311). Though by this time he had attained international status for his selfless devotion and hard-driving manner of achieving humanitarian goals impeded by limited funds, he was still being personally criticized for his arrogance and rudeness. Critics also charged that his philosophy was shortsighted in that local villagers would not be able to maintain his jungle hospitals. But Dooley countered that they could, at least on a level that was higher before he came: "In America doctors run 20th century hospitals. In Asia I run a 19th century hospital. Upon my departure the hospital may drop to the 18th century. This is fine, because previously the tribes lived, medically speaking, in the 15th century" (Dooley, 1960, p.321).

Despite his critics, the sincerity of Dooley's motives and dedication to his work were clearly apparent and frequently outweighed his flaws. His image and mission became one: a sense of compassion, deeply rooted faith, patriotism, and his ability to make one see the Vietnamese as real people and suffering human beings who needed our help (Gallagher, 1965). Dooley and his team were not primarily concerned that their work with the Lao and Vietnamese would earn admiration for themselves and the distant country they represented, but simply and more importantly that these people were the better because we had been there (Dooley, 1960).

Through tape recordings that he felt compelled to make and broadcast to America, he provided American listeners with a feel for everyday life in Laos while urging all Americans to consider the human commonalities they shared with these previously unknown people. He continually impressed that his jungle patients were simply people who needed our help. As such, he was driven not by any private or public agency, but by a highly personal spirituality and a humanitarian vision of an extended family consisting of people whose names he never knew and did not need to know in order to care (Fisher, 1997). He fervently believed that his duties to God and man were the only rule he must heed, and the evidence of his impact was in the thousands of supportive letters he received monthly from likeminded Americans who respected his mission.

"Life with Dooley" was, however, more than challenging. Despite operating a hospital with limited electrical power and equipment, no x-ray facilities, plumbing, or air-conditioning, Dooley and his staff began their seemingly endless day at 6:30 a.m. with a sick-call line that regularly consisted of more than one hundred people daily from local and distant villages for ailments such as tuberculosis, burns, mutilations, dysentery, malnutrition, and pneumonia. Major and minor surgical procedures were performed when necessary throughout the day, as well as "house calls" when merited. The line was closed by 10:30 p.m. which allowed about four more hours of appointed rounds and other duties, followed by a few hours of rest before the next day began (Dooley, 1960). Utilizing a uniquely simple but rigorous practice of medicine, Dooley was the virtual family practitioner of Southeast Asia (Sanchez, 2006). The daily challenges he faced often bordered on the horrific, as related in an incident from Dooley's third and last book that revealed his commitment, anger, fear, and doubt:

Just before dawn, Dooley and his staff were awakened by the shrieks of a screaming woman. She was only a few feet from his window. Seeing several men huddled over something in the bright moonlight, he jumped out of the window to the ground a few feet below, while yelling for his staff to follow him. The group of men raced away, leaving a sagging limp figure on the ground. Dooley bent down and recognized the bloody mass of a young woman he had recently hired as payment for the delivery of her child. Even by moonlight he could tell she had been brutally stabbed with long daggerlike knives that left dozens of deep wounds pumping blood from her body. More tragically, the bundle on the ground by her side was her newborn baby who had also been stabbed.

They carried her bleeding body into the hospital a few feet away and immediately started intravenous fluid in a futile effort to stop the profuse bleeding from all of the stab wounds. But within a few minutes she stopped breathing entirely. The blood loss had been too great. The floor underneath the operating table was soaked with her congealed blood. They then turned their attention to the baby, sewing up the multiple lacerations which tore deeply through the muscles and down to the bone of both an arm and leg. They miraculously saved the infant and gave him to a nurse who removed the child from the tragic scene. Whatever could have prompted such an atrocity, and so close to their house? Was this an indication of hatred for Americans? They carefully wrapped the dead girl's body and buried her the next morning. Her child was adopted by some people in the local neighborhood, but needless to say, the fear provoked by the incident would linger in his mind.

Dooley had no doubt that this incident was a Communist maneuver geared to frighten the American presence out of North Laos. It frightened him indeed, but not out of North Laos (Dooley, 1960).

It seemed that nothing could actually frighten Dr. Dooley, at least not until mid-1959 when he reluctantly returned to America to undergo chest surgery for a malignant melanoma, a rapidly spreading cancer. He initially handled the situation with his usual brashness by downplaying it all and announcing his impatience to return to his jungle hospital. But as a physician, he knew the seriousness of his condition even with the early favorable post-surgical prognosis. It was not to be and his last fifteen months became a race against time, characterized by a relentless drive and sense of urgency to return to his mission. Medicine was his salvation, his hold on life, and his means of expression. Flowing and surging inside him was the passionate desire to tell others of his work, of his kind of medicine, and of his life in the hope that his mission would continue (Dooley, 1960).

He knew time was running out for him as he completed his last book in 1960. The war of Communist aggression was escalating in Southeast Asia and his jungle outpost faced the near-certainty of being overrun by hostile forces. But he steadfastly refused to evacuate. He was not about to abandon what he believed was the correct thing to do in life. His final two months were especially grim as the cancer rapidly consumed him and he was finally convinced to return home. Shortly after his thirty-fourth birthday, Dr. Tom Dooley died in January 1961. More sadly, as Dooley himself would have maintained, MEDICO would virtually die with him despite his deathbed attempts to ensure its survival. Administrative and political squabbles would ultimately kill it without his interventions. But America was about to enter the unsettling 1960s featuring a war in Southeast Asia that would in many respects contribute to Dooley's now-obscure memory.

It is certainly worth exploring why Dooley has been relegated to obscurity in our time. Revered for his work during his short time, his exploits for posterity have been undoubtedly overshadowed by the controversy of America's military involvement in Vietnam, a conflict that proved to be cruelly divisive to our nation's social fabric. His detractors allege that a strong contributing factor may be his shameless showmanship and self-promotion, though this in and of itself would be an unsustainable reason to denigrate a hero's contributions (Sanchez, 2006). In that regard, one would also have to consider the allegation that he was a pawn of the CIA as a spy and of course the ever-lurking specter of his sexual orientation. No hero is without flaws and Tom Dooley certainly had his share. But attacks on Dooley's character still must take into account his positive attributes that were reflective of his considerable achievements and which ultimately symbolized the values of the America Experience.

DISCUSSION GUIDELINE QUESTIONS

1. What values are depicted in the story?
2. Where did Dooley learn his values?
3. What was his greatest character trait?
4. What was his greatest flaw and how did it affect his behavior?
5. Has the importance of his values diminished or stayed the same since Dooley's time?
6. Are Dooley's actions surprising for an American during his time, or are they bound to that time only and have no relevance to conditions today?
7. The story clearly states that Dooley could be arrogant and brash. What is the relationship between personality and character? Does one out-balance the other, or are they one in the same? Can a person have "unpleasant" personality traits and still demonstrate "good" character?
8. Are there any individuals on the scene today who are comparable to Dooley?

REFERENCES

Dooley, T. (1960). *The night they burned the mountain.* New York: Farrar, Strauss & Cudahy.

Fisher, J. (1997). *Dr. America.* Amherst: University of Massachusetts Press.

Gallagher, T. (1965). *Give joy to my youth: A memoir of Dr. Tom Dooley.* New York: Farrar.

Monahan, J. (1961). *Before I sleep: The last days of Dr. Tom Dooley.* New York: Farrar, Strauss & Company.

Sanchez, T. (2006). The forgotten American: A story for character education. *The International Journal of Social Education,* 21 (2): 79-89.

Chapter Nineteen

The Dream Keeper:
Martin Luther King, Jr.

Heroes promote our own potential by encouraging us to follow their lead and adopt their values, a circumstance often unrecognizable because it is considered obvious or inevitable. In that regard, the values we perceive as "new" are merely the "old" values revisited. Despite the breadth of historical time spanning decades or eras, this legacy is timeless. These heroic individuals who have attained such status also share another common circumstance in that "the theme was high, the occasion noble, the stage open to the world's eye, the courage clear and against odds" (Warren, 1972, p.xxvii). Be it a matter of a decade or a moment, the hero's values and actions exist in a social context that transcend historical time and beckon us to seriously contemplate if such values might, never, or must be adopted by us. Amidst the pressures wrought by changing times through perhaps an erroneous tendency toward global perspectives, it is all the more crucial for us to pursue those values that have stood the test of time to define us as "American."

Such a pursuit, however, has sometimes required the ultimate heroic sacrifice to advance the American Experience. But heroic sacrifice is meaningless if the only result is the naming of schools and streets in the hero's memory. Rather, it is only meaningful if it stirs the moral conscience of the nation and changes us for the better. Lincoln's sacrifice is the classic example, but in our more recent past is the sacrifice of Reverend Dr. Martin Luther King, Jr., whose life mission was "to do nothing less than re-create and redeem America itself" (Frady, 2002, p.6). Like many heroic figures, he was a man of contradictions: revered but loathed, fraught with greatness but riddled with frailties, and courageous yet humbly reserved. During one of the most tumultuous social upheavals in our history, he fearlessly spoke out and demanded that his generation take heed to great and uncomfortable truths that could lead to a vision of a better future (Hodgson, 2009). Though he was a man of his time, his courageous witness against racial inequality and injustice through nonviolence has garnered him a heroic place in the American Experience.

Early 20th century America was a decidedly segregationist nation when MLK was born on January 15, 1929, in Atlanta, Georgia, as the middle child to Reverend Martin Luther King, Sr. and his wife Alberta. Racism was prevalent and segregation strictly enforced but Atlanta "was the best possible place to grow up for a young man who was to lead black people on their

troubled and dangerous pilgrimage... to the Promised Land" (Hodgson, 2009, p.22) of freedom. He was a precocious youth who was not especially bright in school, but he saw the dream early: the promise was there for those who had the faith to endure (Ching, 2002).

Inevitably he absorbed from his happy Christian childhood a deep religious faith but he felt burdened with the weight of his father's irrepressible assumption that MLK would join him in the pastorship (Hodgson, 2009). Yet he realized that entering the seminary at age twenty-one was the most promising avenue for his "inner urge to save humanity" (Frady, 2002, p.18), an urge that relentlessly drove him for the rest of his life. In five short years, he was ordained, received his doctorate from Boston University, and became pastor of his first church in Montgomery, Alabama. Quickly establishing a solid reputation for himself, he became immersed in the tumult and conflict of a world in which racial struggle was inevitable, which in turn led him to openly embrace the philosophy of social democracy, a bold move in the 1950s Age of McCarthyism (Hodgson, 2009). Advocating a just and equal society through his deep faith was further inspired by Gandhi's successful activism of nonviolent protest, a philosophy which would prove to be the most enduring trademark in his commitment to the black struggle for civil rights (Thurman, 1981).

Along with his spiritual and intellectual development, his personal life had also changed. While at Boston University, he met Coretta Scott and he was immediately intrigued by her "character, intelligence, personality, and beauty" (Hodgson, 2009, p.36). They soon married and would become the parents of four children. In the years to come, Coretta would be his stalwart and pillar of support during the best and worst of times.

But some things did not change and they would haunt him as his fame grew. At five feet, seven inches tall, MLK had always been vain about his appearance and even as a youth he had been and unfortunately continued to be sexually adventurous (Hodgson, 2009). His infidelity would cause him severe emotional torment, but the vice grew bolder over the years (Frady, 2002). It would lead to a breech between him and Coretta, who was well aware of the situation, but she resigned herself to it and faithfully stood by him. These unflattering traits were obvious frailties, but in an effort to compensate for them, he all the more devoted himself spiritually and physically to "stand up for righteousness, stand up for justice, stand up for truth" (Frady, 2002, p.46). In these efforts he never wavered.

The historic adventure began in Montgomery in 1955 with the Rosa Parks incident, though this was not the first such incident of resisting discrimination and segregation for both Montgomery blacks and Mrs. Parks. Rather, it was a matter or social/political timing to boldly oppose segregation (McMahon, 2004). Drawn into the incident, MLK "sensed himself being gradually enfolded into some wider embrace of fate" (Frady, 2002, p.38) by assuming spiritual and political responsibility to lead a nonviolent bus protest that gained national attention and lasted an astonishing 385 days before it was legally resolved (McMahon, 2004). Its success catapulted him into national prominence in the service of civil rights reform.

The success of the Montgomery boycott validated MLK's philosophy that "nonviolence is a powerful and just weapon… that could win victories without losing wars" (King, 1964, p.26). But realizing that the struggle was in its infancy, he and other activists formed the Southern Christian Leadership Conference (SCLC) as a base operation and political platform for black protest to "meet physical force with soul force" (Frady, 2002, p.39). He would continue to lead the organization until his death. His stance of nonviolent resistance also gave him and his people a new dignity and destiny as he organized and personally led marches to convince America that basic civil rights must be enacted into law (Schofield, 2006). Evoking racial pride and controlling the mission within the SCLC proved difficult and sometimes dangerous, but frequent arrests and continuous threats against his life did not stop him in his life's mission to secure racial equality.

As the 1960s began, MLK used his growing stature to arouse the national conscience against segregation as morally wrong. Widely preaching a political message from a spiritual base, he stressed that "the time is always ripe to do right… for what is best in the American Dream and for the most sacred values in our Judaeo-Chrisitian heritage" (King, 1964, p.86) as promised in the Declaration and Constitution. If segregation was morally wrong and socially unjust, defying it was therefore a moral obligation: "freedom is never voluntarily given by the oppressor; it must be demanded by the oppressed" (King, 1964, p.80). What had to be understood by segregationists was that this demand was immediate. Nonviolent resistance was the most potent vehicle for the demand, but MLK also understood that Gandhi's ensuing assassination might also be his own end as the price to be paid (Hodgson, 2009). A harbinger of that possibility occurred in 1958 when a deranged black woman inflicted a near-fatal stab wound on him. Thus did he have to be diligent of threats from all sides.

Social conditions held the hope of improvement under President Kennedy's New Frontier program, but MLK grew increasingly impatient with Kennedy's apparent hesitation to fully commit to civil rights through legislation. He could also not ignore the rise of other civil rights organizations that were calling for more militant action, a move that threatened to completely undermine his work. African-Americans were now "hungry for change" (Hodgson, 2009, p.74) and by the summer of 1963 his nonviolent stance was creating a growing tension between the social and political goals of the civil rights movement within and among the various organizations. Struggling to control the active protests that continually tested his personal courage, he began advocating the need for social alliance. He truly believed in the depths of his being that black men and women would not be free until white men and women felt a shared destiny with them (Hodgson, 2009). The turning point came with the Birmingham protests.

As a strategic move led by the SCLC to protest business discrimination, the Birmingham episode in 1963 symbolized the ferocious nature with which the American South was resisting change. Spearheaded by MLK's nonviolent protests and boycotts, it became the most crucial vehicle yet in the demand for equal rights and—though not entirely peaceful—began transforming national opinion toward the need for civil rights for black citizens. MLK's subsequent arrest for leading the protests resulted in the writing of his famous "Letter from Birmingham Jail" which passionately related his personal crusade for justice through the sheer and eloquent power of persuasion. If the Montgomery boycott had first put him in the national spotlight, Birmingham solidified his singular stature in the movement. Largely through his courage and daring, it "had become the first, clear, authentic victory actually won in popular confrontation and struggle for King's movement of nonviolent mass protest" (Frady, 2002, p.118). Further, "the moral conscience of the nation was deeply stirred, and, all over the country, [the] fight became the fight of decent Americans of all races and creeds" (King, 1964, p.100). Here was proof that resistance to injustice was a moral responsibility that did not condemn whites but rather prevailed upon them to do the right thing (Hodgson, 2009).

But changing the face of America would still require political action. Originally planned to dramatize prevailing injustice by openly challenging the government's failure to legally safeguard civil rights, the March on Washington for Jobs and Freedom took place on August 28, 1963. It featured more than a quarter million participants—the largest protest in DC history up to that time—specifically demanding their civil and constitutional rights in a voice of quiet moral authority to pressure Congress to act accordingly (Bennett, 2006). The culminating event of the march fittingly took place in front of the Lincoln Memorial when MLK delivered his seventeen-minute "I Have a Dream" speech that enthralled the crowd and the nation. Regarded as one of the most historic examples of American oratory, it was both a stirring sermon and political argument that appealed to all races in realizing the dream of equality. The speech "was a truly cardinal moment in the modern history of the United States" (Hodgson, 2009, p.7) and played a pivotal role in the passage of the Civil Rights Act of 1964.

Progress was not without personal struggle. As the acknowledged religious and political leader of an aroused people, MLK was making more political headway with President Johnson following John Kennedy's assassination, namely with the Civil Rights Act. But on the suspicion of possible communist influence—which he always adamantly denied—he had for some time come under the scrutiny of FBI Director J. Edgar Hoover who ordered surveillance and wiretaps in an ultimate attempt to discredit him (Gilbert, 1990). As Hoover pressed the investigations, MLK feared that if his promiscuity was exposed, it would seriously harm the movement through a contradiction between what he preached and what he practiced and what he preached (Hodgson, 2009). He realized he was no saint, but he could not afford to have his conduct detrimentally affect his mission and in the process suffered "painful and overwhelming guilt" (Garrow, 1981, p.166) as he pressed forward on the strength of his faith. But he was growing increasingly depressed over the rampant underground rumors that Coretta surely heard.

There was also organizational struggle. Though he was still regarded as the most eloquent and leading champion of racial equality, the SCLC was beginning to view his nonviolent strategy as inefficient and he fought for control of the organization, especially as rioting broke out in Mississippi in a virtual firestorm of violence. Many were becoming increasingly convinced that voting rights and not necessarily peaceful protest would prompt progress—a stance he also advocated—while other black leaders such as Malcolm X and the rise of the Black Panthers threatened to seriously consider more militant responses. Some even opined that MLK's continuing leadership was inviting his own violent death (Hodgson, 2009).

But in the midst of perilously navigating between his nonviolent philosophy and the rising anger of other leaders which could have easily unraveled all of his work, 1964 brought three events that significantly affected his position. Two of the events were honors bestowed upon him. Time Magazine selected him as its Man of the Year. He was also awarded the Nobel Peace Prize, becoming the youngest person to be so honored. Both elevated him in stature at a time when he needed it and infuriated his enemies who were bent on toppling him, especially Hoover. The third event was the Tonkin Gulf incident which not only steered America to war in Vietnam, but would also alter MLK's course.

The late 1960s was a season of disillusionment and rage for America. For MLK, it was a time of triumph and frustration. From Atlanta to Selma—but with lesser success in northern cities—his nonviolent actions were part of the continuous fight against friend and foe for integration and equality, and he was greatly encouraged by the passage of the Voting Rights Act of 1965. As he had longed hoped, the country appeared to be at last rallying to his cause (Hodgson, 2009). The militant activist conscience of the movement, however, was steadily pulling away from his philosophy and he was beleaguered in the fight to maintain organizational control, especially with black youth who were more easily influenced by militancy. The constant struggle kept him from realizing that despite all the difficulties and setbacks, the fight he fervently fought in those years established him as a heroic figure of enduring consequence for the character of American life (Hodgson, 2009).

He had totally devoted himself to the cause for over ten years, but now two new components of the fight were added. First, he began speaking for the need for a fundamental change of the economic system in terms of a redistribution of financial resources to compensate for racial injustice which would be intended to benefit the disadvantaged of all races (Washington, 1991; Ling, 2002). The boldness of adding this aspect to the civil rights crusade was "nothing less than a reordering of the very economic and social arrangements of the nation" (Frady, 2002, p.195). MLK's thinking had become more far-sighted in extending the campaign to include all poor people, not just blacks, but it was the second component of the fight that proved to be his undoing.

From the outset, MLK had serious reservations about America's involvement in Vietnam, flatly stating that it was unjust solely on the grounds that the vast sums of money and resources necessary to fund the war should be more appropriately used for his vision of economic compensation (Frady, 2002; Robbins, 2007; Hodgson, 2009). Refusing as always to back down from perceived injustice, his increasingly vocal criticism of the war robbed him of crucially necessary federal support he had formerly utilized and marked an irreversible break with President Johnson. While his anti-war rhetoric did not directly affect the goals of the civil rights movement itself, it indirectly cost him the total support of his constituents.

It all appeared to be crumbling around him. The effects of his ten-plus years of commitment to the cause were taking an inevitable toll on all aspects of his life. In addition to facing a disillusioned constituency, organizational resentment and petty jealousies, and persistent hounding by the FBI, he had been arrested and imprisoned six times. Accustomed to fear, he often acknowledged to his friends and colleagues that he was well aware that his life was constantly at risk (Hodgson, 2009). His personal finances remained shaky, as he habitually gave to the cause most of the vast sums he had earned to the detriment of his own family. His mission had denied him a closer relationship with his children, while his infidelities had seriously strained his marriage. Yet Coretta loyally stayed the course with him despite the humiliation she surely felt. Guilt-ridden as a result, he began drinking heavily to ease his emotional pain (Hodgson, 2009). He remained outwardly upbeat to his followers, but he was fast becoming pessimistic with the perceived stall in the movement and with the country as a whole, somehow feeling responsible for not knowing how to persuade the races to work and live together.

Still he persevered and pressed on. He went to Memphis in that fateful spring of 1968 to lead a nonviolent demonstration in support of striking black sewer workers. The atmosphere there and perhaps everywhere was tense and ominous. On April 4, 1968, he was felled by an assassin's bullet while standing on the balcony of his motel in the company of his organizational lieutenants. Though only thirty-nine-years-old, his autopsy would reveal the burdened heart of a tired man who was far older (Garrow, 1981). National response to his murder was immediate: "…within hours of the assassination, rioting had broken out and ultimately spread to more than a hundred American cities" (Hodgson, 2009, p.205). Civil rights leaders ironically urged nonviolent action as MLK had long demonstrated, while the more militant wing of the movement adamantly called for a forceful retaliation (Manheimer, 2004). For several days we were a nation seemingly out of control and gone mad, as racial violence spun out of hand, a circumstance MLK would have abhorred. A national day of mourning on April 7 helped quell the widespread disturbances and brought back stability as we attempted to make sense of the tragedy.

As with all senseless assassinations, there arose ensuing conspiracy theories over the actual guilt of the convicted assassin, James Earl Ray, which still linger unsubstantiated today (Garrow, 1981; Frady, 2002). Such theories aside, MLK's tragic demise (and in conjunction with Robert Kennedy's equally senseless assassination two months later) immediately called into question the integrity of America in that pivotal moment: skepticism about the power of government, the long-seated attitude of segregation, urban conditions, and the growing anti-war sentiment, all of which contributed to the mood of doubt, frustration, and anger that symbolized 1968 America and an uncertain future.

MLK's legacy as a human rights/civil rights icon began immediately and became an integral part of our national legacy. With the implementation of Martin Luther King, Jr. Day as a nationally observed holiday beginning in 1983, the preacher's son from Atlanta took his place among the immortal heroes of America. The essence of his victory did not truly materialize until after his death, as his legacy of achievement both socially and politically transcended over the criticisms of his own time. The foundation of his message has certainly proven true in that Americans can never truly be free until they accept the equality of all peoples (Hodgson, 2009). The historical timing, of course, had to be right, and though MLK did not create the civil rights movement, the supreme courage of his nonviolent philosophy was the indispensable factor for victory. Despite his inherent flaws, his courageous leadership, oratory, and strength of character ultimately changed America.

It is no exaggeration to assert that in the nearly five decades since his death, African-Americans as well as other minorities have made significant accomplishments in every aspect of American life. With no less exaggeration it can also be stated that such accomplishments would not have taken place without the words and witness of Reverend King (Hodgson, 2009). Perhaps his own words are his most fitting epitaph and they speak volumes of a humble man who did not care for fame, power, or awards: "I'd like someone to mention that day that Martin Luther King, Jr. tried to give his life serving others… that Martin Luther King, Jr. tried to love somebody… And I want you to say that I tried to love and serve humanity" (Manheimer, 2004, p.97). Let his heroism serve as a living testament to the possibilities of the American Dream.

DISCUSSION GUIDELINE QUESTIONS

1. What values are depicted in the story?
2. Where did MLK learn his values?
3. Why are his values still pertinent today?
4. What might have been his greatest character trait?
5. What was his greatest flaw and how did he deal with it?
6. How has the American environment changed due to his efforts?
7. How has the American environment remained the same despite his efforts?
8. Is there anyone currently on the scene who is comparable to him?

REFERENCES

Bennett, S. (2003). *Radical passivism: The war resisters league and Gandhian nonviolence in America, 1915-1965.* Syracuse: Syracuse University Press.

Ching, J. (2002). *The assassination of Martin Luther King, Jr.* New York: Rosen Publishing.

Frady, M. (2002). *Martin Luther King, Jr.: A life.* New York: Penguin Books.

Garrow, D. (1981). *The FBI and Martin Luther King, Jr.* New York: Penguin Books.

Gilbert, A. (1990). *Democratic individuality: A theory of moral progress.* New York: Cambridge University Press.

Hodgson, G. (2009). *Martin Luther King, Jr.* Ann Arbor: University of Michigan Press.

King, M. (1964). *Why we can't wait.* New York: Signet.

Ling, P. (2002). *Martin Luther King, Jr.* New York: Routledge.

Manheimer, A. (2004). *Martin Luther King, Jr.: Dreaming of equality.* New York: Twenty-First Century Books.

McMahon, T. (2004). *Ethical leadership through transforming justice.* New York: University Press of America.

Robbins, M. (2007). *Against the Vietnam war: Writings by activists.* New York: Rowman & Littlefield.

Schofield, N. (2006). *Architects of political change: Constitutional quandaries and social choice theory.* New York: Cambridge University Press.

Thurman, H. (1981). *With head and heart: The autobiography of Howard Thurman.* New York: Harcourt.

Warren, R. (1972). Introduction. In Dixon Wecter (1941), *The hero in America.* New York: Charles Schreiber's Sons.

Postscript

The existence of heroes and heroines is a perpetual reminder of who we are and whom we wish to be. We perceive that our heroes are initially part of us yet paradoxically stand apart from us, that they are cast in a different mold with a passion and sense of duty that stir the impulses of their time, and turn a dream into action. We choose them for various reasons, perhaps mostly because we want to be inspired to grow beyond our self-imposed limitations by adopting the heroic in ourselves. Then and now they carry the weight of our personal and collective aspirations and dreams, a burden they bear by choice and not mandate. From this perspective, we discover that the binding tie is their timeless values that influence us individually and as a culture in that those values distinguish us and make us great. As long as we have a cause worth fighting for, our crises will breed champions whose values, we will not surprisingly discover, mirror those of our past. Their values do not represent the last embers of a bygone era, nor will they usher in a new age. Rather, they will continue to symbolize the essence and timelessness of the American Experience.

Stories that reveal their multi-dimensional strengths and weaknesses not only enhance their heroic exploits but also allow us to analyze the relevance of their values and character in relation to ourselves. Through storytelling and dialogue, the teacher/storyteller can lead students to uncover those common values that endure beyond the context and circumstances of historical time and uniquely define us as "American." Despite their inherent flaws and frailties, heroes and heroines inspire by their example and show us the heroic potential within us all. Thus do they beckon to us across time to follow their lead.

Bibliography

Abrahamson, C. (1998). Storytelling as a pedagogical tool in higher education. *Education, 118(3):* 440-459.

Addams, J. (1961). *Twenty years at Hull house.* New York, NY: New American Library Signet Classic.

Albion, M. (2008). *The Florida life of Thomas Edison.* Gainesville, FL: University Press of Florida.

Alexander, J. (2002). *Samuel Adams: America's revolutionary politician.* Lanham, MD: Rowman & Littlefield.

Anderson, J. (2004). *Inventing flight: The Wright brothers and their predecessors.* Baltimore, MD: Johns Hopkins University Press.

Auerbach, E. (1974). *Mimesis.* Princeton, NJ: University of Princeton Press.

Baldwin, C. (2008). My heroes of history. *News With Views,* 1-4. Retrieved July 9, 2009, from http://www.newswithviews.com!baldwin/baldwin462.html.

Baldwin, N. (2001). *Edison: Inventing the century.* Chicago, IL: University of Chicago Press.

Baker, J. (1987). *Mary Todd Lincoln: A biography.* New York, NY: W.W. Norton and Company.

Bancroft, G. (1866). *History of the United States from the discovery of the American continent.* Boston, MA: Little, Brown.

Baron, S. (1962). *Brewed in America: The history or beer and ale in the United States.* Boston, MA: Little, Brown.

Barton, K.C. & Levstik, L.S. (2004). *Teaching history for the common good.* Mahway, NJ: Lawrence Erlbaum, Associate.

Barton, W. (1922). *The life of Clara Barton, founder of the American Red Cross.* Boston, MA: Houghton Mifflin Company.

Bauer, C.F. (1993). *New handbook for storytellers.* Chicago, IL: American Library Association.

Bennett, S. (2003). *Radical passivism: The war resisters league and Gandhian nonviolence in America, 1915-1965.* Syracuse, NY: Syracuse University Press.

Bloomfield, M. (1975). *Concepts of the hero in the middle ages.* Albany, NY: State University of New York Press.

Blount, H. (1992). Making history live for secondary students: Infusing people into the narrative. *The Social Studies, 83(5):* 220-223.

Bolyston, J. & Wiener, A. (2009). *David Crockett in congress: The rise and fall of the poor man's friend.* Houston, TX: Bright Sky Press.

Boorstein, D. (1982). *The image.* New York, NY: Vintage Books.

Bowers, C. (1980). Curriculum as cultural reproduction: An examination of metaphor as a carrier of ideology. *Teacher College Record, 82:* 270-271.

Brodbelt, S. & Wall, R. (1985). An examination of the presentation of heroes and heroines in current (1974-1984) social studies textbooks. *ERIC Digest No. ID257726.*

Brooks, D. (2000, October 23). Our founding yuppie. *The Weekly Standard,* p.7.

Bryant, H. (2002). *Shutout: A story of race and baseball in Boston.* New York, NY: Rutledge.

Carlyle, T. (1985). *On heroes, hero worship and the heroic in history.* Oxford: Oxford University Press.

Campbell, J. (1988). *The power of myth.* New York, NY: Doubleday.

Carr, W. (1990). *The oldest delegate.* Newark, NJ: University of New Jersey Press.

Casement, W. (1986). Literature, irrationality, and the prospect of didacticism. *The Journal of General Education, 37:* 261-279.

Chan, A. (1987). The art of the storyteller. *The Leader, 1:*1-6.

Channel 2 News (1986). *Interview with Laurence Olivier.* WBBM, Chicago, IL, May 30.

Ching, J. (2002). *The assassination of Martin Luther King, Jr.* New York, NY: Rosen Publishing.

Clark, R. (1977). *Edison: The man who made the future.* London: MacDonald & Jane's.

Clinton, C. (2004). *Harriet Tubman: The road to freedom.* New York, NY: Little, Brown.

Collins, R. (2003). Bridges, bull's-eyes, and dreams: Can the stories we tell make a difference? *Communication Studies, 54(2):*121-131.

Colombo, G., Lisle, B. & Mano, S. (1997). *Framework: Culture, storytelling, and college writing.* Boston, MA: Bedford Books.

Combs, M. & Beach, J. (1994). Stories and storytelling: Personalizing the social studies. *The Reading Teacher, 47(6):* 464-471.

Common, D. (1987). Stories, teaching, and the social studies curriculum. *Theory and Research in Social Studies Education, XV(1):* 41.

Connell, E. (1984). *Son of the morning star.* New York, NY: Harper & Row.

Crisp, J. (2005). *Sleuthing the Alamo: Davy Crockett's last stand and other mysteries of the Texas revolution.* New York: Oxford University Press.

Crouch, T. (2003). *The bishop's boys: A life of Wilbur and Orville Wright.* New York, NY: W.W. Norton and Company.

Cuban, L. (1984). *How teachers are taught.* New York, NY: Longman.

Cushing, H. (ed.) (1908). *The writings of Samuel Adams.* Lanham, MD: Rowman & Littlefield.

Damon, W. (1988). *The moral child.* New York, NY: Free Press.

Dando-Collins, S. (2008). History without heroes: A case in point. *Home Newsletter.* Retrieved October 23, 2009, from http://hnn.us/articles/57696.html.

Davis, A. (1973). *American heroine: The life and legend of Jane Addams.* New York, NY: Oxford University Press.

Davis, W. (1998). *Three roads to the Alamo: The lives and fortunes of Davy Crockett, James Bowie, and William Barret Travis.* New York, NY: Harper Collins.

Denenberg, D. & Roscoe, L. (2006). *Fifty American heroes every kid should meet.* Minneapolis, MN: Millbrook Press.

Derr, M. (1993). *The frontiersman: The real life and many legends of Davy Crockett.* Knoxville, TN: University of Tennessee Press.

Dewey, J. (1934). *A common faith.* New Haven, CT: Yale University Press.

DiClerico, R. (2000). *The American president.* Upper Saddle River, NJ: Prentice-Hall.

Donald, D. (1995). *Lincoln.* New York, NY: Simon and Schuster.

Dooley, T. (1960). *The night they burned the mountain.* New York, NY: Farrar, Strauss & Cudahy.

Douglass, F. (2003). *The life and times of Frederick Douglass.* Mineola, NY: Dover Publications.

Dunn, L. (1991). Teaching the heroes of American history. *The Social Studies, 82(1):* 26-29.

Egan, K. (1989). Memory, imagination, and learning: Connected by the story. *Phi Delta Kappan, 70:* 455-459.

Egan, K. (1990). *Romantic understanding: The development of rationality and imagination, ages 8-15.* London: Routledge.

Eig, J. (2007). *Opening day: The story of Jackie Robinson's first season.* New York, NY: Simon and Schuster.

Ellis, J. (2004). *His excellency George Washington.* New York, NY: Alfred J. Knopf.

Ellyatt, W. (2002). *Learning more about the power of narrative and storytelling.* New York, NY: EBSCO Publishing.

Elshtain, J. (2002). *Jane Addams and the dream of American democracy.* New York, NY: Basic Books.

Evans, R. (1989). Diane Ravitch and the revivals of history: A critique. *The Social Studies, 80:* 85-88.

Falkner, D. (1995). *Great time coming: The life of Jackie Robinson, from baseball to Birmingham.* New York, NY: Simon and Schuster.

Fischer, D. (1994). *Paul Revere's ride.* New York, NY: Oxford University Press.

Fisher, J. (1997). *Dr. America.* Amherst, MA: University of Massachusetts Press.

Fitzgerald, F. (1979). *America revised.* Boston, MA: Atlantic Monthly Press/Little, Brown.

Flexner, J. (1974). *Washington: The indispensable man.* Boston, MA: Little, Brown.

Fowler, W. (1997). *Samuel Adams: Radical puritan.* New York, NY: Longman.

Frady, M. (2002). *Martin Luther King, Jr.: A life.* New York, NY: Penguin Books.

Franklin, B. (2001). *The autobiography of Benjamin Franklin.* New York, NY: Penguin Putnam.

Franklin, J. & Schweninger, L. (1999). *Runaway slaves: Rebels on the plantation.* New York, NY: Oxford University Press.

Freedman, R. (1987). *Lincoln: A photobiography.* New York, NY: Clarion Books.

Freedman, R. (1991). *The Wright brothers.* New York, NY: Holiday House.

Gallagher, T. (1965). *Give joy to my youth: A memoir of Dr. Tom Dooley.* New York, NY: Farrar.

Garrow, D. (1981). *The FBI and Martin Luther King, Jr.* New York, NY: Penguin Books.

Gilbert, A. (1990). *Democratic individuality: A theory of moral progress.* New York, NY: Cambridge University Press.

Gramschi, A. (1983). *Prison notebooks.* New York, NY: International Publishers.

Groneman, B. (1999). *Death of a legend: The myth and mystery surrounding the death of Davy Crockett.* Plano, TX: Republic of Texas Press.

Hakim, J. (2006). Foreward. In D. Denenberg & L. Roscoe, *Fifty American heroes every kid should meet* (p.9). Minneapolis, MN: Millbrook Press.

Hall, E. (1976, July). How cultures collide. *Psychology Today, 2:* 69-75.

Hall, R. (1993). *Patriots in disguise: Women warriors of the Civil War.* New York, NY: Paragon House.

Hamer, L. (2000). Oralized history: History teachers as oral history tellers. *The Oral History Review, 27(2):* 19-37.

Hamilton, M. & Weiss, M. ((1990). *Children tell stories: A teaching guide.* Katonah, NY: Richard C. Owen.

Harris, W. (1987). *Lincoln's rise to the presidency.* Lawrence, KS: University of Kansas Press.

Hechinger, F. (1987). About education and values: Heroes and villains. *Science Times.* Retrieved May 10, 2009, from http://www.nytimes.com/1987/04/28/science/about-education-values-heroes-and-villains.

Henderson, J. (1964). *Ancient myths and modern man.* New York, NY: Doubleday.

Hine, D. & Thompson, K. (1998). *A shining thread of hope: The history of black women in America.* New York, NY: Broadway Books.

Hodgson, G. (2009). *Martin Luther King, Jr.* Ann Arbor, MI: University of Michigan Press.

Hosmer, J. (1980). *Samuel Adams.* New York, NY: Chelsea House.

Howard, F. (1998). *Wilbur and Orville: A biography of the Wright brothers.* Mineola, NY: Dover Publications.

Huggins, N. & Handlin, O. (1980). *Slave and citizen: The life of Frederick Douglass.* Boston, MA: Little, Brown.

Hughes-Hallett, L. (2004). *Heroes, values, traitors and supermen.* London: Fourth Estate.

Humez, J. (2003). *Harriet Tubman: The life and the life stories.* Madison, WI: University of Wisconsin Press.

Isaacson, W. (2003). *Benjamin Franklin: An American life.* New York, NY: Simon and Schuster.

Israel, P. (2000). *Edison: A life of invention.* New York, NY: John Wiley & Sons.

Jacobs, H. & Appiah, K. (2004). *Narrative of the life of Frederick Douglass, an American slave & incidences in the life of a slave girl.* New York, NY: Mass Marketing Paperbacks.

Jakab, P. (1997). *Visions of a flying machine: The Wright brothers and the process of invention.* Smithsonian History of Aviation and Spaceflight Series. Washington, DC: Smithsonian.

Jokinen, A. (1998). Heroes of the middle ages. *Luminarium,* 1-3. Retrieved July 9, 2009, from http://www.luminarium.org/medlit/medheroes.html.

Jones, R. (2006). *In the footsteps of Davy Crockett.* Winston-Salem, NC: John F. Blair.

Jonnes, J. (2003). *Empires of light: Edison, Tesla, Westinghouse, and the race to electrify the world.* New York, NY: Random House.

Kagan, D. (1995, September). Why America dropped the bomb. *Commentary, 100(3):* 17.

Kelly, F. (ed.) (2002). *Miracle at Kitty Hawk: The letters of Wilbur and Orville Wright.* New York, NY: Da Capo Press.

Kennedy, D. (1998). The art of the tale: Storytelling and history teaching. *Reviews in American History, 26(2):* 462-473.

King, M.L. (1964). *Why we can't wait.* New York, NY: Signet Books.

Kirwin, B. (2005). *Out of the shadows: African-American baseball from the Cuban Giants to Jackie Robinson.* Lincoln, NE: University of Nebraska Press.

Knight, L. (2005). *Citizen: Jane Addams and the struggle for democracy.* Chicago, IL: University of Chicago Press.

Knight, L. (2010). *Jane Addams: Spirit in action.* New York, NY: W.W. Norton and Company.

Kohlberg, L. (1958). *The development of modes of moral thinking and choice in the years ten to sixteen.* (Unpublished doctoral dissertation). University of Chicago, Chicago, IL.

LaBarge, S. (2005). Heroism: Why heroes are important. *Markula Center for Applied Ethics.* Retrieved April 21, 2009, from http://www.scu.edu/ethics/publications/ethicsoutlook2005/heroes.html

Larson, K. (2004). *Bound for the promised land.* New York, NY: Ballantine Books.

Leeming, D. (1990). *The world of myth.* New York, NY: Oxford University Press.

Leming, J. (1996). Paradox and promise in citizenship education. In W. Callahan & R. Banaszek (eds.), *Citizenship for the 21*[st] *century.* Bloomington, IN: ERIC.

Levin, P. (1987). *Abigail Adams.* New York, NY: St. Martin's Press.

Levine, R. (1997). *Martin Delaney, Frederick Douglass, and the politics of representative identity.* Chapel Hill, NC: University of North Carolina Press.

Likona, T. (1991). *Educating for character.* New York, NY: Bantam Books.

Lilliback, P. (2006). *George Washington's sacred fire.* Bryn Mawr, PA: Providence Forum Press.

Ling, P. (2002). *Martin Luther King, Jr.* New York, NY: Routledge.

Linge, M. (2007). *Jackie Robinson: A biography.* Westport, CT: Greenwood Press.

Lockwood, A.L. (2009). *The case for character education: A developmental approach.* New York, NY: Teachers College Press.

Loewen, J. (1995). *Lies my teacher told me: Everything your American history textbook got wrong.* New York, NY: Simon and Schuster.

Lofaro, M. (ed.) (1985). *Davy Crockett: The man, the legend, the legacy.* New York, NY: William Morrow and Company, Inc.

Lopez, C. & Herbert, E. (1975). *The private Franklin.* New York, NY: W.W. Norton and Company.

Lorant, S. (1954). *The life of Abraham Lincoln.* New York, NY: New American Library.

Maier, P. (1980). *The old revolutionaries: Political lives in the age of Samuel Adams.* New York, NY: Alfred J. Knopf.

Manheimer, A. (2004). *Martin Luther King, Jr.: Dreaming of equality.* New York, NY: Twenty-First Century Books.

Massey, M. (1966). *Bonnet brigades: American women and the Civil War.* New York, NY: Alfred J. Knopf.

McCullough, D. (1992). *Truman.* New York, NY: Simon and Schuster.

McCullough, D. (2001). *John Adams.* New York, NY: Simon and Schuster.

McLard, M. (1991). *Harriet Tubman and the Underground Railroad.* Englewood Cliffs, NJ: Silver Burdette Press.

McMahon, T. (2004). *Ethical leadership through transforming justice.* New York, NY: University Press of America.

Meltzer, M. (1986). *George Washington and the birth of our country.* New York, NY: Franklin Watts.

Miller, J. (1936). *Sam Adams: Pioneer in propaganda.* Boston, MA: Little, Brown.

Mittelstadt, J. (2003). Why I have spent my time in such ways: The ways of the storyteller. *The Reading Teacher, 56(7):* 680-682.

Monahan, J. (1961). *Before I sleep: The last days of Dr. Tom Dooley.* New York, NY: Farrar, Strauss and Company.

Moorman, C. (1975). *A knight there was: The evolution of the knight in literature.* Lexington, KY: University of Kentucky Press.

Mortimer, G. (2009). *Chasing Icarus: The seventeen days in 1910 that forever changed American aviation.* New York, NY: Walker.

Oakes, J. (2007). *The radical and the republican: Frederick Douglass, Abraham Lincoln, and the triumph of antislavery politics.* New York, NY: W.W. Norton and Company.

Oates, S. (1995). *A woman of valor: Clara Barton and the Civil War.* New York, NY: The Free Press.

Osborne, A. (1989). *Abigail Adams.* New York, NY: Chelsea House.

Paige, S. & Lipman, D. (1993). *Maybe I'll pitch forever: A great baseball player tells the hilarious story behind the legend.* Lincoln, NE: University of Nebraska Press.

Parry, J., Allison, A. & Skousen, W. (2009). *The real George Washington.* New York, NY: National Center for Constitutional Studies.

Paul, R. (1988). Ethics without indoctrination. *Educational Leadership, 45(8):* 10-19.

Peck, J. (1989). Using storytelling to promote language and literacy development. *The Reading Teacher, November:* 138-141.

Percy, W. (1989). Interview. *The Chronicle of Higher Education, May 10, 1989:* A3-A5.

Postman, N. (1989). Learning by story. *The Atlantic, 264:* 119-124.

Pryor, E. (1987). *Clara Barton, professional angel.* Philadelphia, PA: University of Pennsylvania Press.

Puls, M. (2006). *Samuel Adams: The father of the American Revolution.* New York, NY: Palgrave.

Rainey, J. (2007). A time for heroes. *Anderson Independent-Mail.* Retrieved August 2, 2009, from http://www.independentmail.com/news/2007/mar/01/time-heroes.

Rampersad, A. (1997). *Jackie Robinson: A biography.* New York, NY: Ballantine Books.

Raphael, R. (2004). *Founding myths: Stories that hide our patriotic past.* New York, NY: The New Press.

Rawls, J. (1995). Fifty years after Hiroshima. *Dissent, 7(2):* 15-18.

Remini, R. (1967). *Andrew Jackson and the bank war.* New York, NY: W. W. Norton and Company.

Ricouer, P. (1977). *The rule of metaphor: Multidisciplinary studies of the creation of meaning of language.* Toronto: University of Toronto Press.

Robbins, M. (2007). *Against the Vietnam war: Writings by activists.* New York, NY: Rowman & Littlefield.

Robinson, S. (2004). *Promises to keep: How Jackie Robinson changed America.* New York, NY: Simon and Schuster.

Rolfe, D. (2006). Where have all the heroes gone? *The Dove Foundation.* Retrieved May 20, 2009, from http://www.dove.org/news.asp?ArticleID=80.

Ross, I. (1956). *Angel of the battlefield: The life of Clara Barton.* New York, NY: Harper & Brothers.

Rzadkiewicz, C. (2009). What is a hero? The changing concept of heroes. *Personal Development:* 1-2. Retrieved April 21, 2009, from http://personaldevelopment.suite101.com/article.cfm/who_are_our_heroes.

Sanchez, T. (1998). *Heroes/heroines across the life span.* Paper presented at the Indiana Council for the Social Studies Annual Conference, Indianapolis, IN, March 13, 1998.

Sanchez, T. (1998). Using stories about heroes to teach values. *ERIC Clearinghouse for Social
Studies/Social Science Education, EDO-SO-98-10.*

Sanchez, T. (2000). Heroes, values, and transcending time: Using tradebooks to teach values.
Social Studies and the Young Learner, 13(1): 27-30.

Sanchez, T. (2000). It's time again for heroes: Or were they ever gone? *The Social Studies,
91(2), March/April:* 58-61.

Sanchez, T. (2004). Facing the challenge of character education. *International Journal of
Social Education, 19(2), Fall/Winter:* 106-113.

Sanchez, T. (2005). The story of the Boston massacre: An opportunity for character education.
The Social Studies, 96(6): 265-270.

Sanchez, T. (2006). Harry Truman and the atomic bomb: An excursion into character education. *American Secondary Education, 35(1):* 58-65.

Sanchez, T. (2006). The man who could have been king: A storyteller's guide for character
education. *Journal of Social Studies Research, 30(2):* 3-9.

Sanchez, T. (2006). The forgotten American: A story for character education. *The International
Journal of Social Education, 21(2):* 79-89.

Sanchez, T. (2007). The depiction of Native Americans in recent (1991-2004) secondary
American history textbooks: How far have we come? *Equity and Excellence in Education,
40(4):* 311-320.

Sanchez, T. (2009). Tell me a story: Becoming reacquainted with a neglected art form. *Ohio
Social Studies Review, 45(1):* 24-33.

Sanchez, T. (2010). The return of the American hero. *Ohio Social Studies Review, 46(2):* 20-
28.

Sanchez, T. & Mills, R. (2005). Telling tales: Teaching American history through storytelling.
Social Education, 69(5): 269-274.

Sanchez, T. & Stewart, V. (2006). The remarkable Abigail: Storytelling for character education. *The High School Journal, 89(4):* 14-21.

Sanchez, T., Zam, G. & Lambert, J. (2009). Storytelling as an effective strategy for teaching
character education in middle school. *Journal for the Liberal Arts and Sciences, 13(2):* 14-
23.

Santella, A. (1996). *Jackie Robinson breaks the color line.* New York, NY: Children's Press.

Schama, S. (2006). *Rough crossing: Britain, the slaves, and the American Revolution.* New
York, NY: HarperCollins.

Schofield, N. (2006). *Architects of political change: Constitutional quandaries and social
choice theory.* New York, NY: Cambridge University Press.

Schneider, H. (1958). *The Puritan mind.* Ann Arbor, MI: University of Michigan Press.

Scott, D. (2008). America's heroes. *EzineArticles.* Retrieved September 11, 2009, from http://
ezinearticles.com/?Americas-Heroes&id=1063829.

Shackford, J. & Folmsbee, S. (eds.) (1973). *A narrative of the life of David Crockett of the state
of Tennessee.* Knoxville, TN: University of Tennessee Press.

Shaw, P. (1976). *The character of John Adams.* New York, NY: W.W. Norton and Company.

Shenk, J. (2005). *Lincoln's melancholy.* New York, NY: Houghton Mifflin Company.

Simon, S. (2002). *Jackie Robinson and the integration of baseball.* Hoboken, NJ: Wiley.

Sitton, T., Mehaffy, G. & Davis, O. (1983). *Oral history.* Austin, TX: University of Texas
Press.

Smith, P. (1962). *John Adams, volume: 1735-1784.* New York, NY: Doubleday.

Smith, R. (1994). The surprising George Washington. *Quarterly of the National Archives, 26:*
3-11.

Smith, R. (1993). An old moral education method rediscovered. *Education, 113(4):* 541, 550.

Smyth, A. (ed.) (1970). *The writings of Benjamin Franklin.* New York, NY: Haskell House.

Sobol, K. (1974). *Babe Ruth and the American dream.* New York, NY: Ballantine Books.

Still, W. (1970). *The Underground Railroad.* Chicago, IL: Johnson Publishing Company, Inc.

Stoll, I. (2008). *Samuel Adams: A life.* New York, NY: The Free Press.

Storer, D. (1975). *Amazing but true! Stories about the presidents.* New York, NY: Pocket Books.

Strada, M. (1999). *Through the global lens.* Upper Saddle River, NJ: Prentice Hall.

Striner, R. (2006). *Father Abraham: Lincoln's relentless struggle to end slavery.* New York, NY: Oxford University Press.

Stross, R. (2007). *The wizard of Menlo Park: How Thomas Alva Edison invented the modern world.* New York, NY: Random House.

Swindell, L. (1980). *The last hero: A biography of Gary Cooper.* New York, NY: Doubleday.

Thompson, C. (1998). *John Adams and the spirit of liberty.* Lawrence, KS: University of Kansas Press.

Tobin, J. (2004). *To conquer the air: The Wright brothers and the great race for flight.* New York, NY: Simon and Schuster.

Tomlinson, C., Tunnel, M. & Richgels, D. (1993). *The story of ourselves.* Portsmouth, NH: Heinemann.

Truman, H. (1955). *Memoirs, volume 1: Year of decisions.* New York: Doubleday.

Wallace, C. (2004). *Character: Profiles in presidential courage.* New York, NY: Rugged Land.

Warren, R.P. (1972). A dearth of heroes. *The American Heritage, 23(6):* 4-7.

Weber, A. (2009, April 9). What makes a hero? *The Toledo Blade:* B-6.

Webster's new world dictionary (2004). New York, NY: Simon and Schuster.

Wecter, D. (1941). *The hero in America.* New York, NY: Charles Schreibner's Sons.

Wells, G. (1986). *The meaning makers: Children learning language and using language to learn.* Portsmouth, NH: Heinemann.

Wells, W. (1866). *The life and public services of Samuel Adams.* Boston, MA: Little, Brown.

White, R. (2009). *A. Lincoln.* New York, NY: Random House.

Wiesel, E. (2009). My hero's hero: The concept of heroes. *My Hero Project.* Retrieved April 21, 2009, from http://www.myhero.com/myhero/heroprint.asp?hero=Wiesel.

Willis, J. (1992). Lives and other stories: Neglected aspects of the teacher's art. *The History Teacher, 26(1):* 33-43.

Withey, L. (2001). *Dearest friend: A life of Abigail Adams.* New York, NY: Simon and Schuster.

Woodward, W. (1926). *George Washington: The image and the man.* New York, NY: Boni and Liveright.

Zabel, M. (1991). Storytelling, myths, and folk tales: Strategies for multicultural inclusion. *Preventing School Failure:* 32.

Zimbardo, P. (2007). *The Lucifer effect: Understanding how good people turn evil.* New York, NY: Random House.